Understanding Poverty and Environment

CW00403764

Does poverty lead to environmental degradation? Do degraded environments and natural resources lead to poverty? Are there other forces at play? Is the relationship between poverty and the environment really as straightforward as the vicious circle portrayal of 'poverty leading to environmental destruction leading to more poverty' would suggest? Does it matter if the relationship is portrayed in this way?

This book suggests that it does matter. Arguing that such a portrayal is unhelpful and misleading, the book brings together a diverse range of analytical frameworks and approaches that enable a much deeper investigation of the context and nature of poverty–environment relationships. Analytical frameworks and approaches examined in the book are drawn from political ecology, gender, environment and development, institutional analyses, livelihoods and wellbeing, social network analysis and analyses of the governance of natural resources. Key themes running through the analytical frameworks and approaches are highlighted in a concluding chapter, including power, access, institutions and scale.

Nunan draws on material published over the last thirty years as well as key contemporary publications, steering readers towards essential texts within each subject area through annotated further reading recommendations. *Understanding Poverty and the Environment* is unique in critically reviewing a number of frameworks that are often applied within environment and development research. Engaging and accessible, the text will enable students to grasp the key concepts and rationales of the various frameworks and make sense of often complex original sources. The book is a must for students of development studies, environmental studies and related disciplines.

Fiona Nunan is currently Head of the International Development Department at the University of Birmingham, UK. Her research focuses on natural resource governance and livelihoods, particularly in coastal areas and inland fisheries, and relationships between poverty and the environment. She has published papers in a range of journals including *World Development*, *Fish and Fisheries*, *Environmental Management*, *Geoforum* and the *Journal of International Development*.

Understanding Poverty and the Environment

Analytical frameworks and approaches

Fiona Nunan

 Routledge
Taylor & Francis Group

LONDON AND NEW YORK

First published 2015
by Routledge
2 Park Square, Milton Park, Abingdon, Oxon OX14 4RN

and by Routledge
711 Third Avenue, New York, NY 10017

Routledge is an imprint of the Taylor & Francis Group, an informa business

British Library Cataloguing in Publication Data
A catalogue record for this book is available from the British Library

Library of Congress Cataloging in Publication Data
Nunan, Fiona.
Understanding poverty and the environment: analytical frameworks and
approaches / Fiona Nunan.
Includes bibliographical references and index.
1. Poverty—Environmental aspects. 2. Sustainable development.
3. Environmental sociology. 4. Political ecology. I. Title.
HC79.P6N86 2015
339.4′6—dc23
2014043228

ISBN: 978-0-415-70756-5 (hbk)
ISBN: 978-0-415-70759-6 (pbk)
ISBN: 978-1-315-88670-1 (ebk)

Typeset in Times New Roman
by Book Now Ltd, London

Printed and bound in the United States of America by
Edwards Brothers Malloy on sustainably sourced paper

For Ann

Contents

Illustrations

Figures

Tables

Boxes

Preface

The genesis of this book is rooted in my experience in studying, researching, teaching and advising on the environment and natural resources in relation to how people in the Global South manage and benefit from them. The idea for a book that brings together ways of investigating poverty–environment relationships primarily stems from dissatisfaction with the simplistic portrayal of poverty–environment relations as being linked in a 'vicious circle' or 'downward spiral'. There are many constraints on how people use natural resources which are not reflected and acknowledged in the 'vicious circle' and similar portrayals of poverty and the environment. These constraints can be identified and analysed from many perspectives, including analysis of the political economy, governance, gender and institutions. The desire to advocate for the exploration of the context and nuances of poverty–environment relationships prompted the collation of a range of frameworks and approaches that can be used to do just that.

A further rationale for writing this book was to provide a text that can act as a way in to more specialized, complex literature, including literature that was written in the 1980s and 90s that I feel should not be forgotten or ignored. Students may find it challenging to delve straight into journal articles on political ecology or gendered analyses of natural resource situations. This introduction into how frameworks and approaches emerged, their key components and examples of their application, can bridge lectures and specialized books and journal articles.

Beyond the primary concern of this book with challenging simplistic portrayals of poverty–environment relationships, the book is innovative in bringing together a diversity of analytical frameworks and approaches. This should assist students and researchers in appreciating the breadth of concepts, frameworks and approaches that can be employed in investigating people–environment relationships within a development context.

Each chapter concludes with two or three recommended further reading and a list of references. These have not been chosen or drawn on lightly. They constitute a significant resource. Use these as a starting point; there will, of course, be much more literature that can be drawn on. Additional literature should be particularly sought that has been written by the authors of the texts falling within the 'further reading' and references. Work by key authors in each area has been drawn on throughout, providing a rich resource for students and lecturers alike.

My keen interest in how poverty–environment relationships are portrayed and how this dominant portrayal has been challenged was ignited whilst studying for an MA with the School of African and Asian Studies at the University of Sussex. The 'Political Economy of the Environment' module taught by the Institute of Development Studies was particularly instrumental in nurturing this interest.

I have been fortunate to be able to pursue this concern with how poverty–environment relations can be investigated through teaching and research in the International Development Department, University of Birmingham, and working in East Africa for five years on two fisheries management projects, employing livelihoods, institutional and governance analyses.

I would like to thank my colleagues in the School of Government and Society, of which IDD is a part, in providing valuable feedback on draft chapters of this book. Special thanks are due to Tom Hewitt, Emma Foster and Mattias Hjort. I thank Frances Cleaver of Kings College London and anonymous reviewers for their valuable comments. Finally, I thank my family, especially Trevor, Aimée, Éloise and my parents, for their continuous support and encouragement.

Fiona Nunan
Birmingham, September 2014

1 Why poverty and the environment?

Many parts of the world are caught in a vicious downwards spiral: Poor people are forced to overuse environmental resources to survive from day to day, and their impoverishment of their environment further impoverishes them, making their survival ever more difficult and uncertain.

(World Commission on Environment and Development, 1987: 27)

Introduction

The quote above from perhaps the most significant international environment and development report of the twentieth century sums up a common understanding and portrayal of poverty–environment relations. This portrayal suggests that poverty and the environment are linked in a 'vicious circle', where poverty forces many poor people to overuse and degrade the environment on which they depend, leading to environmental destruction which in turn further exacerbates the extent and depth of poverty. Some have described this relationship as a 'downward spiral' – emphasizing that over time, poverty will deepen and the environment will be further degraded.

But, does poverty necessarily lead to environmental destruction? Do degraded and impoverished environmental and natural resources directly lead to poverty? Or, are there other forces at play? Is the relationship between poverty and the environment really as straightforward as the vicious circle portrayal suggests? Does it matter if the relationship is portrayed in this way?

This book suggests that it does matter. The portrayal of the relationship between poverty and the environment as a vicious circle or downward spiral directs efforts to reduce poverty or improve environmental management that may focus only on poverty reduction and/or environmental management in a narrow sense, without taking sufficient account of a multitude of mediating factors, including governance, institutional arrangements and power relationships. These 'mediating factors' influence how people, including poor people, have access to, and control over, the environment and natural resources. Approaches that endeavour to reduce poverty and improve environmental or natural resource management may well achieve more through improving governance, asking who has power and what institutional arrangements constrain or enable access to resources than initiatives that focus directly on poverty or the environment. Whilst it has been argued that thinking about poverty and the environment has largely moved away from the 'vicious circle' portrayal (Reed, 2002), there remains a need for wider adoption of frameworks and approaches that take a more nuanced approach to investigating the linkages.

Tools, approaches and frameworks exist that can be used to investigate how these mediating factors influence and interact with poverty–environment relations. Having appropriate tools and approaches to investigate and generate understanding of poverty–environment relationships is essential because of the significant dependence of many poor people in the developing world on environmental goods and services. Acknowledging and understanding this dependence is even more important in light of the world's growing population and the increasing wealth of powerful individuals and countries who are able to gain access to huge swathes of land and other resources, at times to the detriment of those living in the affected areas. In addition, increasing awareness and experience of the impacts of climate change make understanding of the interactions between poverty and the environment even more critical.

This text provides an introduction to a range of frameworks and approaches from the social sciences that can facilitate a deeper understanding of linkages between poverty and environment. These frameworks and approaches are presented within the following areas of investigation:

- political ecology;
- institutional analysis;
- gender, development and the environment;
- livelihoods and wellbeing;
- social network analysis;
- governance.

Each chapter introduces a number of frameworks and approaches, explaining key concepts and ideas and referencing key material in the development and application of the frameworks and approaches. These frameworks and approaches have not necessarily been developed with the purpose of investigating poverty–environment relationships but have the capacity to be used for this purpose. Examples and case studies of applications of the frameworks and approaches are provided to illustrate how they have been used and what kinds of research questions they may be appropriate for answering. In addition, each chapter identifies key texts to steer readers towards deeper exploration of the theory and assumptions underlying the frameworks and approaches, as well as to further examples of their application. The key readings and the list of references have been carefully and purposefully selected to provide readers with a wide range of important sources and authors in each area reviewed. Readers are encouraged to see the lists of references as both an essential resource and as a starting point for finding further relevant literature.

The discussion of the approaches and frameworks, and the majority of the examples and case studies of their application, relate to and draw on experience in developing countries, and so the book is situated within the multidisciplinary area of Development Studies. Development Studies as an area of academic study is concerned with the normative ambition of improving people's lives and thus has a 'shared commitment to the practical or policy relevance of teaching and research' related to experience 'in "less developed countries" or "developing countries" or "the South" or "post-colonial societies" formerly known as "the Third World"' (Sumner, 2006: 645). Development Studies is a dynamic area of academic study, reflecting the heterogeneity and changes over time in the experience of 'development'. This is reflected in the debate and contention concerned with the classification of countries in relation to development. It is widely acknowledged that the dichotomy of 'developed and developing' in classifying countries is outdated and, at times, unhelpful (Harris *et al.*, 2009). There is no one criterion universally used to categorize countries in relation to their level of 'development' and it is not always clear where countries should be placed (Nielsen, 2013). There is, then, broad consensus that more categories should be used, reflecting different measures of development, changes over time and different purposes of the categorization (Nielsen, 2013; Tezanos and Sumner, 2013). Whilst acknowledging the diversity of development outcomes and experience across countries and the need for more than two categories of countries, the term 'developing country' is used throughout this book. This is because the category of 'developing country' is widely understood as broadly referring to countries with a lower level of economic development and often having a higher level of direct dependence on natural resources than developed countries. This category includes many countries in Asia, Africa and Latin America.

This introductory chapter sets the scene for the book, starting with the broader debate concerning environment and development and the concept of sustainable development, i.e. can the environment be protected whilst also encouraging economic growth and reducing poverty? The chapter goes on to critically review the portrayal of poverty–environment linkages as a vicious circle and downward spiral, before examining different definitions of, and approaches to, poverty and environment. Explanations of key concepts and cross-cutting themes found within the frameworks and approaches in the following chapters are then set out. These are: institutions, social capital, gender, power, property rights and regimes, community, 'access to and control over' natural resources and vulnerability. The structure of the book is then explained, setting out the main themes of each chapter.

Environment and development: the debate

Can you protect the environment and, at the same time, also maintain and even increase development, interpreted for many years as largely equating to economic growth? This question has been the subject of much debate over decades, with evidence providing alleged support for both sides. For many in the developed and developing worlds, a view has prevailed that the environment must wait; economic growth and poverty reduction are the priorities and if the environment is degraded and polluted as a result, then cleaning it up will be less costly in the future than in the present (Clémençon, 2012). This position reflects the environmental Kuznets curve, as shown in Figure 1.1, which suggests that as income increases there comes a point at which environmental degradation will reduce and reverse, as investment in the environment and cleaner technology increases. Before that happens, environmental degradation will increase as per-capita income increases.

Of course, not everyone agrees that the Kuznets curve is correct in its depiction of the relationship between per capita income and environmental degradation (see, for example, Dasgupta *et al.*, 2002 and Stern, 2004). Technology transfer, for example, can enable 'tunnelling through' the curve so that less environmental degradation is experienced than would be predicted. The nature of the relationship may also depend on which pollutants are included in the analysis, what assumptions are made about how the pollutants behave and over what period of time data is available (Stern, 2004). It is not, then, a given that the 'environment must wait'; technology and regulations can be adopted and implemented earlier than may be implied by the Kuznets curve.

Concern about the exploitation of natural resources as a result of development can be traced back to the nineteenth century, when Thomas Malthus voiced concern that as population grew exponentially, food production could not increase at such a rate. Debate about whether the world will run out of natural resources in the face of the increasing global population was highlighted again in the twentieth century with the publication of the report *The Limits to Growth* (Meadows *et al.*, 1972). Reporting on results from computer modelling on a range of scenarios with different levels of population growth, industrialization, pollution, food production and resource depletion, the report presented two scenarios where the global system would collapse and one where stabilization could be reached. Whilst the report received much criticism, questioning the methodology and data used as well as the interpretation of the models, debate

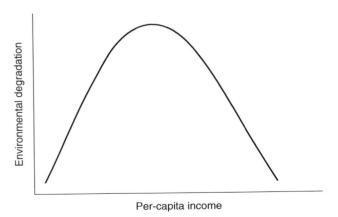

Figure 1.1 The environmental Kuznets curve.

continues into the twenty-first century about whether there will be sufficient natural resources for all, with global population projected to reach 9 billion around 2050. Increasing global population is only part of the picture though, with the rate and nature of consumption in much of the developed world being far from sustainable, as well as inequitable.

The debate about the relationship between environment and development appeared to be settled and even reconciled with the coining of the concept of sustainable development, associated with the 1987 World Commission on Environment and Development report, *Our Common Future*. The WCED was commissioned by the United Nations in 1983 to write a report in response to concern about accelerating environment degradation and the consequences of this degradation for economic and social development. The Commission was chaired by the Norwegian Prime Minister Gro Harlem Brundtland and so the Commission and report is often referred to as the 'Brundtland Commission' and 'Brundtland Report'. The definition of sustainable development given in the 1987 report is the most often cited definition in literature, policy and practice and is set out in Box 1.1.

Box 1.1 Brundtland definition of sustainable development

'Sustainable development is development that meets the needs of the present without compromising the ability of future generations to meet their own needs. It contains within it two key concepts:

- the concept of "needs", in particular the essential needs of the world's poor, to which overriding priority should be given; and
- the idea of limitations imposed by the state of technology and social organization on the environment's ability to meet present and future needs.'
  (World Commission on the Environment
  and Development, 1987: 43)

The concept of sustainable development appears to offer hope that, at last, we can have environmental protection and economic development together. Poverty reduction, or perhaps even elimination, within and between generations is seen as fundamental to the pursuit of sustainable development, as well as sustainable environmental management. However, the concept and very idea of sustainable development has been widely critiqued, with criticisms including:

1 It is far too vague and woolly – anyone can agree with the concept and the definition given in the Brundtland Report whilst having very different understanding of what it means in practice. This has implications for policy and practice, with much being lauded in the name of sustainable development that others may well question as being at all 'sustainable'.

2   Deep ecologists reject the concept on the grounds that it is human-centred, with little, or perhaps no, recognition of the intrinsic right of nature to exist for its own sake, rather than for the sake of humankind. The very term 'natural resources' suggests that nature is there for the survival of humankind, with 'resources' to be used and exploited as necessary.

3   At the other end of the ideological spectrum, it is argued that economic growth must continue unabated and that there are no ecological limits to growth. Not only will more natural resources be discovered, but technology and science will develop new solutions, replacing natural 'capital' with other forms of capital. There is, then, no need for concern, or for limits to be placed on economic growth and development.

It seems then that there are differing views as to whether it is possible to protect and enhance the condition of the environment whilst also encouraging development through economic growth. In reflecting on this, what are the implications for understanding linkages between poverty and the environment?

Poverty and the environment: the vicious circle and downward spiral

As noted at the beginning of this chapter, the relationship between poverty and the environment has traditionally been portrayed as a vicious circle, where poverty leads people to overexploit the environment, leading to degradation and consequently more poverty. The vicious circle of poverty and environmental degradation is shown in Figure 1.2.

The relationship has also been portrayed as a downward spiral, with increasing poverty leading to increasing environmental degradation and hence the situation of both the poor and the environment getting worse and worse. The 'vicious circle' and 'downward spiral' sums up the portrayal of the relationship between poverty and the environment given in the Brundtland Report of 1987:

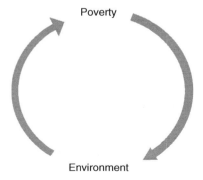

Figure 1.2 Poverty and the environment: a vicious circle.

Environmental stress has often been seen as the result of the growing demand on scarce resources and the pollution generated by the rising living standards of the relatively affluent. But poverty itself pollutes the environment, creating environmental stress in a different way. Those who are poor and hungry will often destroy their immediate environment in order to survive: They will cut down forests; their livestock will overgraze grasslands; they will overuse marginal land; and in growing numbers they will crowd into congested cities.'

(World Commission on the Environment and Development, 1987: 28)

This vicious circle portrayal of poverty and environment has been critiqued using some of the frameworks and approaches set out in this book. A political ecology perspective (see Chapter 2) in particular would argue against some of the statements in the quote above, asking:

- Who is most responsible for a country's deforestation? Is it those engaged in forms of shifting cultivation or the government issuing permits for conversion of forest land to plantations or agriculture to produce crops for animal feed?
- Which areas of land do the poor have access to for grazing their livestock? How has access to land, how much land, where and for how long, changed over time? Who decides who gets access to specific areas of land?
- What is the definition of 'marginal land'? Why do the poor use marginal land; are there alternatives open to them? Who controls access to land?
- Are there alternatives to moving to growing cities and why are these cities congested?

These are the sorts of perspectives and challenges raised by the approaches set out in this book. Asking these kinds of questions brings alternative insights into the relationships between poverty and the environment.

From these reflections on the relationships between poverty and the environment, two questions are identified in relation to the vicious circle portrayal: how accurate is this depiction and how helpful is it? The accuracy of the vicious circle has been questioned in a number of ways:

1   The circle is too simplistic and does not reflect the diversity of poverty–environment linkages and the dynamic, context-specific nature of these linkages.
2   The circle suggests that if the environment is improved, poverty will be reduced, but this may not be the case. There could be many other factors that influence the relationship.
3   The portrayal does not acknowledge any other influencing factors, particularly the wider political and economic situation, which will influence how the poor interact with environmental resources.

In terms of whether the 'vicious circle' portrayal is helpful, concern has already been expressed that it may lead to inappropriate policy responses that do not take into consideration a wide range of 'mediating factors'. One area where this direct circular relationship is taken up is within literature and practice that investigates or pursues the poverty–environment 'nexus', referring to a close connection, link or tie between poverty and the environment, much more tightly defined than a 'relationship' or 'linkage'. The 'poverty–environment nexus' has been defined as 'a set of mutually reinforcing links between poverty and environmental damage' (Dasgupta *et al.*, 2005: 617). The nexus approach is concerned with examining the dependence of the poor on natural resources (World Bank, 2008) and looking for 'win–win' strategies and situations, where poverty will be reduced and the environment improved. Literature on the poverty–environment nexus identifies a set of themes that characterize such relationships. These are:

- the importance of livelihoods (DFID *et al.,* 2002) and assets/income from natural resources for poor people (Bass *et al.*, 2005; World Bank, 2008);
- health, with health outcomes being heavily affected by pollution from, for example, water sources and smoke from cooking stoves, particularly affecting the poor (DFID *et al.*, 2002; World Bank, 2008);
- vulnerability, with poor people being more exposed to environmental hazards and environment-related conflict and having less capacity to cope than non-poor (Bass *et al.*, 2005; DFID *et al.,* 2002).

Such themes suggest areas of correlation between poverty and the environment and, following on from this, potential policy responses and interventions. Even within literature and practice on the poverty–environment nexus, however, it is recognized that the wider context matters. Bass *et al.* (2005: 1) state that 'if poverty and environmental problems persist, it is, in large part because poor people and environmental concerns remain marginalized by – and from – sources of power'. Reed (2006) draws on an approach undertaken by the WWF that stresses the context of poverty–environment relationships. The '3×M Approach' investigates the context of such relationships at micro (local), meso (analysing actors and institutions in between the macro and micro levels) and macro (including macroeconomic policies, sectoral policy reforms and institutional arrangements) levels. Reed (2006: 20) suggests that the 3×M Approach 'distinguishes itself from others' by meeting three standards:

1   including analysis of the complex dynamics between the rural poor and the environment that are specific to localities;
2   interpreting relations between local poverty–environment dynamics and politics and institutions at the meso and macro levels;
3   analysing relations between economic policy and institutional arrangements at the three levels as they affect poverty–environment dynamics.

This approach, and others similar to it (see, for example DFID *et al.*, 2002), have been developed to inform and direct development policy and practice and share concerns and concepts with many of the frameworks and approaches introduced in this text: in particular, the concerns that the context-specific nature of linkages is recognized, that relationships are investigated over time and that the influence of the wider context, at multiple levels, is included in the analysis. The concerns of the poverty–environment nexus literature on livelihoods, health and vulnerability can also be seen in the components and applications of the frameworks and approaches in the following chapters.

Although the idea of a poverty–environment nexus has a place in poverty–environment discussions, this is not the focus of this book. The text instead builds on the critique of the vicious circle portrayal by presenting frameworks that can facilitate analysis of the diversity and complexity of poverty–environment relationships, focusing on factors that mediate between, and influence, these connections. The frameworks and approaches are not, then, seeking to quantify relationships or suggest that certain relationships exist everywhere and at all times, but provide tools for analysis and ways of thinking that go beyond the observation of direct linkages and explanations, enabling deeper analysis of underlying causes and processes.

Definitions and interpretations of poverty

Poverty has often been viewed in monetary terms, that is poverty defined as a per capita income level, or in terms of purchasing power, below which people are viewed as living in poverty (Ravallion *et al.*, 2009). Whilst still dominating many measures of poverty, since the late 1990s it has been more widely accepted that poverty should be viewed as being multi-dimensional, rather than portrayed in monetary terms alone. Different interpretations and understandings of poverty matter for policy, practice and research as they will influence the approaches taken to gathering data and tackling poverty. When investigating the relationships between poverty and the environment, recognition that there is a diversity of experiences and interpretations of poverty, as well as multiple dimensions, is essential.

The recognition of a broader approach to understanding poverty is reflected in the 2000/2001 World Development Report, *Attacking Poverty*. The World Bank (2000: 15) defined poverty as 'pronounced deprivation in wellbeing', with deprivation including vulnerability and exposure to risk, as well as inadequate education, access to health care and material deprivation. The report was informed by a ground-breaking global consultation with people in 23 countries using participatory and open-ended consultation methods to listen to the poor (Narayan *et al.*, 1999, 2000). In analysing the responses in terms of how wellbeing is understood, five key dimensions were identified: material wellbeing, physical wellbeing, security, freedom of choice and action and good social relations (Narayan *et al.*, 1999, 2000). The 'voices of the poor' reinforced the need for a broader view of poverty to be taken, beyond income, and for greater understanding of what makes for, and constrains, wellbeing.

The concept of wellbeing has been interpreted in many ways. Haughton and Khandker (2009: 2) identify three interpretations of the concept: as 'the command over commodities in general, so people are better off if they have a greater command over resources'; in terms of people obtaining enough of a specific type of consumption good ('Do they have enough food? Or shelter? Or health care? Or education?'); and, through the approach taken to wellbeing by Amartya Sen (1999), for whom wellbeing comes from a set of capabilities to function in society, including, for example, having power, voice or access to education. The capability approach suggests that experiencing poverty is associated with a lack of key capabilities. Powerlessness or the absence of rights can as much be associated with the experience of poverty as low income. The capability approach acknowledges that wellbeing is not dependent on money alone, but can be complex to investigate, given the individuality, specificity and complexity of capabilities (Robeyns, 2005).

In theory and in practice, different approaches are taken to understanding and addressing poverty. Laderchi *et al.* (2003) ask whether it matters how poverty is understood and tackled and review three approaches to understanding poverty in addition to the capability approach: monetary, social exclusion and participation. The monetary approach is based on market prices in relation to income and consumption, often for individuals, but the approach can be used for households and communities. It does not attempt to offer explanations for why people are poor, but is generally used as a way of counting the number of people living in poverty at any one time and place, and monitoring how the headcount changes over time and place. It can be difficult to ascertain the level of income or market prices in the developing world, where subsistence living adds complexity to determining equivalent market prices. This is particularly so where people depend in part on natural resources, where water, firewood, other non-timber forest products and fish, for example, may be collected for subsistence as well as for trade.

The concept of social exclusion was developed in the industrialized world in recognition of the extent and nature of the experience of marginalization and deprivation (Laderchi *et al.*, 2003). Social exclusion is socially defined and rather than focusing primarily on individuals, often refers to groups of people, for example racial groups and the aged. It necessarily has a multi-dimensional focus, reflecting on the linkages between different forms of deprivation. Social exclusion is less often applied to analyses of poverty in the developing world, but can be a useful concept in that it reflects structural characteristics of society and distributional issues, and brings attention to these.

Participatory methods of defining and understanding poverty are those which are employed to ask people themselves what it means to be poor and what they understand the magnitude of poverty to be. Rather than externally imposed definitions, then, such an approach enables people to draw on their own experiences and those of people around them. Participatory approaches as pioneered by Robert Chambers (1994, 1997) aim to facilitate discussion and analysis led by people themselves, with the researchers or practitioners listening but not leading. There is a wide range of participatory methods used to facilitate such discussion, including wealth ranking, participatory mapping, seasonal calendars and timelines (see, for example, Mikkelsen, 2005; Narayanasamy, 2009).

Laderchi *et al.* (2003) conclude that it does matter how poverty is defined and understood for developing policies to reduce poverty and that approaches that draw on several of the approaches reviewed is necessary. Building on this consensus that poverty is experienced in a multi-dimensional way and should be addressed through multiple, interacting measures, a Multidimensional Poverty Index (MPI) was developed in the 2000s (Alkire and Santos, 2010). The MPI brings together into one measure ten indicators of deprivation within the categories of health, education and standard of living, and enables a richer depiction of poverty, whilst also enabling comparisons over time and space.

The question of tracking the experience of poverty over time is seen as particularly relevant for research into chronic poverty. The chronically poor are defined by Shepherd (2011: 2) as being

> poor over many years, and may pass their poverty on to the next generation. One of the reasons for interest in the extent to which and why people are poor over long periods of time is that it may become harder to escape poverty the longer you are poor.

The issue of time is emphasized in Addison *et al.*'s (2009) identification of three key dimensions that should inform research into poverty: research should focus on poverty dynamics, being carried out 'over the life course and across generations'; research should include multidimensional concepts and measures of poverty; and, should be cross-disciplinary, bringing insights and methods from different disciplines, including quantitative and qualitative approaches. Insights from research into chronic poverty bring to the fore the need to understand changes in the experience and extent of poverty over time, for individuals, households and different social groups, as well as the multidimensional nature of the experience and manifestation of poverty.

The shift in recognition of the complexity and diversity of the experience of poverty reinforces the need to move beyond the vicious circle portrayal of the relationship between poverty and the environment. Frameworks are needed that facilitate a more nuanced understanding of the linkages, reflecting diversity in the nature and experience of poverty and wellbeing, between individuals and groups and over time.

The environment and natural resources

Poor people in developing countries, particularly in rural areas, are more directly dependent on their immediate environment than most other people (Barbier, 2010). We are all dependent on the environment, but the dependence of poor, especially rural, people in developing countries is more critical for their daily survival. Opportunities for employment and income-generating activities that do not involve natural resources are limited. It is essential then, if poverty is to be addressed, that the interactions of poor people with their environment are understood.

The natural environment can be seen as providing people with a range of services, including provision of natural resources, a sink for many types and forms of waste (including carbon dioxide and other greenhouse gases) and regulatory functions, where ecological processes such as regulating water flow and recycling essential elements, enables life to continue on our planet. The environment, then, is a broad term and includes natural resources, which can be either renewable (they can replenish themselves, providing the stock, or population, is above a certain limit, or threshold), such as fisheries, forests and grazing land, or non-renewable, that is, the resource cannot replenish itself, such as oil, coal and minerals. The term 'environment' also includes other goods and services, such as clean air, beautiful landscapes and water regulation.

Since the mid-1980s, the term 'environmental services' has broadly been replaced by 'ecosystem services' (Lele *et al.*, 2013), which the Millennium Ecosystem Assessment defines as 'the benefits people obtain from ecosystems', with an ecosystem defined as 'a dynamic complex of plant, animal, and microorganism communities and the nonliving environment, interacting as a functional unit' (MA, 2005: V). The MA identifies four categories of ecosystem services, as shown in Table 1.1.

There are other ways of categorizing ecosystem services and the MA acknowledges that there are overlaps between the service categories, but argue that this categorization enables a broad range of services vital for human well-being to be recognized. The use of the term 'services' is considered contentious by some as ecosystem functions are not universally viewed as services (see Lele *et al.*, 2013 for a review of the debates). In addition, the language and analyses of ecosystem services have become closely associated with economic valuation, where economic values of the different services are estimated as a way of showing their value to human welfare and informing decision-making. This is also contentious, partly because not everyone agrees that placing economic values on nature is appropriate but also because of the difficulties encountered in some of the methods and approaches of economic valuation (Lele *et al.*, 2013).

Nevertheless, the categorization of ecosystem services into the four broad categories provides an overview of the types of relationships people have with the environment, and how and why people interact with the environment, to inform readers of what is meant by the environment in this text. The term 'natural resources' is also widely used in the book, referring to resources such as water, land, forests and fisheries. There is an emphasis within the book on renewable natural resources as these are particularly important in the everyday lives of many people in the developing world, especially in rural areas. There is a close relationship between natural resources and the environment, or environmental resources, and both terms are used in the book.

Table 1.1 Types of ecosystem services

Ecosystem service category	Examples
Provisioning	Food, water, wood for timber and fuel
Regulating	Water purification, regulation of the climate
Cultural	Spiritual, aesthetic, recreation
Supporting	Soil formation, nutrient cycling, primary production

Source: MA (2003: 37).

The condition and availability of environmental resources is of importance to poverty–environment relationships, but is not covered in detail in this book. There are many textbooks available that look at the condition of land, water, fisheries and forests, for example.

Cross-cutting themes

Before examining the frameworks and approaches in detail, there are a number of concepts and terms that are relevant to most, if not all, the following chapters, which require definition and review so that key interpretations taken, and characteristics assumed, in this book are clear. These concepts and terms are:

1   institutions;
2   social capital;
3   gender;
4   power;
5   property rights and regimes;
6   community;
7   'access to and control over' natural resources;
8   vulnerability.

Institutions

Analysing institutions is central to many of the frameworks and approaches included in this book. But what is meant by the term 'institution'? In keeping with broader literature and the analytical frameworks, institutions are understood to be 'rules of the game', as espoused in Douglas North's 1990 classic text *Institutions, Institutional Change and Economic Performance*. More fully, North defined institutions as 'the rules of the game in a society, or more formally, are the humanly devised constraints that shape human interaction', which 'reduce uncertainty by providing a structure to everyday life' (North, 1990: 3). Another classic definition of institutions was given by March and Olsen (1989: 22) as 'the routines, procedures, conventions, roles, strategies, organizational forms, and technologies around which political activity is constructed. We also mean beliefs, paradigms, codes, cultures and knowledge, that surround, support, elaborate, and contradict those roles and routines'. This definition highlights the vast diversity of institutions that mediate and influence decision-making and behaviour in people's lives. Institutions are not, then, the same as organisations and can be a bit elusive and hard to identify, understand and analyse. Taking an institutional approach to analysis recognizes that focusing on organizations alone is insufficient for gaining a full picture of how linkages and interactions develop and are maintained.

Within literature on accessing natural resources, Leach *et al.* (1997: 5) define institutions as 'regularized patterns of behavior between individuals and groups in society' and Cleaver (2012: 8) as 'arrangements between people which are reproduced and regularised across time and space and which are subject to constant processes of evolution and change'. The latter definition is particularly useful as it acknowledges that institutions may change over time and space, reminding analysts to investigate the dynamics of institutional arrangements. Institutions are intricately linked to management and governance systems and structures, enabling (or constraining) access to, and control over, natural resources. Institutions are often referred to as being classified in two categories: formal and informal, or modern and traditional. Cleaver (2002) suggests that it is more accurate to use the terminology of 'bureaucratic' and 'socially-embedded' institutions and offers the following definitions:'Bureaucratic institutions are those formalised arrangements based on explicit organisational structures, contracts and legal rights, often introduced by governments or development agencies. Socially embedded institutions are those based on culture, social organisation and daily practice' (Cleaver, 2002: 13).

It is this categorization of institutions that is drawn on and used throughout the book, recognizing that institutions at times referred to as 'traditional' or 'informal' may be misleading as they may be quite recently developed or modified and may be considered quite formal within a particular setting. Some institutions may bridge the two categories, so distinct boundaries between bureaucratic and socially-embedded institutions may not always be clear.

'Institutions' encompass a broad range of relations, rules and arrangements that both constrain behaviour and decision-making as well as in other situations reduce transaction costs and make things easier to happen. Institutions play a critical role in mediating linkages between poverty and the environment and can range from formal policies of the state to local norms, gender relations and taboos. The frameworks reviewed in this book, particularly critical institutionalism, the Environmental Entitlements approach, the Institutional Analysis and Development framework and the Sustainable Livelihoods framework, highlight the role of institutions and provide ways of thinking about and investigating these roles.

Social capital

Managing natural resources very often requires collective action, which, in turn requires that people work together to make and enforce rules. Collective action is assisted by the existence of trust and feelings of reciprocity between those involved in managing a natural resource. This is referred to as 'social capital', a concept that arises in relation to several of the frameworks examined in this book, but particularly in relation to the Sustainable Livelihoods framework and social network analysis. One of the most often cited definitions of social capital is that put forward by Putnam, who refers to social capital as 'connections among individuals – social networks and the norms of reciprocity and trustworthiness that arise from them' (2000: 19). Social capital can be seen as an asset that people can access and draw on. Think of your family, friends and colleagues you could turn to in times of need; these relations contribute to your social capital. Social capital is best viewed in relational terms rather than as something one can possess individually, without interaction with others.

Several types of social capital are identified in the literature (see Woolcock, 2001, for example):

- *Bonding capital:* these are the linkages between people sharing similar objectives and characteristics, such as relations among family members and close friends.
- *Bridging capital:* refers to individuals and groups having links with others who do not have the same objectives, such as relations among more distant friends, associates and colleagues.
- *Linking capital:* refers to the ability of groups to engage with external agencies, with connections across different levels within a hierarchy.

Pretty and Ward (2001) identify four key aspects of social capital, forming a framework that can enable investigation and understanding of the characteristics and manifestations of social capital:

- *Relations of trust:* trust is critical for cooperation and so is an important element of social capital. It takes time to build trust, but this is needed if there is to be belief that someone will act as they have agreed to act and social obligation is to be created. Trust can be easily broken and cooperation in natural resource governance will not be easy, or even possible, in the absence of trust.
- *Reciprocity and exchanges:* reciprocal behaviour and exchange of resources contribute to increasing trust over time.
- *Common rules, norms and sanctions:* these need to be mutually agreed or handed-down and are essential for putting in place norms that put group interests above those of the individual.
- *Connectedness, networks and groups:* there are different types of connections that support social networks. The number of linkages within a social network will also be important in influencing how these connections contribute to, or enable, social capital.

Social capital is difficult to identify and measure, making the use of proxy indicators necessary, such as membership of groups or networks, or manifestations of trust in others. Social capital has an important role to play within poverty–environment relations, providing a means through which benefits from natural resources can be accessed and maintained.

Gender

Gender is a form of social differentiation and gender relations form a type of institution that is critical in many analyses of poverty–environment relationships, closely related to the distribution of power within a society. Gender is different from being male or female, i.e. it is different to sex. Gender analysis is concerned with analysing gender relations, that is, roles and relationships amongst and between men and women that are socially constructed. These relationships are often, even usually, unequal in power and equality, and therefore have implications for how men and women use, access and make decisions about natural resources. The analysis of gender relations is not then solely concerned with how men and women use natural resources differently, but with analysing who makes decisions, how these decisions affect women and men, how gender relations beyond the natural resource influence access to and control over natural resources. Awareness and analysis of gender is therefore critical in much analysis of poverty–environment relations and forms part of the approaches to analysing these interactions covered in many of the chapters.

Power

Why is power a matter of concern and interest in investigating and analysing poverty–environment relations? Power matters because power can be exercised to gain access to, and control over, environmental resources, or, more precisely, over people and their rights over, and access to, environmental resources. Power can be productive, enabling decisions to be made, resources to be managed and livelihood benefits gained from those resources. It can also, however, be manipulative and destructive, preventing people from having adequate access to land, water and forests, for example. Although identifying and locating power is critical for understanding many poverty–environment relations, it is a difficult concept to define, identify and research (Few, 2002).

Power is often seen as a relational concept, that is, an individual, organization or group may only have, or be able to exercise, power over certain other individuals, organizations or groups, or at certain times and places. Power may not be intrinsic; someone may only hold power depending on the circumstances and relationships. It may come with position, status or gender. Analysis of poverty–environment relations, then, may involve the identification and analysis of power relations. This involves identifying who makes what decisions, why they are the ones to make those decisions and how these decisions impact on other people accessing, or wanting to access, environmental resources. Power relations are a category of social relations and in some situations may be closely related to gender relations, where, for example, men may control the determination of, or dominate negotiations over, which natural resource products from a forest can be gathered by women and which by men.

Power relations form part of the institutional arrangements that enable or constrain access to environmental resources. Power relations may be part of the 'rules of the game' that shape access to and control over environmental resources and so are subject to institutional analysis in investigating poverty–environment relations. Investigating power relations is also critical for political ecology and analysis of the arrangements and performance of governance. Whilst the concept of power is discussed in many of the chapters in this book, the concept is further reflected on in Chapter 8, where further literature and interpretations of the concept are reviewed.

Property rights and property regimes

Natural resources are governed by different types of property regimes. Understanding what type of regime is in place is essential for understanding whether and how people may benefit from a resource and who is responsible for looking after that resource. To clarify, property is an economic term that has been defined by Bromley (1991: 2) as 'a benefit or income stream', rather than a tangible object. He goes onto define a property right as 'a claim to a benefit or income stream that the state will agree to protect' (1991: 2). Having rights is one thing, but rights come along with duties as well, so rights are constrained and enabled by rules. A property regime refers to how rights are structured and to the rules under which rights can be realized. Understanding poverty–environment relationships will often involve an analysis of the property regimes and of the property rights that people have within that regime. Four types of property regimes are identified in the literature: private, common, state and open, with different types and characteristics of rights and duties within each regime (Hanna *et al.*, 1996). Perhaps the most famous narrative on natural resource property regimes is that of Garrett Hardin's 'tragedy of the commons' (TofC) (1968). This is explained in Box 1.2.

Box 1.2 Hardin's 'tragedy of the commons'

Hardin (1968) argued that common ownership of a resource cannot succeed, because there is innate human desire to maximise individual benefits that will inevitably cause overuse and eventually resource degradation. He gave a metaphor of herders sharing common grazing land. Each herder wants to get as much out of the grazing land as they can, so they put as many animals out to graze on the land as they desire. This may be fine for many years, but at some point, the land will be overgrazed and degraded, leading to individual ruin. Hardin's metaphor has been used to explain overgrazing and other examples of environmental degradation (e.g. the emission of greenhouse gases into the atmosphere) ever since, and has informed many natural resource management approaches.

Critics of the TofC suggest that Hardin confused an open-access regime with a common property regime. Within an open access regime anyone can come along and use the resource and there are no rules defining how much of a resource someone can take and how they can take it. In a common property regime, however, there are rules that not only exclude non-members from drawing on the resource, but there may also be rules about how much people can take, when and how. The metaphor of a tragedy is also criticized for failing to recognize the possibility that resource users might work together and come up with an agreement about how many animals to graze, for example. There have also been accusations that the metaphor does not reflect how common pool resources have been used throughout history. What is perhaps most important about this metaphor, however, are the implications. The wide acceptance of the tragedy has contributed to a perception that private property rights or state ownership were the only solutions for managing common pool resources. Land should be parcelled up and individuals given rights over grazing or for farming, rather than sharing land.

Partly inspired by a rejection of the TofC, other researchers in the 1970s and 1980s investigated how groups of people have come together to agree on how resources should be shared and used. Fikret Berkes (1989) and Elinor Ostrom (1990) are key theorists in the field of common property theory. This body of theory challenges the TofC thesis that suggests that common property management necessarily leads to the abuse of natural resources. Instead, the theory recognizes that many natural resources are actually governed by regulations agreed by groups of users, rather than set down in state law. Many natural resources are governed under common property regimes; a collective of people with rights over a resource, able to prevent people from outside their group from using the resource. This might be the case in pastureland, forests and irrigation systems. Common property is different from 'open access' where there are no rules or limits on who can extract resources, such as in many marine or inland fisheries and where the TofC may indeed apply.

There are no natural resources that are inherently common property, as any resource could be managed by more than one type of regime, but they may be common pool. 'Common pool' refers to the characteristics of resources, whereas 'common property' refers to the governing arrangements. The key characteristics of common pool resources are the difficulty of excluding people from their use (they are 'non-excludable') and by the fact that extraction by one person affects the availability of the resource for others (they are 'subtractable'). There is then, a difference between common pool resources and common property regimes, but unhelpfully both are 'CPR's! You will even find the term 'common property resources' used, yet another CPR, but this is not often used, as regime is more accurate to use than resources in this context, with no resources being inherently common property. Within a common property regime, it is possible to exclude people from using the resource, so identification of the rules is important for understanding who benefits from resources and why. Very often, it is the poor who are very dependent on resources held within a common property regime, whether this is a forest where they collect firewood and medicinal plants or pastureland where their animals are grazed. If the management regime of such resources changes, the poor may suffer further hardship.

In many situations, however, it is difficult to determine which type of property regime exists and, in fact, the property regime could be a hybrid, that is, a mix of regime types. Take, for example, a lake fishery in a low-income country, which is state property, held in trust by government for the people. In addition to being within a state-governed regime, there could be elements of open access, as the government does not want to limit access and it is difficult and costly to police the entire lake. There could also be elements of a common property regime, as certain procedures have to be followed to gain access to the lake, within rules created by the resource users themselves. A new fisher might have to get permission from a community leader to fish, as well as buy a permit and be employed on a boat, and comply with locally agreed rules and regulations. So, it is not always easy to determine which regime dominates.

Community

Two dimensions are examined with respect to the concept of 'community'. First, the shift towards greater participation of resource users in the management of natural resources and therefore a focus on 'communities', and second, key critiques of the concept of community. These are two significant areas of debate and concern within literature and practice associated with poverty–environment relationships.

Since at least the 1980s, there has been a shift in approach to the management of natural resources in developing countries, from more centralized control, with the exclusion of local people from management and use, to more participatory forms. This shift resulted from the broader trend towards decentralization of government functions, the growing emphasis on participation in development practice and the concern that central government had failed to sustainably manage natural resources. The shift towards more community-based natural resource management (CBNRM) has largely occurred through top-down projects (usually donor funded) and policies, in contrast to more bottom-up common property regimes.

CBNRM is a term particularly used to refer to the participation of local people in national park management, but there are other forms of CBNRM such as community-based forest management. In addition, there are related forms of collaborative management, with users of the natural resource working collaboratively with government, such as Joint Forest Management in India and fisheries co-management. Central to CBNRM is the belief that natural resources can be sustainably managed and conserved through the participation of local communities and resource users in decision-making. The approach has been particularly attractive for the donor community as there has been a perception that such approaches offer the potential for 'win–win' outcomes, i.e. both the conservation of the natural resource and improved livelihoods of local communities. This is often far from realized in practice (Blaikie, 2006; Dressler *et al.*, 2010).

There are multiple reasons given in the literature as to why so many CBNRM initiatives have failed to deliver on both conservation and improved livelihoods, or perhaps even either. Such reasons include the lack of genuine devolution of power and resources to decentralized structures (Larson and Ribot, 2004) and the desire for those in power to keep control over resources that can yield wealth and influence, thereby preventing 'real' participation of the poor in decision-making and management and benefits to the poor (Nelson and Agrawal, 2008). In addition, inadequate understanding of who local people are, who uses the natural resources and should have a say in management, and of the power dynamics within local areas, has often led to inappropriate design of management structures, leading to elite capture and even cases where poor people's access to natural resources was further limited. This can in part be attributed to inappropriate use and understanding of the concept of 'community'.

The notion of a community is as contentious and difficult in the area of natural resource management and environment as it is in other spheres of social concern. The reason for this is because the term has been used in a way that gives an impression that local people dependent on a natural resource can be spatially defined and have a homogeneous social structure and shared norms (Agrawal and Gibson, 1999). Of course, this is not the case for almost any community. There will inevitably be divisions within a group of people, and diverse and complex power relations; also, households dependent on a particular resource may not be easily defined in a spatial sense, particularly in areas where there is migration. It is difficult, however, to avoid using the word 'community'. When it is used, it should encompass recognition of social and economic diversity, with investigation of the range of actors and interests within a community, how these influence decision-making and who is excluded and marginalized from such decision-making. This implies investigation into how power is distributed and manifested within 'communities'. This could be carried out, for example, by identifying and analysing institutions, by mapping social relations through the use of social network analysis or by taking a political ecology approach, as set out in the following chapters.

'Access to and control over' natural resources

Fundamental to the question of whether or not, and how much, people benefit from natural resources around them is whether they have access to those resources and to what extent they exercise control in terms of deciding how much to extract, when and how. In analysing the relationship between poverty and the environment, the question of access will often arise. Ribot and Peluso (2003: 153) define access as 'the ability to benefit from things – including material objects, persons, institutions, and symbols'. They suggest that access is about the *ability to benefit* rather than about rights as in property theory because this highlights the range of social relationships that can constrain or enable people to benefit from resources. It is not just property relations that will facilitate or constrain benefit, but also kinship, employment and gender, for example. Property, then, is one type of access relationship, but there are others. These factors will also influence the degree and nature of 'control' that people have in relation to managing natural resources, influencing the access that other people have and the condition of natural resource.

The frameworks set out in this book enable the analysis of access, with recognition of different forms of access and that not everyone will have direct access to a natural resource, but may have to gain and maintain access through others.

Vulnerability

Vulnerability is an important concept in the analysis of poverty–environment relationships as there are multiple sources and manifestations of vulnerability, both physical and social, that will impact on how people access and use environmental resources or are affected by changes in such resources. As sources, and scale, of vulnerability will change over time and space, the dynamic nature of vulnerability must also be taken into consideration. The concept of vulnerability has particularly become a focus of concern within studies and policy on climate change adaptation. Adger (2006: 270) suggests that vulnerability is most often conceptualized as 'being constituted by components that include exposure and sensitivity to perturbations or external stresses, and the capacity to adapt. Exposure is the nature and degree to which a system experiences environmental or socio-political stress'. Critical to understanding the nature and degree of vulnerability, then, is identifying sources of stress, their magnitude, frequency, duration and the area over which they are found. The capacity to cope with and adapt to change will also influence the level and nature of vulnerability.

A note on 'frameworks'

The chapters in this book do not include or discuss theories and models, but focus on frameworks and approaches. It would be a good idea, then, to be clear what is meant by a 'framework' as opposed to a theory or model. A framework identifies key variables and shows how these are structured and linked in relation to a particular issue. It does not, however, provide a mechanism to make predictions on what might happen given a set of variables or conditions. A framework is more of a tool for analysis. Miles and Huberman (1994: 18) state that a conceptual framework 'explains, either graphically or in narrative form, the main things to be studied – the key factors, constructs or variables – and the presumed relationships among them. Frameworks can be rudimentary or elaborate, theory-driven or commonsensical, descriptive or causal'.

A theory, in contrast, includes a set of assumptions about the relationship between variables and outcomes in an attempt to explain cause and effect. Schutt (2012: 37) defines theory as 'a logically interrelated set of propositions that helps us make sense of many interrelated phenomenon and predict behaviour and attitudes that are likely to occur when certain conditions are met'.

In turn, models are more concerned with making predictions than theory is and often rely on mathematical tools. They may require a lot of data to be able to construct reliable and useful predictions based on past behaviour and observations, and data relating to variables identified as important for offering explanation and prediction.

Frameworks are, then, less ambitious and looser. They offer a tool to help a researcher answer questions, but do need to be used with care, so that cause-and-effect conclusions are not made which cannot be justified. A framework may help a researcher to find a way into a complex situation by breaking it down into components, providing a structure for the key variables and mapping out how these variables may be connected. A researcher may focus on one part of a framework within a study rather than investigate and use the entire framework. This may be particularly appropriate for investigating a particular variable or context of a framework in depth. Frameworks are not static, but are constantly being adapted and modified to reflect developments in theory and concepts, but also to reflect research findings and new research contexts. References to examples of modifications to the frameworks included in this book are noted in the chapters, but other modifications and additions can be found and will continue to be made.

Not all of the chapters focus on frameworks, but include broader approaches, or ways of thinking, for example social network analysis includes many types of tools and methods but overall is best thought of as a perspective or approach that focuses on the relations among actors rather than on actor attributes. Approaches and frameworks are informed by theory and models and can be used in conjunction with these too. These are referred to where relevant in each chapter.

Frameworks for the analysis of poverty–environment and people–environment relationships are numerous and there are many more than are presented in this book. Fisher *et al.* (2013) review nine frameworks that enable examination of poverty–environment relationships as part of their research into investigating linkages between ecosystem services and poverty alleviation. From this review, Fisher *et al.* (2014) develop their own framework that identifies how a range of ecosystem services are accessed and contribute to poverty reduction and poverty prevention, both seen as contributing to overall wellbeing, understood in terms of the five dimensions of wellbeing set out by Narayan *et al.* (1999, 2000). Fisher *et al.*'s (2013, 2014) interest in poverty and ecosystem services reflects recent interest in ecosystem services arising from the Millennium Ecosystem Assessment (MA, 2005) and research under the Ecosystem Services for Poverty Alleviation programme (www. espa.ac.uk), and builds on frameworks and approaches used to investigate poverty–environment relationships.

Structure of the book

The review of frameworks and approaches begins in Chapter 2 with an exploration of the complex and diverse area of political ecology. This is an 'umbrella' term for a broad range of approaches drawing on diverse disciplines to investigate people–environment interactions, particularly in relation to environmental degradation. At the heart of political ecology is the recognition that power matters and that power will influence how people access natural resources and whether, or to what extent, they are able to control, or manage, those resources. The chapter provides an introduction to the field, identifies key themes and draws on case studies to identify the characteristics of a political ecology approach and what such an approach can reveal about poverty–environment relationships. The approach taken to political ecology in this chapter is influenced by Blaikie (1985) and Leach and Mearns (1996), amongst others, situated within development studies, examining and challenging 'dominant narratives' and 'received wisdom'.

Chapter 3 focuses on institutional analysis, beginning with a reminder of what institutions are understood to be and reviewing why they matter. Although institutions form part of many other analytical approaches and frameworks covered in other chapters, for example the Sustainable Livelihoods framework in Chapter 5, this chapter focuses on Critical Institutionalism (Cleaver, 2012), the related

'Environmental Entitlements' approach developed by Leach *et al.* (1997, 1999) and the Institutional Analysis and Development (IAD) framework developed by E. Ostrom (see, for example, Ostrom *et al.*, 1994). These are explained in detail, and case study examples illustrate how they have been applied and what they reveal about how people interact with the environment on which they depend.

The cross-cutting concept of gender is investigated within Chapter 4. Whilst gender is a concern and dimension to be acknowledged and investigated within many other approaches and frameworks, including the Sustainable Livelihoods framework for example, it is worthy of a dedicated chapter to examine in more detail the emergence and development of thinking and literature in relation to the environment. Understanding of the key issues and concepts from the literature on gender, development and environment is of critical importance in being able to effectively use many of the frameworks in this book. As observed earlier, gender is one source of influence on the relationships between people and the environment; gender relations act as institutions that enable or constrain access to and control over natural resources. Thinking on these relationships has, however, changed over time and these changes are traced in Chapter 4. The chapter advocates the use of gender as a 'lens' to investigate how men and women access and are affected by environmental resources, with literature on gender and land, forestry and fisheries reviewed. No one approach or framework is advocated for or specifically reviewed in this chapter, though the work of Cornwall (see, for example, 2007) and Agarwal (1994, 2010) is particularly drawn on.

The analysis of livelihoods and wellbeing is the subject of Chapter 5, focusing particularly on the Sustainable Livelihoods approach (SLA) and framework (SLF) (Carney, 1998; Scoones, 1998), the Millennium Ecosystem Assessment (MA) frameworks (MA, 2003) and the Wellbeing in Developing Countries approach (White, 2010). The SLA and SLF were developed in the 1990s in recognition of the complexity of poverty and livelihoods and the need for a deeper analysis of how livelihood strategies are developed and maintained to inform the development and implementation of more effective poverty reduction interventions. Natural resources form part of the assets that an individual may possess or have access to. Their role in livelihood strategies and how access to and control over natural resources are influenced by policies, institutions and processes can be analysed using the SLF. A focus on wellbeing in relation to poverty–environment relationships is much more recent and as a consequence there are a limited number of examples of the application of the Wellbeing in Developing Countries approach to people–environment interactions, though examples in the fisheries sector illustrate the utility of the approach. Reference to the MA frameworks has led to particular interest in the interactions between ecosystem services and poverty and wellbeing (see Fisher *et al.*, 2013, for example).

The nature of relationships between people and the environment is influenced by social relations, therefore social network analysis, the subject of Chapter 6, is included as it provides an approach to map and investigate social relations within a defined group of actors, or to investigate the personal relations of individual actors. Through such mapping, relationships of influence and importance on a particular matter, such as access to forests or fisheries, can be identified and investigated. The chapter provides an introduction to social network analysis, focusing on how the approach has been used within natural resource settings in the global South. Bodin and Prell's (2011) edited volume examining the application of social network analysis in natural resource settings is a particularly useful resource for exploring the potential use of this analytical approach.

Governance is an overarching concern of many of the frameworks and so forms the focus of Chapter 7. The chapter introduces governance, good governance and principles of governance. There are many examples of the decentralization of natural resource governance throughout the world and key concerns related to the limited success associated with such decentralization are identified, namely accountability and representation. Several frameworks for analysing natural resource governance are then reviewed: Franks and Cleaver's (2007) framework for analysing water governance, the Interactive Governance and Governability approach (Kooiman *et al.*, 2008) and Batterbury and Fernando's (2006) governance analysis components. Key challenges within governance are then explored, of power, scale and coping with change (i.e. adaptive governance).

The book concludes by reflecting on what the frameworks and approaches suggest really matters in an analysis of poverty–environment relationships and identifies key common themes. These common themes and concepts are then reviewed, building on how they are used in the frameworks and approaches, focusing on power, institutions, access, poverty, livelihoods and wellbeing, gender, narratives/myths and scale. The chapter introduces key data collection methods associated with many of the frameworks and approaches, focusing on ethnographic, mixed and participatory methods. Finally, the book closes with a few observations on the nature and use of frameworks and approaches.

Summary of key points

1   The portrayal of poverty and the environment being linked in a vicious circle or downward spiral is too simplistic and unhelpful. Such portrayals fail to acknowledge the underlying and wider factors that influence choice, access and livelihoods. Theories and frameworks exist that can be used to analyse how the poor interact with the environment in specific contexts and generate a deeper level of understanding. These analytical frameworks and approaches include the analysis of gender relations, institutions, livelihoods, power, social networks and governance.

2   The portrayal of poverty and the environment as a vicious circle reflects wider attitudes to the relationship between environment and development, where it has been argued that environmental protection cannot be prioritized until there is more economic development in a country. Such a position has been challenged by the concept of sustainable development, though limited progress has been made in working towards a more sustainable approach to development.

3   At the heart of poverty–environment linkages is the question of who has 'access to and control over' environmental resources. Access is dependent on a range of institutions, from gender relations to having power and influence, and may vary over time. 'Control over' refers to having the power to manage environmental resources, making decisions over how much and what can be extracted, and when and where resources can be extracted.

4   Recognition that poverty is multi-dimensional, complex and dynamic is important for analysing and understanding poverty–environment relationships. Poverty is much more than having a low income; the multi-faceted nature of poverty and the range of individual experiences mean that in investigating poverty–environment relationships, assumptions about the nature of poverty cannot be made. In addition, the nature of poverty–environment relations will be multi-dimensional, with relationships with health, education and vulnerability, for example.

5   The environment can be seen as providing a range of products and services that people everywhere rely on. Many poor people in developing countries, particularly in rural areas, however, rely directly and substantially on natural resources, whether that is soil, forests, grazing land, water or fisheries.

6   A number of concepts and variables cut across the frameworks included in the book. These include: institutions, social capital, gender, power, property rights and regimes, community, access to and control over resources and vulnerability. No doubt other cross-cutting concepts and themes could be identified, but these are sufficient for embarking on an examination of analytical frameworks that can be used to generate an informed understanding of poverty–environment relations.

Further reading

There are a number of key texts that further develop some of the key concepts and arguments presented in this chapter. There are of course many others, some of which are referred to and drawn on in subsequent chapters.

Adams, W.M. (2009) *Green Development: Environment and Sustainability in a Developing World*, 3rd edition, London: Routledge (see also 1990 and 2001 editions).
Green Development is an excellent text, providing a critical reflection on how the relationship between environment and development has been understood and responded to, particularly through the concept of sustainable development, both in theory and practice. The text sets out the origins and uptake of the concept, exploring mainstream approaches to sustainable development through ecological modernization and environmental economics, for example, and more radical critiques. In doing so, it introduces key approaches and concepts to analysing environment and development interactions, including ecological economics and political ecology. It goes on to apply the concept to ecosystems or sectors such as drylands, forests, biodiversity conservation, water and urban and industrial development. The text concludes by examining the opportunities for reforming 'green development' or offering a more radical response through resistance and protest.

DFID, EC, UNDP and the World Bank (2002) *Linking Poverty Reduction and Environmental Management*, Washington, DC: World Bank.

This is a policy-oriented text, written for the 2002 World Summit on Sustainable Development (WSSD) held ten years after the 1992 United Nations Conference on Environment and Development, produced by the UK's Department for International Development, the European Commission, the United Nations Development Programme and the World Bank. The text is included here as a key reading because it challenges the vicious circle portrayal of poverty–environment relationships, arguing that poverty–environment linkages are dynamic and context specific and that poor people should be viewed as part of the solution to environmental problems, rather than part of the problem. The report explores the importance of the environment for livelihoods and health, and in the context of vulnerability, as well as for economic growth. The report, then, is not radical in the sense that it does not challenge economic growth, but it sets out a framework for understanding the role of environmental management in tackling poverty. In doing so it goes beyond a focus on poverty and environment to recognize the importance of governance in how poverty and environment linkages are manifested and responded to, as well as the need to 'improve' the quality of growth and reform international and industrial country policies to support improved management of the environment and reduced poverty.

References

Adams, W.M. (2009) *Green Development: Environment and Sustainability in a Developing World*, 3rd edition, London: Routledge.

Addison, T., Hulme, D. and Kanbur, R. (2009) 'Poverty dynamics: Measurement and understanding from an interdisciplinary perspective', in Addison, T., Hulme, D. and Kanbur, R. (eds), *Poverty Dynamics: Interdisciplinary Perspectives*, Oxford: Oxford University Press.

Adger, W.N. (2006) 'Vulnerability', *Global Environmental Change*, 16: 268–281.

Agarwal, B. (1994) *A Field of One's Own: Gender and Land Rights in South Asia*, Cambridge: Cambridge University Press.

Agarwal, B. (2010) *Gender and Green Governance: The Political Economy of Women's Presence Within and Beyond Community Forestry*, Oxford: Oxford University Press.

Agrawal, A. and Gibson, C.C. (1999) 'Enchantment and disenchantment: The role of community in natural resource conservation', *World Development*, 2(4): 629–649.

Alkire, S. and Santos, M.E. (2010) 'Acute multidimensional poverty: A new index for developing countries', *OPHI Working Paper No. 38*, Oxford: Oxford Department of International Development, Queen Elizabeth House, University of Oxford.

Barbier, E.B. (2010) 'Poverty, development, and environment', *Environment and Development Economics*, 15: 635–660.

Bass, S., Reid, H., Satterthwaite, D. and Steele, P. (2005) *Reducing Poverty and Sustaining the Environment: The Politics of Local Engagement*, London: Earthscan.

Batterbury, S.P.J. and Fernando, J.L. (2006) 'Rescaling governance and the impacts of political and environmental decentralization: An introduction', *World Development*, 34(11): 1851–1863.

Berkes, F. (1989) *Common Property Resources*, London: Belhaven Press.

Blaikie, P. (1985) *The Political Economy of Soil Erosion in Developing Countries*, London: Longman.

Blaikie, P. (2006) 'Is small really beautiful? Community-based natural resource management in Malawi and Botswana', *World Development*, 34(11): 1942–1957.

Bodin, Ö. and Prell, C. (eds) (2011) *Social Network Analysis and Natural Resource Management*, Cambridge: Cambridge University Press.

Bromley, D. (1991) *Environment and Economy: Property Rights and Public Policy*, Oxford: Basil Blackwell.

Carney, D. (ed.) (1998) *Sustainable Rural Livelihoods: What Contribution Can We Make?* London: Department for International Development.

Chambers, R. (1994) 'The origins and practice of participatory rural appraisal', *World Development*, 22(7): 953–969.

Chambers, R. (1997) *Whose Reality Counts? Putting the First Last*, London: Intermediate Technology Publications.

Cleaver, F. (2002) 'Reinventing institutions: Bricolage and the social embeddedness of natural resource management', *European Journal of Development Research*, 14(2): 11–30.

Cleaver, F. (2012) *Development Through Bricolage: Rethinking Institutions for Natural Resource Management*, London: Earthscan.

Clémençon, R. (2012) 'Welcome to the Anthropocene: Rio+20 and the meaning of sustainable development', *Journal of Environment & Development*, 21(3): 311–338.

Cornwall, A. (2007) 'Revisiting the "gender agenda"', *IDS Bulletin*, 38(2): 69–78.

Dasgupta, S., Laplante, B., Wang, H. and Wheeler, D. (2002) 'Confronting the environmental Kuznets curve', *Journal of Economic Perspectives*, 16(1): 147–168.

Dasgupta, S., Deichmann, U., Meisner, C. and Wheeler, D. (2005) 'Where is the poverty-environment nexus? Evidence from Cambodia, Lao PDR, and Vietnam', *World Development*, 33(4): 617–638.

DFID, EC, UNDP and the World Bank (2002) *Linking Poverty Reduction and Environmental Management*, Washington, DC: World Bank.

Dressler, W., Büscher, B., Schoon, M., Brockington, D., Hayes, T., Kull, C.A., McCarthy, J. and Shrestha, K. (2010) 'From hope to crisis and back again? A critical history of the global CBNRM narrative', *Environmental Conservation*, 37(1): 5–15.

Few, R. (2002) 'Researching actor power: Analyzing mechanisms of interaction in negotiations over space', *Area*, 34(1): 29–38.

Fisher, J.A., Patenaude, G., Meir, P., Nightingale, A.J., Rounsevell, M.D.A., Williams, M. and Woodhouse, I.H. (2013) 'Strengthening conceptual foundations: Analysing frameworks for ecosystem services and poverty alleviation research', *Global Environmental Change*, 23(5): 1098–1111.

Fisher, J.A., Patenaude, G., Giri, K., Lewis, K., Meir, P., Pinho, P., Rounsevell, M.D.A. and Williams, M. (2014) 'Understanding the relationships between ecosystem services and poverty alleviation: A conceptual framework', *Ecosystem Services*, 7: 34–45.

Franks, T. and Cleaver, F. (2007) 'Water governance and poverty: A framework for analysis', *Progress in Development Studies*, 7(4): 291–306.

Hanna, S., Folke, C. and Mäler, K-G. (1996) 'Property rights and the natural environment', in Hanna, S., Folke, C. and Mäler. K-G. (eds), *Rights to Nature: Ecological, Economic, Cultural and Political Principles*, Washington, DC: Island Press, pp. 1–10.

Hardin, G. (1968) 'The tragedy of the commons', *Science*, 162(3859): 1243–1248.

Harris, D., Moore, M. and Schmitz, H. (2009) 'Country classifications for a changing world', *IDS Working Paper 326*, Brighton: Institute of Development Studies.

Haughton, J. and Khandker, S.R. (2009) *Handbook on Poverty and Inequality*, Washington, DC: World Bank.

Kooiman, J., Bavinck, M., Chuenpagdee, R., Mahon, R. and Pullin, R. (2008) 'Interactive governance and governability: An introduction', *The Journal of Transdisciplinary Environmental Studies*, 7(1).

Laderchi, C.R., Saith, R. and Stewart, F. (2003) 'Does it matter that we do not agree on the definition of poverty? A comparison of four approaches', *Oxford Development Studies*, 31(3): 243–274.

Larson, A. and Ribot, J.C. (2004) 'Democratic decentralisation through a natural resource lens: An introduction', *European Journal of Development Research*, 16(1): 1–25.

Leach, M. and Mearns, R. (eds) (1996) *The Lie of the Land: Challenging Received Wisdom on the African Environment*, Oxford: The International African Institute, London, in association with James Currey.

Leach, M., Mearns, R. and Scoones, I. (1997) 'Environmental entitlements: A framework for understanding the institutional dynamics of environmental change', *IDS Discussion Paper*, no. 359, Brighton: Institute of Development Studies.

Leach, M., Mearns, R. and Scoones, I. (1999) 'Environmental entitlements: Dynamics and institutions in community-based natural resource management', *World Development*, 27(2): 225–247.

Lele, S., Springate-Baginski, O., Lakerveld, R., Deb, D. and Dash, P. (2013) 'Ecosystem services: Origins, contributions, pitfalls, and alternatives', *Conservation and Society*, 11(4): 343–358.

March, J.G. and Olsen, J.P. (1989) *Rediscovering Institutions: The Organizational Basis of Politics*, New York: Free Press.

Meadows, D., Meadows, D., Randers, J. and Behrens III, W.W. (1972) *The Limits to Growth: A Report for the Club of Rome's Project on the Predicament of Mankind*, New York: Universe Books.

Mikkelsen, B. (2005) *Methods for Development Work and Research: A New Guide for Practitioners*, 2nd edition, New Delhi: Sage.

Miles, M.B. and Huberman, A.M. (1994) *Qualitative Data Analysis*, Thousand Oaks, CA: Sage.

Millennium Ecosystem Assessment (MA) (2003) *Millennium Ecosystem Assessment, Ecosystems and Human Wellbeing: A Framework for Assessment*, Washington, DC: Island Press.

Millennium Ecosystem Assessment (MA) (2005) *Ecosystems and Human Wellbeing: Synthesis Report (Millennium Ecosystem Assessment)*, Washington, DC: Island Press.

Narayan, D., Chambers, R., Shah, M.K. and Petesch, P. (1999) *Global Synthesis: Consultations with the Poor*, Washington, DC: World Bank.

Narayan, D., Chambers, R., Shah, M.K. and Petesch, P. (2000) *Voices of the Poor: Crying Out for Change*, Oxford: Oxford University Press.

Narayanasamy, N. (2009) *Participatory Rural Appraisal: Principles, Methods and Application*, New Delhi: Sage.

Nelson, F. and Agrawal, A. (2008) 'Patronage or participation? Community-based natural resource management reform in Sub-Saharan Africa', *Development and Change*, 39(4): 557–585.

Nielsen, L. (2013) 'How to classify countries based on their level of development', *Social Indicators Research*, 114: 1087–1107.

North, D.C. (1990) *Institutions, Institutional Change and Economic Performance*, Cambridge: Cambridge University Press.

Ostrom, E. (1990) *Governing the Commons: The Evolution of Institutions for Collective Action*, Cambridge: Cambridge University Press.

Ostrom, E., Gardner, R. and Walker, J. (1994) *Rules, Games and Common-Pool Resources*, Ann Arbor: University of Michigan Press.

Pretty, J. and Ward, H. (2001) 'Social capital and the environment', *World Development*, 29(2): 209–227.

Putnam, R.D. (2000) *Bowling Alone: The Collapse and Revival of American Community*, New York: Simon & Schuster.

Ravallion, M., Chen, S. and Sangraula, P. (2009) 'Dollar a day revisited', *The World Bank Economic Review*, 23(2): 163–184.

Reed, D. (2002) 'Poverty and the environment: Can sustainable development survive globalization?', *Natural Resources Forum*, 26: 176–184.

Reed, D. (2006) *Escaping Poverty's Grasp: The Environmental Foundations of Poverty Reduction*, London: Earthscan.

Ribot, J.C. and Peluso, N.L. (2003) 'A theory of access', *Rural Sociology*, 68(2): 153–181.

Robeyns, I. (2005) 'The capability approach: A theoretical survey', *Journal of Human Development and Capabilities*, 6(1): 93–117.

Schutt, R.K. (2012) *Investigating the Social World: The Process and Practice of Social Research*, Thousand Oaks, CA: Sage.

Scoones, I. (1998) 'Sustainable rural livelihoods: A framework for analysis', *IDS Working Paper, 72*, Brighton: Institute of Development Studies.

Sen, A. (1999) *Commodities and Capabilities*, New Delhi: Oxford University Press.

Shepherd, A. (2011) *Tackling Chronic Poverty: The Policy Implications of Research on Chronic Poverty and Poverty Dynamics*, Manchester: Chronic Poverty Research Centre, University of Manchester.

Stern, D.I. (2004) 'The rise and fall of the environmental Kuznets curve', *World Development*, 32(8): 1419–1439.

Sumner, A. (2006) 'What is development studies?', *Development in Practice*, 16(6): 644–650.

Tezanos, S. and Sumner, A. (2013) 'Revisiting the meaning of development: A multidimensional taxonomy of developing countries', *Journal of Development Studies*, 49(12): 1728–1745.

White, S. (2010) 'Analysing wellbeing: A framework for development practice', *Development in Practice*, 20(2): 158–172.

Woolcock, M. (2001) 'The place of social capital in understanding social and economic outcomes', *Isuma: Canadian Journal of Policy Research*, 2(1): 11–17.

World Bank (2000) *World Development Report 2000/01: Attacking Poverty*, Washington, DC: World Bank.

World Bank (2008) *Poverty and the Environment: Understanding Linkages at the Household Level*, Washington, DC: World Bank.

World Commission on the Environment and Development (1987) *Our Common Future*, Oxford: Oxford University Press.

2 Political ecology

Introduction

In Chapter 1 it was suggested that relationships between poverty and the environment are complex and context specific. Being 'context specific' suggests that the political and economic situation matters. A multitude of political and economic factors from the household to the global level can affect how people gain and maintain access to natural resources, what benefits they derive and the condition of those resources. The influence of such factors on the status of natural resources, and on who benefits and how, can be investigated through taking a 'political ecology' approach.

Of all the frameworks and approaches considered in this book, political ecology is particularly difficult to define and pin down. It can be viewed as an umbrella term, that is, an overarching term encompassing a diverse range of conceptual analyses and underlying assumptions. At its heart is a concern with the nature and influence of power in influencing how environmental degradation is understood, explained and manifested. In taking a political ecology approach, a researcher recognizes that natural science understanding and solutions will not suffice on their own. Science, knowledge and policy are influenced by power, political processes and economic factors – in combination forming 'political ecology'. Political ecology has strong roots within rural environmental issues in developing countries, having been used to investigate and challenge dominant explanations of the causes of soil erosion, desertification and forest degradation. It can, however, be used in many settings, in any part of the world.

This chapter reviews definitions of the term 'political ecology', identifies key characteristics of the approach and provides examples of its application. It then goes on to examine how environmental science and ecology is viewed within a political ecology perspective. Political ecology analysis is often premised on a critique of dominant thinking (Robbins, 2012; Stott and Sullivan, 2000). Examples of such dominant thinking are set out, with three key themes identified from these. Explanation of the political ecology critique of these themes follows. Political ecology analysis may be undertaken and presented as a 'chain of explanation', bringing out the local, national and global context of people–environment relations. The discussion on 'chains of explanation' is followed by a reflection on feminist political ecology. A more detailed example of political ecology critique of dominant thinking is then presented for the case of desertification, followed by shorter examples of application of political ecology analysis. The chapter concludes by identifying key debates and issues that have arisen within the broad area of political ecology, before a summary of key points. Box 2.1 gives examples of the types of questions that might be asked in undertaking research that adopts a political ecology approach.

Box 2.1 **Questions that might be addressed by a political ecology approach**

- Why was a decision made to demarcate strict boundaries around a national park and how are people living in the area affected by this decision?
- Why were nomadic pastoralists evicted from an area and prevented from grazing their livestock and accessing water in that area?
- How have people living in an area responded to environmental change over time and why have they responded in that way? Are there reasons why other decisions could not, or were not, made?

What is political ecology?

As there are many ways of taking a political ecology approach to the analysis of environmental change, there are inevitably different views as to what constitutes political ecology. A definition given by Stott and Sullivan summarizes key characteristics of the approach, defining political ecology as

> a concern with tracing the genealogy of narratives concerning "the environment", with identifying power relationships supported by such narratives, and with asserting the consequences of hegemony over, and within, these narratives for economic and social development, and particularly for constraining possibilities for self-determination.
>
> (Stott and Sullivan, 2000: 2)

A key theme in the definition is the identification and investigation of 'narratives', or stories, that explain the status of the environment. The definition suggests that there could be more than one explanation of an environmental problem and that such explanations are not only informed by natural science but by political and economic factors and interests. These factors influence the type of evidence sought and used, and how such evidence is interpreted and understood. This implies that human–environment interactions are far from easy to understand and respond to. A more concise definition is given by Blaikie and Brookfield, who suggest that the term 'political ecology' brings together 'the concerns of ecology and a broadly defined political economy' (1987a: 17). Box 2.2 explains what is generally understood by the term 'political economy'.

Box 2.2 What is 'political economy'?

The term 'political economy' is used in many contexts and has been, and can be, used to refer to different approaches and experiences. Yet at its core, political economists are interested in the relationship between politics (be it political elites or community groups involved in lower level governance) and economics (for example in relation to markets, trade relations and production). In using the term, it is generally assumed that an interdisciplinary study is being undertaken that draws on economics and political science in investigating how political institutions, the political environment and the economic system interact and influence a certain context. A study of the political economy will involve an investigation into the exercise and distribution of power and of the broad economic context, identifying key trends, values and property regimes.

The recognition of there being multiple explanations of environmental problems within political ecology is just one reason why this field of thinking and activity is hard to define and understand. There are other characteristics of political ecology that contribute to this, including:

1   The approach draws on a range of academic disciplines, including anthropology, sociology, geography, environmental sociology and political science (Bryant, 1998; Robbins, 2012). It has therefore been influenced by different concepts and assumptions and used in different ways, with different points of emphasis and concern.

2   There is, then, no one way of 'doing' political ecology. It is not possible to set out a list of stages that one must go through in carrying out a political ecology analysis and there are no specific methodologies that must be employed. Political ecology is not a theory or body of theory and does not refer to a particular set of methods either (Robbins, 2012).

3   Political ecology takes on the challenge of scale. Local 'environmental problems' are to be seen in the context of local, national and international influence, such as the effects of the world trading system on input and crop prices and national policies on land tenure. This makes the potential scope of analysis very wide and challenging (Zimmerer and Bassett, 2003).

4   Knowledge is not viewed in a positivist sense of there being one, objective, explanation of environmental degradation. Knowledge is seen as being influenced by social and political context and processes and therefore knowledge

about the environment is influenced by power structures, in terms of what that knowledge is, what explanations it provides about environmental change and what types and sources of knowledge are accepted.

Very often one view of what explains environmental degradation may prevail, becoming the *dominant narrative*, with strong influence on policy, yet often resulting in adverse consequences for resource users. Identifying and analysing how dominant narratives have come about in different settings is a key feature of undertaking political ecology analysis. Following on from this is a concern within political ecology for social justice for resource users adversely affected by policy informed by ill-conceived dominant narratives.

Dominant narratives are seen as being those explanations that have drowned out alternative explanations of environmental degradation; they may reinforce other assumptions about the environment and society and be influenced by power relations between actors, both in terms of the content of the narrative and which narrative becomes dominant. The problem with there being dominant narratives is that they may not be true in all situations and may lead to inappropriate, ineffective and unfair policies. Such narratives have proved to be persistent and hard to challenge. Leach and Mearns refer to dominant narratives as 'received wisdom', which 'obscures a plurality of other possible views, and often leads to misguided or even fundamentally flawed development policy in Africa' (1996a: 3). Examples of dominant narratives and explanation of how they have come about are given in this chapter.

Adger *et al.* (2001) view the identification and analysis of narratives as being part of a broader analysis of *discourses* in taking a political ecology approach. They define a discourse as 'a shared meaning of a phenomenon' (2001: 683) and discourse analysis as involving 'analysis of regularities in expressions to identify discourses; analysis of the actors producing, reproducing and transforming discourses; and social impacts and policy outcomes of discourses' (Adger *et al.*, 2001: 684). Within an analysis of discourses then, a narrative is viewed as being a 'story with a chronological order' and bringing about 'a particular structure with respect to a 'cast' of actors' (Adger *et al.*, 2001: 685). An analysis of narratives takes place within an analysis of discourses concerning an environmental issue, identifying key actors, interests and issues, and investigating how these are portrayed, understood and composed.

Contemporary interpretations of political ecology trace its origins to the 1970s, though some commentators trace the origins back much further. Political ecology is seen as being closely related to the area of 'cultural ecology' (Peet and Watts, 1996), defined by Forsyth (2003: 7) as 'research focusing on local environmental practices often in anthropological fashion'. Political ecology has strong Marxist foundations, challenging power relations, seeking justice in relation to poverty and the environment and investigating inequalities (Bryant, 1998). Political ecology has diverse roots and branches, with Robbins suggesting that political ecology can best be seen as a 'community of practice', referring to there being a wide group of people who engage in a 'global conversation revolving around a set of specific themes, one that adopts a specific sort of critical attitude' (2012: 85).

There are several defining texts on the development and application of political ecology in an international development context, such as Piers Blaikie's (1985) *The Political Economy of Soil Erosion*, Piers Blaikie and Harold Brookfield's (1987b) *Land Degradation and Society* and Melissa Leach and Robin Mearns' (1996b) *The Lie of the Land: Challenging Received Wisdom on the African Environment*. These are defining in the sense of setting out key themes, approaches and examples of political ecology investigation and analysis. Blaikie's review of approaches to explaining and addressing soil erosion in the developing world challenged colonial views on the agricultural practices of small-scale farmers and the policies and interventions associated with these. In Blaikie and Brookfield's edited volume, they begin by declaring that 'land degradation should by definition be a social problem' (1987a: 1), challenging purely technical approaches to understanding and addressing land degradation. They go on to explain that 'natural' environmental processes such as leaching of nutrients and erosion of soil occur with or without human interference, but for there to be 'degradation' of the environment, there must be a source of human interference. This then implies that social, political and economic forces are relevant in seeking explanations of how environmental resources are used, managed and degraded through human action, whether direct or indirect. The volume edited by Leach and Mearns was defining in terms of the range of cases brought together in one book to provide evidence that challenges dominant narratives on environmental degradation in the developing world.

In summarizing the defining features of political ecology, it is useful to identify key words and phrases associated with the approach. Such key words illustrate some of the language of political ecology and are listed in Box 2.3.

Box 2.3 Key words associated with political ecology

- environmental degradation
- dominant narrative
- power
- knowledge
- political economy
- equilibrium and non-equilibrium ecology
- social justice

Environmental science and ecology

Undertaking a political ecology approach implies that an investigation is interdisciplinary, drawing on natural and social sciences, investigating human–environment interactions over time. There are several key issues or debates regarding the natural science focus in political ecology. These are whether the science of a situation or issue should be well understood or known before action is taken, or whether science is informed by, and emerges, as debate on the nature of environmental degradation continues; to what extent nature is seen as having its own intrinsic value within political ecology; and, whether equilibrium or non-equilibrium explanations are given emphases within the ecological analysis.

The first issue on the level, timing and availability of scientific knowledge concerning an environmental matter relates not only to there being potentially *competing* explanations, but also *incomplete* explanations, where uncertainties exist in explaining what is going on in the environment and why. This recognition suggests that policy to address environmental issues cannot necessarily wait until there is scientific certainty and consensus, but that debate about the cause and extent of environmental degradation should be part of the political discussion as much as the response itself. This is a key characteristic of Forsyth's 'critical political ecology' (2003). He argues that

> instead of approaching environmental debates as though the science is already agreed, scholars of environment need to focus more on the mechanisms by which knowledge about environment is produced and labelled, then used to construct "laws", and the practices by which such laws and lawmakers are identified as legitimate in political debate.
>
> (Forsyth, 2003: 10)

This is not so easy in practice, where politicians want scientific certainty to inform policies and legislation or may exploit uncertainties in science to justify a particular decision.

A second key issue in relation to environmental science is the status of nature in political ecology. Some commentators believe that political ecology has placed too much emphasis on the social construction of the environment, to the detriment of seeing nature independently of human preference, with its own intrinsic value (Forsyth, 2003). Such a concern is perhaps inevitable given the focus of political ecology on human–environment interactions, but is important to note as the value and role of ecosystems goes beyond human needs and desires.

Finally, a further key theme in political ecology has been interest in 'non-equilibrium ecology', challenging previous emphasis on equilibrium ecology, which assumes stability in ecosystems, where any change that occurs would be corrected to bring the system back to the original state (Forsyth, 2003; Zimmerer, 2000). Non-equilibrium ecology suggests that this does not necessarily happen, but that change in ecosystems can be chaotic and non-linear. The introduction of the concept of 'resilience' as opposed to 'stability' in relation to ecosystems contributed to the acceptance of non-equilibrium thinking (Holling, 1973). It has been suggested that some political ecologists have given too much attention to non-equilibrium ecology, to the neglect of the potential of ecosystems to be stable and move back to equilibrium. In studying and undertaking political ecology, attention should be paid to explanations of how ecosystems cope with and respond to change, yet very often political ecologists are not trained in natural sciences, suggesting a need for interdisciplinary studies.

Challenging dominant narratives: three key themes

The idea of there being dominant narratives that are accepted as providing the most robust explanation of environmental change implies that the nature of the environment and associated change has been 'constructed' (Blaikie, 1995a). This challenges the idea of there being one objective truth for the condition of an environment and how it came to be in that condition. There may instead be a number of explanations of the condition of the environment and how it came to be in that condition. The idea of the environment being 'constructed' is important within political ecology, as it means that investigation is needed into how and why the environment is understood in a certain way, how it came to be perceived in that way and who, or what interests, dominated in the 'construction' of the environment.

The construction of the environment and its associated change is reflected in the nature of dominant explanations of environmental change, or dominant narratives. Table 2.1 sets out examples of 'myths' of environmental change that have, in particular, received attention from political ecology, challenging 'received wisdom'. Key characteristics of each narrative are set out in the second column, followed by examples of typical policies that follow on from these explanations of environmental change. Examples are then given in the final column of how political ecology has challenged the narratives and of key sources that can be consulted for more detailed discussion of the political ecology perspectives and analyses. The sections below identify key themes from the dominant narratives, associated policy responses and political ecology critiques.

Dominant narratives can also be presented as thematic, as found in Robbins (2012), where he identifies five dominant narratives found within the broad area of political ecology. These dominant narratives are: degradation and marginalization; conservation and control; environmental conflict and exclusion; environmental subjects and identity; and political objects and actors. The themes of 'degradation and marginalization' and 'conservation and control' are reflected in the narratives examined in Table 2.1, whilst the other theses are beyond the scope of this introductory chapter on political ecology. Robbins' (2012) presentation of thematic narratives is also reflected in the key themes of political ecology analysis identified below.

Perceived causes of environmental change: common themes

Three key common themes can be identified from Table 2.1 within the column of perceived causes of environmental change. These themes are: overpopulation/population pressure causing environmental degradation; users of natural resources portrayed as both victims and agents of environmental change; and, existence of a 'tragedy of the commons'. These key themes found within dominant narratives of environmental degradation emerge from a political ecology critique and understanding of such themes is essential in undertaking, or studying, a political ecology approach. Each theme is explained below, before going on to examine the nature of political ecology critiques.

Table 2.1 Examples of dominant environment development narratives

Environmental change narrative	Perceived causes of environmental change	Associated response	Political ecology perspectives and questions and key political-ecology-related sources
Desertification Overgrazing and overstocking of livestock in dryland areas causes the spread of the desert	• Overpopulation in area • Overstocking of animals, contributing to overgrazing • Degradation is attributed to the 'tragedy of the commons'	• Encouragement of nomadic pastoralists to settle • Control over livestock numbers • Changes in institutional arrangements regarding access to grazing land and water	• The desertification thesis has been challenged through examination of historical data on the climate and vegetation of the concerned areas • Rules and regulations imposed upon pastoralist communities, for example preventing access to traditional grazing land, contribute to the perceived overstocking and overgrazing (Adams, 2009; Mortimore, 1989; Swift, 1996)
Deforestation Slash-and-burn farmers ('shifting cultivation') have caused the destruction of vast areas of forest in the global South	• Overpopulation in the vicinity puts pressure on land, requiring the opening up of new agricultural land • Inappropriate agricultural practices lead to the loss of forest cover	• Limits put in place to reduce or prevent access to forests by local communities • This may be through state control or community-based forest management, which has also at times reduced access to forest resources	• Shifting cultivators follow loggers and oil prospectors along new roads, which open up new areas for cultivation and ranching. A focus on shifting cultivation alone would provide an incomplete, and often inaccurate, explanation of deforestation • Forest management very often reflects the interests of powerful actors, reflecting the economic value of timber and land • The knowledge and interests of forest dwellers/forest dependent communities should be drawn on (Adams, 2009; Agrawal, 2005; Fairhead and Leach, 1998; Ribot, 1999)

(Continued)

Table 2.1 (Continued)

Environmental change narrative	Perceived causes of environmental change	Associated response	Political ecology perspectives and questions and key political-ecology-related sources
Woodfuel crisis The demand for woodfuel in the form of firewood and charcoal outstrips supply, leading to a 'woodfuel crisis' and deforestation	• Overpopulation leads to overexploitation of trees through felling for firewood and charcoal leading to deforestation • Comparison of current consumption with current standing stock leads to crisis conclusion	• Tree planting on a vast scale, with government and project interventions to enable this to happen • Introduction of fuel-efficient cooking stoves to reduce demand for woodfuel	• Woodfuel does not usually come from live trees • Estimates of standing trees may ignore other sources of woodfuel, such as shrubs, smaller trees and bushes • Local responses such as reducing fuel consumption and planting trees may suffice to address perceived shortage • Issues of access to, and control over, wood resources should be investigated to understand decision-making • Changes in vegetation over a long period of time must be examined • External pressure for woodfuel, from urban areas for example, require investigation into the effects of government policy and the local economy (Leach and Mearns, 1988; Mearns, 1995; Ribot, 1999)
Land degradation Population pressure and poor agricultural practices leads to erosion and degradation of land	• Population pressure leads to intensification of agriculture and farming on marginal land • Poor agricultural practices lead to loss of soil and lower productivity	• New land-use management practices encouraged • Changes in tenure systems encouraged, especially to privatization and state ownership	• Land degradation is both a result and cause of social marginalization • Increasing population does not necessarily mean degradation; it can lead to innovation – there is no inevitability about increasing population leading to degradation (Blaikie, 1985; Blaikie and Brookfield, 1987b; Boserup, 1965, 1981; Tiffen et al., 1994)
Pastoralism Nomadic pastoralism often seen as unsustainable, with overgrazing and land degradation	• Overpopulation leads to an increase in livestock numbers leading to overgrazing and land degradation • Typically a 'tragedy of the commons' scenario is portrayed	• Control over numbers of livestock introduced • Pastoralism blamed for land degradation and water shortages, leading to removal of pastoralists from certain areas • Control over movement, particularly in relation to national parks, with consequences for access to grazing land, including through transhumance corridors	• Common property regimes have been shown to have rules and processes that control numbers and movement of livestock • Movement of livestock and pastoral communities offers a sustainable livelihood in dryland areas • The wider political economy reduces access to suitable land and leads to overstocking and overgrazing (Scoones, 1996; Catley et al., 2012; Moritz et al., 2013)

1   *Overpopulation/population pressure.* Concern about resource-dependent populations increasing to an unsustainable level are based on neo-Malthusian assumptions about society and environmental change. The term 'neo-Malthusian' refers to thinking and interpretations of situations informed by concern about population growth and the impact of such growth on the availability of environmental resources. The term is named after Thomas Malthus, noted in Chapter 1 as the nineteenth-century scholar who raised concern about the capacity for agricultural production to keep pace with growing populations. A neo-Malthusian view would call for the control of population growth or for the control over access to environmental resources, linking population growth with environmental degradation and neglecting any alternative explanations there could be. Such a perspective pervades dominant narratives about environmental change in development contexts, as shown in Table 2.1.

2   *Natural resource users as victims and agents of environmental change.* Within the dominant narratives of environmental change, resource users are often portrayed as being both victims of the environmental change, that is they are shown to be adversely affected by land degradation or deforestation for example, and as being responsible for that environmental change. This portrayal reflects the 'poverty–environment cycle' discussed in Chapter 1, where poverty is seen to lead to environmental degradation and environmental degradation then leads to deepening and more pervasive poverty, with a reinforcing relationship or perhaps a downward spiral of worsening poverty and environmental degradation. Such a portrayal simplifies the complexity of poverty–environment relations, neglecting the wider political-economy context of the resource and its users and suggests that people in poverty are, through necessity, both victims and agents of environmental degradation. Portraying users as agents of environmental change has often led to a view that the existing land-use practices must change so that practices are less destructive. Within this theme, resource users are seen as being risk-averse and being more concerned with the short-term than investing in resource management for future benefits.

3   *Tragedy of the commons (TofC).* The narrative of Garrett Hardin's 'tragedy of the commons' was explained in Chapter 1. The TofC set out by Hardin (1968) suggests that common management of natural resources cannot work because people are incentivized to use the resource for maximum individual gain at the long-term expense of the sustainability of the resource. According to this narrative, there will come a point at which the resource cannot sustain the level of exploitation and will thus degrade and perhaps not be able to recover to its former, more productive, state. The tragedy can be seen in all of the dominant narratives reviewed in Table 2.1, which explains similarities in the portrayal and response to the situations of environmental change.

Responses to environmental change

Such understanding and portrayals of causes of environmental change that reflect these themes have led to policy responses that also have common themes, as seen in Table 2.1. These include imposing control over access to natural resources and privatizing ownership of land and forests. Regulations to control access to natural resources have taken the form of closing off areas for grazing livestock, such as the 'fences and fines' approach of conservation of wildlife areas through many national park policies up until the 1980s (see Adams and Hulme, 2001); removing pastoralists and their livestock from defined areas; and, limiting access to forests and forest products in response to concerns about deforestation. Such approaches are informed by wide acceptance of Hardin's 'tragedy of the commons', where responses to perceived tragedies include the privatization or state control of common pool resources.

A further response has been to encourage the adoption of new land-use practices which are seen to be less destructive than 'traditional' practices such as 'slash and burn'. The push for more 'modern' forms of agricultural practices has, however, at times led to further environmental degradation and reductions in productivity with adverse consequences for livelihoods (Leach and Mearns, 1996a).

Challenges to dominant narratives from political ecology

Political-ecology-informed critiques of these narratives do not seek to deny that there are concerns about the condition of the environment, but to examine how the state of the environment is understood and by whom, and how the dominant explanations given for the condition of the environment were constructed and by whom. Such understanding and explanations have implications for the types of policy responses developed, with subsequent implications for the livelihood strategies and outcomes of the affected resource users.

Researchers taking a political ecology approach to investigating environmental change can be seen to be responding to the common themes identified in the dominant narratives: overpopulation; users as victims and agents of environmental change; and the perception of the 'tragedy of the commons'. This section examines what political ecologists have concluded within these areas in response to the dominant narratives.

Population: are there too many people and does it matter?

The question of the population of direct and indirect resource users is clearly a major concern in considering the nature, extent and implications of environmental change. The number of indirect resource users can have an impact on the demand for food, firewood, charcoal and livestock products, encouraging direct users to demand more of the resources on which they depend. For some, poverty may encourage people to have larger families so that they have children to look after them in older age and to increase the chances of them having children that live into adulthood, as well as extra pairs of hands to help with domestic, agricultural and other work. Yet, the relationship between population and the state of the environment is complex and not easy to draw clear conclusions about. Blaikie and Brookfield (1987c: 29) observe that for there to be concern about 'overpopulation', as there is in many narratives of the causes of environmental change, there must be a critical population density, 'often described as the "carrying capacity" of the land, a notion which applies to human populations a principle that is well-established among animal populations'. They refer to the thesis concerning population and land degradation as 'population pressure on resources' or PPR.

The idea of there being a carrying capacity of land that can be calculated, to indicate how many people can be supported by a given area of land, has been challenged by a number of analysts. Ester Boserup, who will be referred to again in Chapter 4 in relation to her influence in raising awareness about gender and development, developed an alternative hypothesis to the view that population pressure inevitably leads to environmental degradation.

The Boserup hypothesis (1965, 1981) challenged the neo-Malthusian view of resource degradation, drawing on evidence to show how output from a given area can increase more than adequately in response to additional labour inputs than the neo-Malthusian view would suggest. The hypothesis then goes on to assert that as population increases, changes are made in agricultural practices that enable an increase in productivity, whether that is through technological innovations or intensification of labour inputs, or both. Despite being widely accepted, the hypothesis did not really result in changes in prevailing policy, which tended to side with views that modern 'green revolution' type innovation was required rather than intensification of labour (Blaikie and Brookfield, 1987a).

A further often cited example of a study that challenges the neo-Malthusian thesis concerns an examination of rural population growth and environmental sustainability through the major historical study of Machakos District in Kenya by Mary Tiffen and others. Their book, entitled *More People, Less Erosion* (Tiffen *et al.*, 1994), charts innovation in agricultural practices in the district resulting from the increase in population leading to increases in output. Their study was carried out in that particular district in response to the perception that population increase in the area had led to severe soil erosion through damaging agricultural intensification practices. Tiffen *et al.* (1994) undertook a historical study of the area and their findings showed that rather than there being extensive degradation of land, the increasing population had provided the impetus and labour for innovation and sustainable intensification of agriculture.

Perhaps what can be concluded from this debate about the nature and implications of population growth for the environment is that whilst concern is understandable and at times justified, there are no absolutes and population pressure does not always lead to environmental degradation. As concluded by Blaikie and Brookfield,

> degradation can occur under rising PPR, under declining PPR, and without PPR. We do not accept that population pressure inevitably leads to land degradation, even though it may almost inevitably lead to extreme poverty when it occurs in underdeveloped, mainly rural, countries.
>
> (Blaikie and Brookfield, 1987a: 34)

The responsibility of resource users

The theme of resource users as 'victims and agents of environmental change' sees poor resource management practices as contributing to land degradation. The ignorance and conservatism of peasant farmers are seen as explaining the lack of uptake of more modern, efficient and productive resource management practices. A political ecology perspective challenges these assumptions and calls for a more nuanced understanding of small-scale farmers' perspectives. The knowledge, attitudes and practices of small-scale farmers may be informed by different time and spatial scales compared with specialized government extension workers, making it difficult for mutual understanding to develop. Questions have been raised through political ecology analysis of the nature and extent of soil erosion, for example questioning the timescale studied and the interpretation of data that led to conclusions attributing blame solely to resource users (Blaikie, 1985). A political ecology perspective challenges assumptions about certain practices that have been particularly subject to criticism, such as rotational grazing and shifting cultivation, which are not inherently unsustainable but need sufficient land over which they can be employed.

A further consideration raised by a political ecology perspective with regard to the practices of small-scale farmers in the global South is the influence not only of national and regional policies but of international trade agreements and the policies of other countries. For example, subsidies to farmers in Europe and the USA affect food prices and influence access to, and benefits from, agricultural markets, in turn influencing the practices of many farmers around the world (Anderson *et al.*, 2011).

Is there necessarily a 'tragedy of the commons'?

Responses to the 'tragedy of the commons' thesis were outlined in Chapter 1 where it was explained that common property theory was developed in response to this thesis. Common property theory was developed through the identification and analysis of empirical cases that show how resource users have managed resources sustainably through collective decision-making, challenging the 'tragedy of the commons' thesis. A political ecology perspective supports such theory, focusing on the institutional arrangements that enable the management of common pool resources, but also examining government and international policies that influence decisions by, and practices of, common pool resource users. For example, institutions within some pastoralist communities influence how many livestock people have, when they move with their livestock and where they move to, including the route taken (Homann *et al.*, 2008; Swift, 1991). There is communication and cooperation between pastoralists for effective grazing. A political ecology perspective, however, recognizes that such communication and cooperation can be undermined by external influences such as government policies to restrict movement and livestock numbers.

A 'tragedy of the commons' cannot be assumed to occur in all commons situations, though care should be taken in distinguishing between common and open access regimes (as discussed in Chapter 1). In many resource management situations, there may be a mix of elements of open, common and state management regimes, reflecting the scale of resources and the challenge for governments to fully and effectively implement their policies over vast areas and with limited resources.

Chains of explanation within political ecology

It has been established that political ecology is often used to critique dominant narratives that purportedly explain environmental degradation and have led to particular policy responses. In undertaking such critique, key themes have been identified of the nature and influence of population pressure, resource users as victims and agents of environmental change and the reality, or otherwise, of the tragedy of the commons. A further way of presenting a political ecology analysis was developed by Blaikie and Brookfield (1987c), who presented their political ecology analysis of land degradation as a 'chain of explanation', moving from one set of relations to another. They explained that land degradation

> starts with the land managers and their direct relations with the land (crop rotations, fuelwood use, stocking densities, capital investments and so on). Then the next link concerns their relations with each other, other land users, and groups in the wider society who affect them in any way, which in turn determines land management. The state and the world economy constitute the last links in the chain.

> (Blaikie and Brookfield, 1987c: 27)

This descriptive account was subsequently illustrated in a chain of explanation by Blaikie (1995b), showing the stages through which a political ecology explanation would proceed, as shown in Figure 2.1. A more specific chain of explanation was also provided by Blaikie (1995b), in relation to land degradation, as shown in Figure 2.2. Both figures are shown in an adapted form from Adams (2009).

The 'chain of explanation' illustrates the linkages between physical processes and the political-economic context, with linkages identified between multiple levels of influence, including influences at the global level. Such portrayal of an explanation of environmental degradation suggests a clear linear relationship, which may not always be accurate or very helpful, with linkages between seemingly unconnected parts of the chain not apparent, for example between stage G

Figure 2.1 Political ecology chain of explanation.

Source: Adams, 2009: 206, adapted from Blaikie, 1995b: 18.

A	Physical changes in soil and vegetation	• Sheet and gully erosion • Bush/weed encroachment
B	Economic symptoms at a specific place	• Falling crop yields • Increased mortality and mortality of cattle • Increased yield variability
C	Specific land-use practices at that place	• Insufficient fallowing • Overstocking • Felling too many trees
D	Land users, resources, skills, assets, time horizon and technology	
E	The nature of agrarian society	• Distribution of rights to land • Laws of inheritance • Gender division
F	Nature of the state	• Official laws on land tenure (common and private property) • Weak or strong government (ability to enforce laws) • Abilities of administration • Government stance on transnational corporations in forestry and plantations
G	The international economy	• The foreign debt crisis • Oil prices • IMF restructuring

Figure 2.2 The chain of explanation of land degradation.

Source: Adams, 2009: 207, adapted from Blaikie, 1995b: 19.

(political-economy factors at the international level) and stage B (the 'symptoms'). The reality could be much messier and chaotic, with interrelationships between and within many levels, but the 'chain of explanation' does help to bring a level of clarity to a political ecology analysis. Whilst potentially providing a useful guide for some forms of political ecology investigation, the 'chain of explanation' approach should be seen as providing a way into political ecology and used with caution, as it may lead researchers in particular directions.

Feminist political ecology

A gendered approach to political ecology is not found explicitly in much of the writing, but may often be implied in investigating the political economy of environmental change. In observing this, Rocheleau *et al.*'s (1996) text *Feminist Political Ecology: Global Issues and Local Experience* promoted the development of a 'feminist political ecology'. The book invited political ecology scholars to investigate gendered relations as part of their analysis of power and to extend their analysis to the household level, reflecting the importance of intra-household relations in influencing access to, and benefits from, environmental resources.

Despite this promising start, Elmhirst (2011) observes that there is little literature that explicitly refers to feminist political ecology. She suggests, however, that much literature can be found that could be regarded as incorporating a feminist political ecology approach, even if this term is not used and the study is not labelled as such. She cites examples of such literature as including literature on gender dynamics in community-based institutions associated with natural resource management, gendered environmental knowledge and gender and policy discourses. Elmhirst (2011) also explains the lack of explicit use of the term 'feminist political ecology' as a reflection of the 'decentring' of gender, where gender has come to be seen as one dimension of social difference that should be considered alongside other dimensions, such as caste, race and sexuality. In a related vein, Mollett and Faria (2013) are critical of feminist political ecology, and of political ecology more broadly, for failing to explicitly engage with race, racism and racialization. They urge that race and gender should be seen as mutually constituted, viewing race as a 'shifting web of social signification that gives meaning to and represents social struggles and interests by highlighting human differences' (Mollett and Faria, 2013: 117).

Feminist political ecology is seen by some as a re-emerging field of enquiry, with particular potential to draw on developments within feminist and gender theories of the interrelatedness of axes of difference and the need to include multiple levels and locations in a political ecology analysis, including a focus on intra-household relations. Understanding of, and approaches to, gender and the environment are explored in more detail in Chapter 4, where the place and potential of feminist political ecology is further considered.

Desertification: a classic case study of a dominant narrative and political ecology critique

The narrative of 'desertification' is touched on in Table 2.1, where the dominant understanding of, and explanation for, desertification is listed as a narrative that has dominated thinking and policy in relation to dryland management, often with adverse consequences for dryland communities, particularly nomadic pastoralists. This section describes the development of the dominant narrative of desertification in more detail and sets out the political ecology critique, to provide a more detailed example of how a dominant narrative may come about and with what consequences.

The 1994 United Nations Convention to Combat Desertification defines desertification as 'land degradation in arid, semi-arid and dry sub-humid areas resulting from various factors, including climatic variations and human activities' (UNGA, 1994: 5). This seems a reasonable definition and desertification a reasonable cause for concern. Yet, desertification is one of the most contested processes of environmental change. Concern about how desertification is portrayed and explained, and about many of the policy prescriptions resulting from such portrayal and understanding, has arisen through analysis of what is really happening in dryland areas and of the impacts of associated policies.

Concern about desertification arose in the 1920s and 30s when French colonialists became aware of the apparent drying out of large areas of their Sahelian colonies. Such concern spread to English-speaking colonies in the 1930s. A British forester, E. P. Stebbing, is viewed as being particularly influential in interpreting the processes at work at that time. He toured West Africa after spending years in Indian drylands and was influenced by his own experience in interpreting what he saw. Thinking at that time was also influenced by the Dust Bowl of the American Great Plains, where widespread dust storms were experienced between 1933 and 1938, causing severe wind erosion in areas where wheat cultivation had only relatively recently begun. This resulted in tens of thousands of families abandoning their homes and suffering great hardship.

The understanding and explanation of desertification at this time is seen to have included the following characteristics (Swift, 1996; Thomas and Middleton, 1994):

1   The movement of the desert is a natural process, but human action has led to further and faster expansion of the area under desert.
2   Human action is seen to contribute to desertification through practices that encourage surface water to be dried up, the water table to be lowered and rainfall to decrease – referred to as desiccation. Such desiccation is seen to result from practices such as shifting cultivation, increase in nomadic grazing pressure and bush fires. Thomas and Middleton (1994: 67) summarize the perceived causes as falling under the headings of 'overgrazing, overcultivation and deforestation'.
3   An increase in local populations, resulting from the ending of local warfare and improvements in health, contributed to the expansion of practices leading to desiccation and subsequently desertification.

Livestock-based livelihoods are particularly important in dryland areas and often these involve pastoral-nomadic systems, with people moving their livestock within certain areas, taking well-used routes, in response to the availability of water and grazing land. In seeking explanations of the causes of desertification, then, the number of livestock and the approaches taken to grazing them has come under close scrutiny, with policy measures at times developed to control numbers and movement. It is not just the consumption of plants that is seen as a cause for concern, but the trampling of plants and disturbance of root systems resulting from grazing. As part of the dominant narrative of desertification, concern was expressed about 'overstocking' of livestock, exceeding the perceived 'potential carrying capacity' (PCC). In practice, it is far from easy to determine a PCC and the interaction between biomass availability, rainfall and optimal livestock levels are complex and variable. Deforestation has also been linked to desertification, with clearance for agriculture and pasture land and increasing demand for fuelwood and charcoal being associated with increasing desertification. The interpretation of the processes and causes of desertification led to policies that sought to control numbers of livestock and confine them to certain areas, encouraging the permanent settlement of nomadic pastoralists, and to the creation of forest reserves, controlling access to forest resources by local communities.

Concern about desertification resurfaced in the 1970s in response to a series of major droughts in the Sahelian region and in Sudan, leading to the 1977 United Nations Conference on Desertification (UNCOD) and subsequently the United Nations Convention to Combat Desertification, agreed at the 1992 UN Conference on the Environment and Development.

Critiques of the narrative have been developed and espoused over the years. These do not deny that degradation is sometimes happening but argue that the perceived causes and processes leading to degradation within the dominant narrative of desertification have prevented more appropriate responses from being considered. Swift (1996) critiques the narrative of desertification in terms of encompassing three related, but distinct, phenomena: drought, desiccation and dryland degradation, and explains the differences between these phenomena as follows.

- Drought is defined as two or more years of rainfall well below average and reduces primary production substantially, especially in drier areas. The vegetation can quickly recover when there is better rain, without any long-term damage to productivity.
- Desiccation refers to more general drying out over time, resulting from extended drought over decades. This will have more substantial impact than drought, though such impacts are felt gradually, over a long period of time.
- Dryland degradation refers to a decrease in the productivity in vegetation and soils resulting from land use leading to physical changes irrespective of rainfall.

It can be difficult to distinguish between these effects, though this is important given the types of policies and actions resulting from interpretations of ecological changes. Thomas and Middleton (1994) also suggest that the general portrayal of desertification as the 'spread of the desert' does little to reflect the complexity and range of processes at work within dryland areas.

Alternative explanations to the dominant narrative of desertification link degradation much more closely with soil erosion and productivity variations with rainfall variations and, in contrast to the dominant narrative, recognize the high productivity of extensive nomadic pastoralism and how indigenous technical knowledge and customary institutions can inform more appropriate responses to dryland degradation (Binns, 1990; Swift, 1996). Critiques of the dominant narrative of desertification have also suggested that insufficient data over long enough periods of time and space have been used to support the desertification thesis. Concern about the narrative also arises from its underlying premise of neo-Malthusian assumptions concerning population growth and environmental productivity. The desertification thesis remains contested and controversial, in part reflecting the diversity of 'proximate causes and underlying forces' associated with dryland degradation (Geist and Lambin, 2004: 817).

In a detailed and impressive book setting out longitudinal research carried out in the 1970s and 80s, Mortimore (1989) took a political ecology perspective in questioning the bleak portrayal of African drylands as plagued by drought, poor soils and poor land management, and investigated the impact of external political-economic factors. His study into famine, drought and desertification experienced in northern Nigeria challenges the desertification thesis by acknowledging the adaptive capacity and resilience of people in the face of considerable adversity. He questioned whether people can continue to adapt to change as they have done in the past, and called for greater support for communities living in 'high-risk environments' (1989: 230).

Political ecologists have interrogated the desertification thesis, identifying key themes that characterize accounts of the narrative as follows: inclusion of inaccurate assumptions about the ecology of the areas by early colonial scientists; holding increasing populations of people and livestock responsible for dryland degradation; and relying on 'tragedy of the commons' thinking about resource management, particularly of traditional management systems, to inform beliefs and policies.

Other examples of the application of political ecology

The case of desertification is a classic area of study within political ecology and an often cited example of where political ecology has challenged 'received wisdom'. There are, however, many other examples of the application of political ecology. A few of these are drawn on in Table 2.2. In the table, the dominant narrative for each case is identified, with reasons given for the development of the narrative, and how that narrative was sustained over time. The questions raised by the political ecology analysis are then identified to illustrate how political ecology has been, and can be, used. The key characteristics of political ecology of critiquing a dominant narrative, giving recognition to multiple environmental 'knowledges', particularly of resource users, and investigating power relations with respect to how the environment is perceived and interpreted can be seen in each case.

Political ecology approaches have also been used to investigate global environmental concerns, such as overfishing, energy security and climate change (Adger *et al.*, 2001; Newell and Bumpus, 2012; Peet *et al.,* 2011), demonstrating its potential to go beyond local and individual case studies to provide a framework to analyse the global manifestation of human–environment interactions.

Debates and issues within political ecology

Within the broad area of political ecology, controversies and debates have inevitably arisen over time. Key examples of such debates and concerns include whether there has been sufficient focus on politics; whether much political ecology work

Table 2.2 Examples of the application of political ecology

Study	Dominant narrative	How did the narrative come about?	Political ecology analysis
Mangrove forest conservation in Central Sulawesi, Indonesia (Armitage, 2002)	• Conversion of mangrove forests for aquaculture is economically efficient and part of the wider development agenda	• Local resource use and management regimes are inefficient • Range of 'services' of mangrove forests not valued in the same way as aquaculture despite the multiplicity of benefits	• High costs associated with the conversion of mangrove forests for aquaculture development are prohibitive for most local individuals and communities, so the majority of benefits from conversion go to people from outside the locality • It is in the interests of government staff to grant permits for conversion to gain revenue • Unclear legal frameworks, including lack of recognition of common property regimes, act in favour of conversion
Farmer–herder conflict in Tanzania (Benjaminsen et al., 2009)	• Herders overgraze their own village lands and enter farmers' territory to feed ever-growing herds of livestock • Local narrative reflects dominant national narrative on pastoralism	• Policy support for increase in agriculture • National government policy of modernization, with land titling, enclosure of commons and permanent settlements • Pastoralists consistently told to reduce livestock numbers	• Access to wetlands, important for grazing, lost due to expansion of agriculture and conservation; associated with a border dispute • Struggle for control over land has become a struggle between different narratives • Modernization policies marginalize pastoralists • Conflict exacerbated by corruption and nature of governance; pastoralists pay bribes to graze livestock
Jatropha plantations for biodiesel in Tamil Nadu, India (Ariza-Montobbio et al., 2010)	• Jatropha is a pro-poor and 'pro-wasteland' development crop	• Refrain of 'energy security' • Opportunity to rehabilitate degraded or drylands, the so-called 'wastelands', without competing with food crops • Argued that agrofuels have the potential to alleviate poverty	• Questions the concept of 'wastelands'; argues that the term is value-laden and subjective • In practice, Jatropha had displaced groundnut crops • Short maturation period argued to be good for income generation for poor farmers, but maturation period is contested • Irrigation necessary for good yields, but is beyond the reach of poor farmers

(Continued)

Table 2.2 (Continued)

Study	Dominant narrative	How did the narrative come about?	Political ecology analysis
Native property rights and natural resource management in Sabah, Malaysia (Doolittle, 2010)	• Native shifting cultivators are responsible for more forest destruction than any other group • Natives in Sabah seen as ignorant, backward and responsible for environmental degradation	• Narrative holds power since colonial times • Colonial administrators viewed shifting cultivation as wasteful and unscientific; the practice was problematic for the expansion of valuable plantations	• Resource governance continues to be centralized for the benefit of powerful elite at the expense of local livelihoods • Tangled legacy of land rights left behind at end of colonialism with contestation over land continuing for many decades • Maintaining the rhetoric of destructive and backward traditional practices keeps the focus away from other activities that may be destructive, such as copper mining, oil palm plantations and logging
Environmental degradation narratives in Madagascar (Pollini, 2010)	• Madagascar was a pristine forested island before human settlement • Deforestation resulted from traditional agricultural practices of shifting cultivation and use of forest fires as a management method	• Colonial interpretations of the ecosystems and of environmental change • Colonial views persisting of the damaging effects of shifting cultivation	Pollini explores different political ecology narratives, as follows: • Environmental degradation is largely a myth Malagasy ecosystems are changing rather than degrading • Alternative political ecology narrative: the cause of any environmental degradation is unwise policies that create conflict over resources. Traditional land management practices are not to blame Political ecology needs to critique its social construction of the environment to 'correct its own biases about the way it addresses ecological processes' (2010: 721). The case of the Malagasy highlands may be better explained by drawing on multiple narratives

sufficiently reflects an emphasis on ecology; why political ecology rarely provides alternative narratives and from these specific policy advice; and the lack of guidance on how to carry out political ecology research. Such concerns have arisen over different periods of time, reflecting changes in emphases and approaches. In the 1980s, political ecology was broadly criticized for not engaging sufficiently with politics, yet with a shift towards more poststructuralist political ecology in the 1990s, with a much stronger analysis of politics, some argued that this was a shift too far, with too much attention paid to environmental politics and insufficient engagement with the science of ecology (Walker, 2005).

Walker (2006) identifies a further area of concern for political ecologists as being the lack of engagement with making practical policy recommendations. This might, he suggests, be partly explained by the fact that although political ecology successfully challenges dominant narratives regarding people–environment relations, 'as a whole, political ecology has not been notably successful in creating effective counter-narratives' (Walker, 2006: 385). Other reasons put forward for this lack of policy focus includes the dominance of studies on individual case studies, making scaling-up findings challenging, and the Marxian roots of the field of study, having a concern with power, justice and inequality, making the approach unpalatable for some policy-makers.

In relation to there being insufficient guidance in the literature on political ecology on how to conduct such research, Doolittle suggests that 'little attention is paid to how research is carried out and how research materials are produced' (2010: 68). She contributes to remedying this through providing a detailed account of how she planned for, collected and analysed data for her study on natural resource management in Sabah, Malaysia. The lack of guidance on 'how to do' political ecology may reflect its diversity of disciplinary roots, each discipline recognizing certain theory, approaches and methods above others. Many reports on studies do, however, contain information on how the study was planned for, data collected and interrogated, providing a range of examples of what a study taking a political ecology approach may involve, which may remedy the lack of more generic advice on 'how to do' political ecology.

Summary of key points

Key points that arise from this introduction to political ecology are:

1   There is no one way of undertaking political ecology. There is no single approach to, or categorical definition of, political ecology.
2   The nature, distribution and influence of *power* on how human–environment interactions are understood, defined and responded to is at the core of political ecology.
3   Interrogating discourses and narratives that purport to explain environmental change is a key objective of a political ecology approach.
4   A political ecology approach can be particularly illuminating in investigating poverty–environment relations as it stresses the need to work with resource

users, including poorer resource users, in investigating the causes and processes of environmental degradation.

5   Taking a political ecology approach to the analysis of environmental issues
     implies an investigation of the broad historical, social, economic and politi-
     cal context of how people interact with the natural environment, why and
     with what consequences. Snapshots of situations are to be avoided, with data
     over time sought to allow for more contextual analysis.

6   A political ecology analysis would also explore connections between local
     and global phenomena in relation to the political economy as well as in terms
     of environmental functions.

7   Seeking social justice is a key aim of undertaking political ecology analysis.

Further reading

Blaikie, P. (1985) *The Political Economy of Soil Erosion in Developing Countries*,
    London: Longman.
This is a seminal text by one of the key proponents of taking a political economy approach
to the analysis of environmental issues in the pursuit of social justice. The book is concerned with asking why soil conservation programmes in developing countries rarely
succeed. Blaikie portrays soil erosion as a political-economic issue because it is a site of
conflict – it is not a neutral issue that can be treated purely as a technical process, with clear
technical solutions. There are conflicts of interest that come from multiple sources, such as
land tenure systems, legislation and markets. Blaikie examines perceptions of soil erosion
held by different actors, such as government officials and administrators, in the context of
the 'colonial' or classic model of soil conservation in which the problem is seen as an environmental issue rather than a socio-environmental problem. In seeking to understand why
soil erosion occurs, Blaikie presents a scheme to investigate decision-making at multiple
levels and then presents an analysis of the political economy associated with that decision-
making. The elements of political economy examined include social relations of production
and exchange, the world economic system, marginalization, proletarianization and incorpo-
ration, and spatial marginalization, private property and the commons. The book was
seminal in undertaking such an analysis of the political economy of an environmental issue,
challenging perceptions of environmental issues as being purely technical and of there
being one type of understanding of the issue and how it should be approached. The case of
soil erosion illustrates the complexity of the issue, being affected by so many interests, areas
of policy and a range of market forces. Blaikie concludes from his analysis that 'soil erosion
in lesser developed countries will not be substantially reduced unless it seriously threatens
the accumulation possibilities of the dominant classes' (1985: 147), reflecting the influence
and role of interests and perceptions on this very political-economic issue.

Leach, M. and R. Mearns (eds) (1996) *The Lie of the Land: Challenging Received Wisdom
    on the African Environment*, Oxford: The International African Institute, London, in
    association with James Currey.
This edited volume was innovative in its time, bringing together a range of case studies of
explanations of environmental degradation from across Africa and challenging orthodox
explanations of degradation in the context of range management, soils, dryland, game
reserves, forestry and agricultural land. The volume is premised on concern that much

environmental policy is based on a set of powerful images of environmental change that are not always fair, helpful or accurate. Such images identified and addressed in this book include 'overgrazing', 'desertification' and the 'woodfuel crisis'. The editors, Leach and Mearns, argue that such images have acquired the status of conventional wisdom, yet may be deeply misleading and that a more critical approach is needed to investigating and responding to situations of environmental degradation. They urge for analysis that draws on the broad historical, political and institutional context of science and policy. The editors summarize the scope of the book as addressing three central questions (p. 6):

> First, how does received wisdom about environmental change in Africa become established, get reproduced, and in some cases persist even in the face of strong counter-evidence? Second, how is it put to use and with what outcomes? And third, what alternative approaches for policy and applied research are suggested by countervailing views?

Forsyth, T. (2003) *Critical Political Ecology*, London: Routledge.
Forsyth sets out a 'critical' approach to political ecology which advocates for the recognition of the construction of environmental knowledge through social and political processes, meaning that analysis that adopts a political ecology approach should investigate how scientific explanations of environmental degradation are constructed, understood, accepted or contested within the political realm. In this significant contribution to the literature on political ecology, Forsyth draws on political philosophy and sociological thinking to inform analysis of the construction of environmental knowledge and portrayal of environmental issues. He examines social framings of environmental science, the coproduction of environmental knowledge and what could be achieved through 'democratizing' explanations of environmental issues and contributions to environmental science. Forsyth argues that 'environmental science and politics should be seen as *coproduced* – or as mutually reinforcing at every stage' (2003: 266) and urges for political ecology to 'conduct critical analysis of the political factors that underlie competing definitions and explanations of environmental reality' (2003: 278). The book contains examples of environmental orthodoxies, such as understanding and explanations of desertification and deforestation, that can be challenged on the grounds of how politics and scientific understanding are enmeshed and mutually reinforcing.

Robbins, P. (2012) *Political Ecology*, 2nd edition, Chichester: Wiley-Blackwell.
Robbins provides a comprehensive review of the development and key themes of the broad area of political ecology. The conceptual and theoretical underpinnings of political ecology are reviewed, before examining five key themes: degradation and marginalization, conservation and control, environmental conflict and exclusion, environmental subjects and identity, and political objects and actors. Each theme is the subject of a separate chapter through which the application of a political ecology perspective is examined.

References

Adams, W. (2009) *Green Development: Environment and Sustainability in a Developing World*, 3rd edition, London: Routledge.
Adams, W. and Hulme, D. (2001) 'Conservation and community: Changing narratives, policies, practices in African conservation', in Hulme, D. and Murphree, M.W. (eds), *African Wildlife and Livelihoods: The Promise and Performance of Community Conservation*, Martlesham: James Currey, pp. 9–23.

Adger, W.N., Benjaminsen, T.A., Brown, K. and Svarstad, H. (2001) 'Advancing a political ecology of global environmental discourses', *Development and Change*, 32: 681–715.

Agrawal, A. (2005) *Environmentality: Technologies of Government and the Making of Subjects*, London: Duke University Press.

Anderson, K., Cockburn, J. and Martin, W. (2011) 'Would freeing up world trade reduce poverty and inequality? The vexed role of agricultural distortions', *Policy Research Working Paper 5603*, Washington DC: World Bank.

Ariza-Montobbio, P., Lele, S., Kallis, G. and Martinez-Alier, J. (2010) 'The political ecology of Jatropha plantations for biodiesel in Tamil Nadu, India', *Journal of Peasant Studies*, 37(4): 875–897.

Armitage, D. (2002) 'Socio-institutional dynamics and the political ecology of mangrove forest conservation in Central Sulawesi, Indonesia', *Global Environmental Change*, 12: 203–217.

Benjaminsen, T.A., Maganga, F.P. and Abdallah, J.M. (2009) 'The Kilosa killings: Political ecology of a farmer–herder conflict in Tanzania', *Development and Change*, 40(3): 423–445.

Binns, T. (1990) 'Is desertification a myth?', *Geography*, 75(2): 106–113.

Blaikie, P. (1985) *The Political Economy of Soil Erosion in Developing Countries*, London: Longman.

Blaikie, P. (1995a) 'Changing environments or changing views? A political ecology for developing countries', *Geography*, 80(3): 203–214.

Blaikie, P. (1995b) 'Understanding environmental issues', in Morse, S. and Stocking, M. (eds), *People and the Environment*, London: UCL Press, pp. 1–30.

Blaikie, P. and Brookfield, H. (1987a) 'Defining and debating the problem', in Blaikie, P. and Brookfield, H. (eds), *Land Degradation and Society*, London: Methuen, pp. 1–26.

Blaikie, P. and Brookfield, H. (1987b) *Land Degradation and Society*, London: Methuen.

Blaikie, P. and Brookfield, H. (1987c) 'Approaches to the study of land degradation', in Blaikie, P. and Brookfield, H. (eds), *Land Degradation and Society*, London: Methuen, pp. 27–48.

Boserup, E. (1965) *The Conditions of Agricultural Growth: The Economics of Agrarian Change Under Population Pressure*, Chicago: Aldine.

Boserup, E. (1981) *Population and Technology*, Oxford: Blackwell.

Bryant, R.L. (1998) 'Power, knowledge and political ecology in the third world: A review', *Progress in Physical Geography*, 22(1): 79–94.

Catley, A., Lind, J. and Scoones, I. (eds) (2012) *Pastoralism and Development in Africa: Dynamic Change at the Margins*, London: Routledge.

Doolittle, A. (2010) 'Stories and maps, images and archives: Multimethod approach to the political ecology of native property rights and natural resource management in Sabah, Malaysia', *Environmental Management*, 45: 67–81.

Elmhirst, R. (2011) 'Introducing new feminist political ecologies', *Geoforum*, 42: 129–132.

Fairhead, J. and Leach, M. (1998) *Reframing Deforestation: Global Analysis and Local Realities: Studies in West Africa*, London: Routledge.

Forsyth, T. (2003) *Critical Political Ecology*, London: Routledge.

Geist, H.J. and Lambin, E.F. (2004) 'Dynamic causal patterns of desertification', *BioScience*, 54(9): 817–829.

Hardin, G. (1968) 'The tragedy of the commons', *Science*, 162(3859): 1243–1248.

Holling, C.S. (1973) 'Resilience and stability of ecological systems', *Annual Review of Ecology and Systematics*, 4: 1–23.

Homann, S., Rischkowsky, B., Steinbach, J., Kirk, M. and Mathias, E. (2008) 'Towards endogenous livestock development: Borana pastoralists' responses to environmental and institutional changes', *Human Ecology*, 36(4): 503–520.

Leach, G. and Mearns, R. (1988) *Beyond the Woodfuel Crisis: People, Land and Trees in Africa*, London: Earthscan.

Leach, M. and Mearns, R. (1996a) 'Environmental change and policy: Challenging received wisdom in Africa', in Leach, M. and Mearns, R. (eds), *The Lie of the Land: Challenging Received Wisdom on the African Environment*, Oxford: The International African Institute, London, in association with James Currey, pp. 1–33.

Leach, M. and Mearns, R. (eds) (1996b) *The Lie of the Land: Challenging Received Wisdom on the African Environment*, Oxford: The International African Institute, London, in association with James Currey.

Mearns, R. (1995) 'Institutions and natural resource management: Access to and control over woodfuel in East Africa', in Binns, T. (ed.), *People and Environment in Africa*, Chichester: John Wiley, pp. 103–114.

Mollett, S. and Faria, C. (2013) 'Messing with gender in feminist political ecology', *Geoforum*, 45: 116–125.

Moritz, M., Catherine, B.L., Drent, A.K., Kari, S., Mouhaman, A. and Scholte, P. (2013) 'Rangeland governance in an open system: Protecting transhumance corridors in the Far North Province of Cameroon', *Pastoralism: Research, Policy and Practice*, 3: 26.

Mortimore, M. (1989) *Adapting to Drought: Farmers, Famines and Desertification in West Africa*, Cambridge: Cambridge University Press.

Newell, P. and Bumpus, A. (2012) 'The global political ecology of the clean development mechanism', *Global Environmental Politics*, 12(4): 49–67.

Peet, R. and Watts, M. (1996) 'Liberation ecology: Development, sustainability, and environment in an age of market triumphalism', in Peet, P. and Watts. M. (eds), *Liberation Ecologies: Environment, Development, Social Movements*, London: Routledge.

Peet, R., Robbins, P. and Watts, M. (eds) (2011) *Global Political Ecology*, London: Routledge.

Pollini, J. (2010) 'Environmental degradation narratives in Madagascar: From colonial hegemonies to humanist revisionism', *Geoforum*, 41: 711–722.

Ribot, J. (1999) 'A history of fear: Imagining deforestation in the West African dryland forests', *Global Ecology and Biogeography*, 8: 291–300.

Robbins, P. (2012) *Political Ecology*, 2nd edition, Chichester: Wiley-Blackwell.

Rocheleau, D., Thomas-Slayter, B. and Wangari, E. (eds) (1996) *Feminist Political Ecology: Global Issues and Local Experience*, London: Routledge.

Scoones, I. (1996) 'Range management, science and policy: Politics, polemics and pasture in Southern Africa', in Leach, M. and Mearns, R. (eds), *The Lie of the Land: Challenging Received Wisdom on the African Environment*, Oxford: The International African Institute, London, in association with James Currey, pp. 34–53.

Stott, P. and Sullivan, S. (2000) 'Introduction', in Stott, P. and Sullivan, S. (ed.) *Political Ecology: Science, Myth and Power*, London: Arnold, pp. 1–11.

Swift, J. (1991) 'Local customary institutions as the basis for natural resource management among Boran pastoralists in Northern Kenya', *IDS Bulletin*, 22(4): 34–47.

Swift, J. (1996) 'Desertification: Narratives, winners and losers', in Leach, M. and Mearns, R. (eds), *The Lie of the Land: Challenging Received Wisdom on the African Environment*, Oxford: The International African Institute, London, in association with James Currey, pp. 73–90.

Thomas, D.S.G. and Middleton, N.J. (1994) *Desertification: Exploding the Myth*, Chichester: John Wiley.

Tiffen, M., Mortimore, M. and Gichuki, F. (1994) *More People, Less Erosion: Environmental Recovery in Kenya*, Chichester: Wiley.

United Nations General Assembly (1994) *United Nations Convention to Combat Desertification*, New York: United Nations.

Walker, P.A. (2005) 'Political ecology: Where is the ecology?', *Progress in Human Geography*, 29(1): 73–82.

Walker, P.A. (2006) 'Political ecology: Where is the policy?', *Progress in Human Geography*, 30(3): 382–395.

Zimmerer, K.S. (2000) 'The reworking of conservation geographies: Nonequilibrium landscape and nature-society hybrids', *Annals of the Association of American Geographers*, 90(2): 356–369.

Zimmerer, K.S. and Bassett, T.J. (2003) 'Future directions in political ecology: Nature–society fusions and scales of interaction', in Zimmerer, K.S. and Bassett, T.J. (eds), *Political Ecology: An Integrative Approach to Geography and Environment-Development Studies*, London: The Guilford Press, pp. 274–295.

3   Analysing institutions

Introduction

A wide range of factors influence whether, how and to what extent people derive benefits from natural resources. Such factors might include the prevailing climate, terrain and the condition of the resources, but will also include national policies and legislation, local rules and norms and intra-household relations. These latter kinds of factors can be viewed as institutions. In Chapter 1, institutions were defined as 'rules of the game', referring to different types of arrangements that mediate access to benefits from resources. They can be rather elusive and difficult to identify and understand, but there are many tools and approaches that have been developed to investigate the nature and roles of institutions in mediating people–environment relations. Some of these frameworks and approaches are reviewed in other chapters, such as taking a gendered lens in Chapter 4 and the Sustainable Livelihoods Approach in Chapter 5. This chapter focuses on three frameworks and approaches that have institutions at the heart of their analysis of how natural resources are governed, accessed and benefited from. These are Critical Institutionalism, associated with Frances Cleaver (2012), the Environmental Entitlements approach, developed in the 1990s by Melissa Leach, Robin Mearns and Ian Scoones, all at that time based at the Institute of Development Studies, and the Institutional Analysis and Development (IAD) framework, developed principally by the late Elinor Ostrom of the Workshop in Political Theory and Policy Analysis at Indiana University, USA. A further development of the IAD framework, the Social-Ecological System (SES) framework, is also introduced.

The chapter begins by examining why institutions matter in poverty–environment relations, before reviewing each of the approaches set out above. Examples of the application of each approach provide illustration of the kinds of questions that may be asked and what kind of data is collected. The chapter concludes with a comparison of the frameworks and approaches. There are many other approaches to an analysis of institutions, stemming from different disciplines, such as political science, economics and sociology. The frameworks in this chapter draw mainly from sociology and economics, but there are other traditions within these disciplines that focus on institutions. The three approaches reviewed in this chapter were selected because of their concern with people–natural resources interactions, and there being examples of their use in developing country settings.

Within natural resource literature, a number of categorizations have been put forward in relation to institutional analysis. These include Johnson's (2004) distinction between collective action and entitlement scholars, Agrawal's (2005) distinction between common property and political ecology scholars and Lewins' (2007) distinction between Leach *et al.*'s (1997) institutional analysis through the Environmental Entitlements approach and those taken through New Institutional Economics and Common Property Resources theory. These categorizations share the distinctions identified by Cleaver (2012), who places institutional analysis within natural resource settings into two categories of Mainstream Institutionalism and Critical Institutionalism. Mainstream Institutionalism is associated with the common property scholarship of Elinor Ostrom, including the IAD and SES frameworks, broadly concerned with making predictions about governance to inform the design of institutions for sustainability. 'Design principles' or 'conditions' for natural resource governance are identified, such as user representation, mechanisms for conflict resolution and devising and applying sanctions. Critical Institutionalism, with which the Environmental Entitlements framework is associated, does not seek to be predictive or identify essential conditions, but seeks to acknowledge and investigate the complexity of institutional arrangements that mediate access to benefits from natural resources. These contrasting approaches to the analysis of institutions within natural resource settings have different starting points, disciplinary backgrounds and objectives, and employ quite different data collection and analysis methods. The choice of approach would depend on the scholar, the questions being asked and the research context, though it is also possible to draw on elements of both categories of approaches. Box 3.1 sets out examples of the types of questions that could be asked within institutional analysis.

Box 3.1 Questions addressed by institutional analysis

As the types of questions addressed by the different frameworks will vary, examples are given for each framework/approach.

Critical Institutionalism

- How does governance function in an area and with what implications for different types of resource users?
- How are bureaucratic and socially embedded institutions drawn on in the governance of natural resources?

Environmental Entitlements

- How do people get access to and control over particular natural resources? Which institutions mediate access and control?
- How does natural resource use by different social actors lead to changes in different components of the environment?

Institutional Analysis and Development

- What types of rules would lead to the sustainable use of fisheries in a given context?

Social-Ecology System framework

- Why are some social-ecological systems sustainable whereas others collapse?

Why do institutions matter in poverty–environment relations?

Institutions play a role in every part of our lives. From how we interact with our parents, our peers and our employers to how we behave in public and how we are affected by government policies and regulations. Institutions must, then, play a role in how people get access to environmental resources, how much they can extract, when and how. Understanding the nature and influence of institutions is particularly important when new policies or projects are planned for a natural resource and/or for people using a natural resource. Managing natural resources requires much more than having the right knowledge about different types of trees and fish species, about their reproduction and extraction techniques and rates, for example. Understanding is needed regarding who it is that is extracting or harvesting the natural resources, when and why those people, who makes decisions and why. Institutions can be hard to identify and research, particularly those more indirect in their influence, for example kinship and gender relations affecting access to forest resources. The focus of this chapter then is to explore how institutions can be identified and their role in influencing decisions and behaviour in relation to people–environment relations understood. Box 3.2 summarizes why and when you might want to focus on institutions in an investigation of poverty–environment relations.

Box 3.2 **Why and when would you focus on institutions for investigating poverty–environment relations?**

- When you want to understand how formal and informal arrangements affect how people interact with environmental resources;
- to investigate arrangements beyond those associated with natural resources that may have a bearing on how people access natural resources, e.g. marriage and power relations;
- to investigate how people have cooperated to manage natural resources and what rules have been developed for this management.

The section on definitions and categorizations of institutions in Chapter 1 should be referred to and recalled throughout this chapter, particularly the definitions of bureaucratic and socially embedded institutions taken from Cleaver (2002).

Critical Institutionalism

Critical Institutionalism refers to a broad range of approaches to the analysis of institutions that mediate access to, and control over, natural resources, bringing together insights from a range of disciplinary perspectives, including social theory, political ecology, legal pluralism and history (Cleaver, 2012). Whilst there are many ways of approaching institutional analysis within a Critical Institutionalism perspective, they share key characteristics, as set out in Table 3.1 and compared with characteristics of Mainstream Institutionalism.

The types of characteristics of Critical Institutionalism are summarized by Hall *et al.* (2014: 73) as forming three areas of emphasis: '(i) complexity of institutions entwined in everyday social life; (ii) their historical formation; and (iii) the interplay between the traditional and the modern, formal and informal arrangements'.

In contrast to Mainstream Institutionalism, a Critical Institutionalism approach gives greater recognition to institutions that mediate access to, and control over, natural resources but are not necessarily 'designed' or 'developed' with natural

Table 3.1 Key features of institutional thinking

Features	Mainstream Institutionalism	Critical Institutionalism
Nature of institutions	Formal/public institutions in nested layers with horizontal and vertical linkages	Blurring of boundaries and of scales, blending of institutional logics and forms (e.g. formal/informal)
Formation of institutions	Institutions formed through crafting: design principles characterize robust institutions	Institutions pieced together through practice, improvisation, adaptation of previous arrangements
Nature of decision-making	Decision-making and negotiations mainly conducted in public fora	Decision-making and negotiations embedded in everyday life, shaped by history and politics
Models of agency	'Bounded rationality' models of agency as strategic and purposeful – individuals as resource appropriators	Agency as relational, exercised consciously and non-consciously – individuals with complex social identities and emotions
Factors shaping human behaviour in institutions	Information, incentives, rules, sanctions and repeated interactions	Social structures and power dynamics, relationships, norms, individual creativity
Outcomes	Institutions can be crafted to produce efficient resource management outcomes	Institutions evolve to 'socially fit': functioning may result in access to *or* exclusion from resources

Source: Cleaver (2012: 16).

resource governance in mind. Such institutions are, instead, closely associated with social life and interactions, power relations, kinship and gender. Therefore, the identification and analysis of institutions that matter, why and how for poverty–environment relations, is a challenging task. As Cleaver observes, 'rules, boundaries and processes are "fuzzy"; people's complex social identities and unequal power relationships shape natural resource arrangements and outcomes' (2012: 9). The boundaries of formal and informal, or bureaucratic and socially embedded, institutions become blurred, making distinctions between them difficult, as institutions are interpreted, adapted and negotiated. In this array of institutions, Critical Institutionalism also recognizes that not only do people have different degrees and types of access to natural resources, they also differ in how much, or whether, they can influence the nature of institutions, i.e. who sets the rules. The nature of power relations within a group of people, and between groups, is therefore of particular interest to Critical Institutionalism. This diversity of institutions and the importance of social identities and relations make understanding their background and rationale critical. The nature of, and change in, institutions over time should be explored, taking an historical approach, as well as analysing the political and economic context and implications of institutions.

The interplay of institutions is given particular attention in Critical Institutionalism through the coining of the term 'institutional bricolage', where people draw on bureaucratic and socially embedded institutions to find a way through institutional arrangements to make things happen (Cleaver, 2002). Cleaver (2012: 45) refers to institutional bricolage as

> a process in which people consciously and non-consciously draw on existing social formulae (styles of thinking, models of cause and effect, social norms and sanctioned social roles and relationships) to patch or piece together institutions in response to changing situations.

de Koning and Cleaver (2012: 281) adjust this definition, describing institutional bricolage as 'a process through which actors consciously and unconsciously reshape or piece together different arrangements at hand'. Bricolage is a useful term for reflecting the dynamism, complexity and diversity of institutional arrangements; it gives emphasis to the importance of both bureaucratic and socially embedded institutions and how these interact and are used pluralistically by different actors for a range of purposes.

Examples of investigations informed by Critical Institutionalism and institutional bricolage are given by de Koning (2011) and Cleaver *et al.* (2013). de Koning (2011) takes a Critical Institutionalism approach to investigate forest governance in the Amazon investigating how 'institutions, either introduced or locally embedded, affect the forest practices of small farmers in the Amazon region of Bolivia and Ecuador' and how these smallholders reshape these institutions (de Koning, 2011: 38). de Koning (2011) examined the nature and influence of rules, norms and beliefs within bureaucratic and socially embedded categories of institutions, observing that new forest governance institutions, designed for example for community-based forest management, are introduced into settings that are already governed by socially embedded institutions and existing bureaucratic institutions. The new arrangements are not likely to remain as they were designed but are adapted in various ways, reflecting the existing institutions. Different types of 'bricolage practices' are identified in different locations, resulting in different combinations and manifestations of institutions. These 'bricolage processes' are categorized as aggregation ('recombination of various institutional elements'), alteration ('the adaptation or reshaping of both bureaucratic and socially embedded institutions') and articulation ('emphasising local rules, norms, and beliefs because of disagreement with bureaucratic institutions') (de Koning, 2011: 32–33). New structures, rules and processes are adjusted, adapted and interpreted differently in different settings, with the nature and extent of the response informed by existing institutions. The subsequent management structures, rules and systems will consequently differ between locations, with potential for different outcomes for both people and natural resources. Distinguishing between different processes or practices of bricolage can guide an analysis of the interactions between institutions and enable understanding of what may happen when new governance arrangements are introduced or an institutional context is altered in some way. An examination of the bricolage practices also sheds further light on how people navigate their way through different forms and sources of institutions to access benefits from natural resources.

The example provided by Cleaver *et al.* (2013) investigates the practices and implications of local governance in relation to pastoralists in the Usangu Plains in southwest Tanzania. The context of the case study is of national-level concern regarding the drying-up of the Ruaha River in the 1990s and of conflict regarding access to land and water between farmers and pastoralists. The drying-up of the river was commonly blamed on the pastoralists and their cattle, culminating in government-initiated removal of the pastoralists from much of the plains in 2006–07. Cleaver *et al.* (2013) identify and examine how bureaucratic and socially embedded institutions are interwoven in responses by members of the pastoralist communities to the conflict and removal. The examples include how a village council kept a woman and her child 'hostage' to encourage her pastoralist husband, accused of allowing his cattle to trample over a farmer's crops, to surrender to the council. This 'extralegal' practice of keeping the pastoralist's wife and child hostage was undertaken when efforts to arrest the pastoralist more formally had failed. Negotiations were subsequently planned between the farmer and the pastoralist by the village council, rather than taking the pastoralist to the police to be charged and tried. A range of responses were available to, and used by, the village council to reach a conclusion that was satisfactory to the farmer and reasonable given the lack of strong evidence and vehement denial by the pastoralist.

A further example is of the operation of Sungusungu, a 'militia' group that had taken on broader governance roles during Cleaver *et al.*'s initial research period of 1999–2002 in addition to guarding cattle in the area due to the perceived lack of state ability to ensure law and order. These groups of young and elder pastoralists and agriculturalists had either replaced or supplemented the formal village defence committees, expanding their role of guarding cattle to patrolling the area and reporting to the village committees. By 2011, as a result of the conflict and eviction, the Sungusungu had lost its semi-formal status and members were meeting more clandestinely but the group was still important as an ethnic identity organization and part of the wider governance network in the pastoralist communities. Cleaver *et al.* (2013: 184) conclude that using the lens of institutional bricolage enables understanding of the 'pattern in which mobile pastoralism as a livelihood strategy is being squeezed out' in the area. The lens enables recognition of the plurality of institutional arrangements that exist in many situations and of the influence of power relations on the form, functioning and outcomes of institutional arrangements.

Identifying and investigating a range of institutions and how these interact and are reshaped in a certain situation and over time is a challenging task. A broad, yet deep, investigation is needed, to be able to capture the range of institutions that may influence natural resource governance, going well beyond institutions designed for that purpose. Institutions to be investigated may include kinship relations, cultural norms and taboos, and gender norms and relations, including within marriage and households, as well as rules regarding how natural resources are used and who can use them, when and how. Making generalizations about natural resource governance from a Critical Institutionalism analysis would therefore be difficult. This approach is, however, particularly useful for an analysis of natural resource governance through its recognition of the plurality and diversity of relevant institutions and how these interact and may be reshaped and combined to form new and diverse institutional arrangements.

The Environmental Entitlements approach

The Environmental Entitlements approach, developed by Leach, Mearns and Scoones (1997, 1999), provides a framework for understanding the role of institutional dynamics in environmental change. The approach takes a Critical Institutionalism perspective, though it predates the coining of the phrase 'Critical Institutionalism'. It does this through recognizing diversity and complexity in the range and nature of institutions that influence how people access natural resources, rather than aiming to design new, or reshape existing, institutions. The approach assumes that endowments are drawn from environmental goods and services, where endowments refer to 'the rights and resources that social actors have' and entitlements refer to 'legitimate effective command over alternative commodity bundles' (Leach *et al.*, 1997: 16–17). Leach *et al.* go on to define environmental entitlements as 'alternative sets of utilities derived from environmental goods and services over which social actors have legitimate effective command and which are instrumental in achieving wellbeing' (1997: 17).

The approach draws on Amartya Sen's analysis of the causes of famine in the 1980s, from which he developed the concept of entitlements in the context of people not having sufficient food despite food being available locally in the market. Sen defined entitlements as 'the set of alternative commodity bundles that a person can command in a society using the totality of rights and opportunities that he or she faces' (1984: 497). The use of the concept of entitlements recognizes the complexity of accessing resources and the interplay of rights and opportunities in commanding access to resources. Leach *et al.* (1997, 1999) set out the connections between endowments, entitlements and capabilities in a diagram. This is shown in Figure 3.1, with explanations of each dimension added for clarity.

The Environmental Entitlements framework was developed in response to a critique of community-based natural resource management (CBNRM) initiatives, which Leach *et al.* suggest have 'frequently fallen short of expectations' (1999: 226). They suggest that the lack of success of CBNRM is in part due to the lack of recognition of diversity and complexity within 'communities'. Such initiatives had, they argued, assumed that everyone in a community had equal say, rights and assets and were able to engage with, and benefit from, CBNRM.

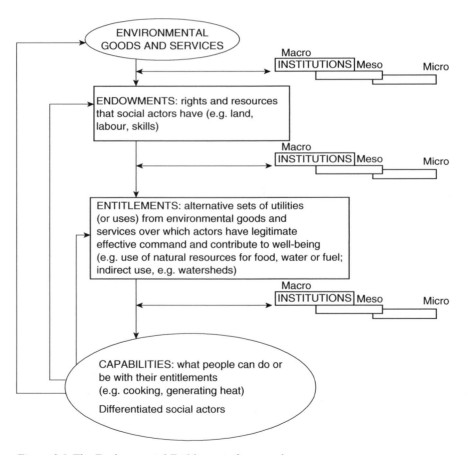

Figure 3.1 The Environmental Entitlements framework.

Source: Adapted from Leach *et al.*, 1999: 234.

The Environmental Entitlements approach does not make such an assumption and instead recognizes diversity in the endowments and entitlements that people have. It builds on this recognition through analysing the nature and extent of endowments and entitlements and how these may or may not be used and benefited from given the types of institutions that influence use and benefits. Institutions are identified and their role and influence analysed at three levels: micro (household and local), meso (between government level and local, including district government) and macro (including macro-economic policies and global agreements).

The framework aims to assist in improving CBNRM initiatives by promoting a focus on institutions as 'mediators of people–environment relations' (1999: 226) rather than focusing on organizational structures for natural resource governance and on recognizing how institutions influence the endowments and entitlements people have and benefit from. The nature of endowments and entitlements in turn influence use and management of natural resources. The approach was also developed on the premise that landscapes transform over time, responding to a concern that environmental change was being labelled as degradation where 'transformation' was a more appropriate label.

The approach is seen as being useful in that it:

1   recognizes and shows that many institutions play a role in natural resource management, some of which are not dedicated to the use or management of natural resources, such as marriage or kinship, but are 'important in mediating the endowments and entitlements of certain social actors' (Leach *et al.*, 1999: 240);
2   reveals how people rely on different institutions to support their claims to environmental goods and services;
3   incorporates the reality that many of the institutions involved are informal and dynamic.

The framework is intended to reflect the dynamic context within which environmental goods and services can be accessed, as institutions change over time and space and are not to be viewed as static. Leach *et al.* (1999) draw on several case studies to illustrate the application of the framework, including two villages in the Wenchi District of Ghana which were studied to investigate institutions that mediate access to forest resources. The leaves of *Marantaceae* plants are given as an example of endowments that people have as rights can be gained over them, with women collecting the leaves and either using or selling them for wrapping food, kola nuts and other products. The nature of the endowment depends on whether the plants are inside or outside of government-reserved forests. Outside of the reserved forests, the leaves are usually common property, with village rules and norms influencing access to them. If the plants are on farmland, access would depend on negotiation with the land-holding or farm household. Within a reserved forest, access would depend on getting a permit from the Forest Department. A range of institutions exist, then, to control access, largely depending on the location of the plants. Entitlements derived from the leaves, or endowments, include direct use or cash income from the sale.

Environmental entitlements and fisheries resources in Uganda

A further example of the application of the Environmental Entitlements framework was given in an article published on my own analysis of fisheries in Uganda (Nunan, 2006). My application of the Environmental Entitlements framework was undertaken with respect to the introduction of co-management within the fisheries sector in lake fisheries. Fisheries co-management is defined as 'an arrangement where responsibility for resource management is shared between the government and user groups' (Sen and Raakjær Nielsen, 1996: 406) and has been widely adopted within the sector. The rationale for this widespread adoption is partly due to the shift towards decentralization and participation in all spheres of government within a development context, but also due to there often being inadequate resources to manage fisheries at the scale and depth needed. The analysis undertaken in Nunan (2006) uses the Environmental Entitlements framework to show how institutional arrangements may change with the introduction of co-management, but it was too soon after the introduction of the approach to assess whether such changes had in fact materialized. The aim of the analysis was to illustrate the diversity and nature of institutional arrangements influencing access to, and benefits from, fisheries and how these could be challenged by co-management.

The fisheries sector in Uganda is significant, providing employment to an estimated 1–1.5 million people and has been at times the second highest foreign exchange earner within agricultural commodities (after coffee). There have, however, and continue to be, concerns about declining stocks and catches in the lakes of Uganda and in the early 2000s the Government embarked on the implementation of the new policy of implementing fisheries co-management. Nunan (2006) includes an analysis of institutions that mediate access to, and benefits from, fisheries resources prior to and after the adoption of co-management. This is illustrated in Figure 3.2, which follows the Environmental Entitlements framework in identifying institutions at the macro, meso and micro levels that mediate the nature and extent of endowments from environmental goods and services and entitlements from these endowments. Examples of institutions mediating access to the fisheries include:

- Policies and legislation on fishing gear and methods and on licensing methods and processes. The scope and impact of these on access is limited however, as demonstrated by belief that there are widespread illegalities across the inland lakes, catching undersized and immature fish.
- Relationships of power and influence between stakeholders, particularly between boat owners and boat crew, and between local government Fisheries Officers and fishermen. Boat owners are generally wealthier and more powerful than the boat crew they employ. Without employment, the boat crew cannot get into a boat and benefit from access to the fisheries. They therefore need good relations with boat owners and a good reputation for catching fish. Payment may come in the form of sharing the catch, or the income from the

catch, requiring negotiation, trust and accepted norms of behaviour in terms of fishing methods, use of gear and the sale of catch.

- Gender relations mediate access to fishing and to fish for processing and trading. It is generally considered taboo for a woman to fish from a boat, though some have successfully challenged that belief, and so women are more likely to be processors or traders.
- The relationships among and between fish processors, fishmongers (traders) and boat owners and crew are institutions that affect benefits and management. Those with entitlements to buy fish from a fisher may include his wife, relatives, especially those who have helped the fisher in the past, and traders who have provided credit. The nature and dynamics of these relationships will be affected by power and gender relations, social norms and other factors.
- The existence of local leaders, known as Gabungas, who were not elected but passed down the role through generations. These were supplemented by the formation of Landing Site Committees and Taskforces in the 1990s and early 2000s, and then replaced by Beach Management Units (BMUs) with the introduction of co-management in the 2000s. It is possible that the influence of the 'Gabunga' survived through election of powerful individuals onto the BMU Committee.

Prior to the introduction of co-management, the fisheries were more difficult to access for boat crew and women than boat owners, though boat owners rely on crew for catch and often on women for processing and trading the fish. Institutional arrangements favoured access to the fisheries by boat owners, with their dominant positions as Gabungas and latterly as members of other fisheries committees. The introduction of co-management did not drastically change these institutions overnight, but created opportunity for greater empowerment of women and boat crew through their required participation in BMUs. Participation in new natural resource governance structures does not, however, necessarily equate to having new power and may result in very limited, if any, change. The analysis only points to where challenges to institutional arrangements exist and how efforts to empower previously marginalized stakeholders may create opportunities for better access to natural resources. The institutions prior to the introduction of co-management and how they could change with the introduction are set out in Table 3.2, together with an analysis of how the changes could lead to benefits for actors. Subsequent to initial implementation, the effectiveness of co-management structures and processes has differed between areas and concern about stock levels continues (Kjær *et al.*, 2012).

The example of fisheries co-management in Uganda shows how institutions exist at multiple levels and are interconnected, with institutions at one level impinging on other levels, and that institutions beyond the sector, such as marriage and kinship, impact on how people may gain and maintain access to natural resources.

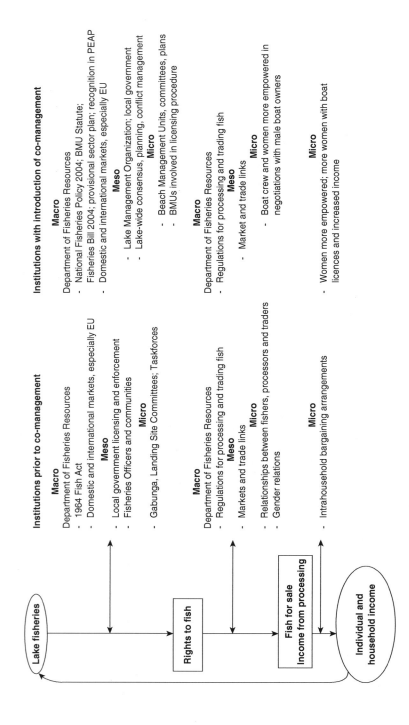

Institutions prior to co-management

Macro

Department of Fisheries Resources
- 1964 Fish Act
- Domestic and international markets, especially EU

Meso
- Local government licensing and enforcement
- Fisheries Officers and communities

Micro
- Gabunga, Landing Site Committees; Taskforces

Macro

Department of Fisheries Resources
- Regulations for processing and trading fish

Meso
- Markets and trade links

Micro
- Relationships between fishers, processors and traders
- Gender relations

Micro
- Intrahousehold bargaining arrangements

Institutions with introduction of co-management

Macro

Department of Fisheries Resources
- National Fisheries Policy 2004; BMU Statute; Fisheries Bill 2004; provisional sector plan; recognition in PEAP
- Domestic and international markets, especially EU

Meso
- Lake Management Organization; local government
- Lake-wide consensus, planning, conflict management

Micro
- Beach Management Units, committees, plans
- BMUs involved in licensing procedure

Macro

Department of Fisheries Resources
- Regulations for processing and trading fish

Meso
- Market and trade links

Micro
- Boat crew and women more empowered in negotiations with male boat owners

Micro
- Women more empowered; more women with boat licences and increased income

Figure 3.2 Environmental Entitlements diagram for fisheries co-management, Uganda.

Source: Nunan, 2006: 1325.

Table 3.2 Changes in fisheries institutions in Uganda in the 2000s

Pre-existing institution	New institutions	Impact on stakeholders from changes
1964 Fish Act and statutory instruments on fishing methods and gear, fish size and vessel licensing	Decentralized fisheries licensing 2004 National Fisheries Policy 2003 Fish (Beach Management Rules)	Roles of communities and local governments changed; more power given to communities; legal role of communities in planning and management
Gabungas, Taskforces and Landing Site Committees hold power over access to and use of fisheries within fisheries communities	All stakeholders participate in decision-making and negotiations within new structures (Beach Management Unit Committees and Assemblies, and Lake Management Organizations)	Power of boat owners challenged and reduced; women, boat crew, fish mongers and processors, and other fisheries stakeholders have more voice in decision making
Mistrust between local government Fisheries Officers and fisheries communities; extraction of informal 'tax' on fisheries activities	Co-management changes relationship between fisheries communities and Fisheries Officers: requires greater co-operation, information sharing and collaboration	BMU members should have greater influence on local government through participation in planning, revenue generation, information collection and enforcement
Gender relations: women rarely involved in decision making and very few women owned boats	Legislation requires women to have at least 30% of BMU Committee places; licensing process on lakes Edward and George had target to promote women with boat licences	Women empowered, with greater influence on decision-making, able to speak out on issues affecting women. Greater access to boat licences and consequently increase in income
Boat owners more powerful than crew, with more influence on decision-making	Legislation requires crew to have 30% of places on BMU Committee; licensing process on lakes Edward and George had target to promote access for boat crew to obtain boat licences	Boat crew empowered, with greater influence on decision-making, able to speak out on issues affecting boat crew. Greater access to boat licences and consequently increase in income

Source: Adapted from Nunan (2006: 1326).

Institutional Analysis and Development framework

The IAD framework was developed by Ostrom and others in the 1980s onwards (Ostrom, 2011) as a tool for understanding institutional arrangements and interactions with natural resource systems. It sits firmly within common property scholarship, categorized above as Mainstream Institutionalism. The focus is on how institutions have evolved to govern common property and on investigating and testing design principles that enable sustainable and effective common property management. There are, to date, many more examples of the framework being applied in a developed world context, but the framework and associated scholarship on common property reflects many government- and donor-sponsored approaches to natural resource management in the developing world, where the emphasis is often on creating new structures and processes for natural resource management and identifying and learning from 'what works'. There are, though, examples of application of the framework in a developing country context and its application by Clement (2010) in Vietnam is provided as an example of this.

The IAD framework can be used in combination with many theories and models, but is most closely associated with classical economics and rational choice theory, which assumes that actors will act rationally in their own self-interests. It may be used with game theory for example, to simulate how actors may respond under certain conditions and within specified rules.

- The framework consists of a set of external variables in three categories: physical/material conditions, attributes of the community and rules-in-use.
- These external variables influence the action arena in which the action situations and actors interact.
- The action arena feeds into patterns of interactions, leading to outcomes.
- Evaluative criteria can be used to assess the performance of the institutions, process and system.

The framework is shown in Figure 3.3, with an explanation of each of the variables given in Table 3.3. The IAD framework suggests that outcomes of the action arena are shaped both by the outputs of the action situation and by exogenous factors (McGinnis, 2011: 172). The framework is portrayed as a process, with feedback from the outcomes going back into the exogenous variables before being fed back into the action situation to inform further

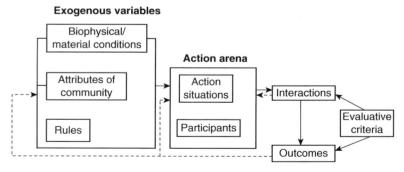

Figure 3.3 The Institutional Analysis and Development framework.

Source: Adapted from Ostrom, 2005: 15.

Table 3.3 Variables in IAD

Type of variable	Explanation
Physical or biophysical conditions	How are the resources characterized in terms of: • Subtractibility – does consumption by one unit lower that available to others? • Exclusion – how costly is it for one unit to exclude others from using the resource? Resources are categorized as: • Private – subtractibility and low costs of exclusion • Public – nonsubtractibility and high costs of exclusion • Toll – nonsubtractable and low costs of exclusion • Common pool – subtractibility and high costs of exclusion
Attributes of the community	• Trust – how far do community members believe that everyone will keep to the rules and cooperate? • Reciprocity – will members cooperate with others who have cooperated in previous encounters? • Common understanding – to what extent do members have the same goals and values? • Social capital – of an individual that can be drawn on in relying on others to help in times of need; and, of a group, generated by stable networks of important interactions among members of that community • Cultural repertoire – strategies, norms, rules, organizational templates and other remembered or imagined practices that are drawn on in processes of deliberation and implementation
Rules-in-use	• May include rules that are formal (i.e. laid down and agreed), that result from strategies, norms and rules being used on a regular basis by participants and property rights • Property rights take different forms, including access, withdrawal, management, exclusion and alienation, and understanding is needed of the nature of the property rights system • Seven categories of rules identified: position, boundary, choice, aggregation, information, payoff and scope
Evaluative criteria	• Efficiency – in how resources are used • Equity – in how outcomes and processes are distributed • Legitimacy – as perceived by participants • Participation – what is the nature and extent of participation, as participation is considered to be associated with legitimacy? • Accountability – to whom are the structures accountable and how are the structures accountable to direct users? • Adaptability, resilience, robustness or sustainability – how much can a system suffer a disturbance and yet recover and continue to function, not losing its structural or functional integrity?

Source: McGinnis (2011).

decision-making based on the nature and implications of the outcomes and changes in the variables, as shown in Figure 3.3. Ostrom (2009: 9) referred to the IAD framework as a 'multi-tier conceptual map', one which sets out concepts relevant to an institutional setting. The framework is used not only for understanding institutional arrangements, but also for predicting decisions and actions.

Action arena

The IAD framework has as its unit of analysis an 'action arena', which includes those individuals and organizations that make resource management decisions. As can be seen from Figure 3.4, the analysis is concerned with how actions are linked to possible outcomes and the different costs and benefits associated with certain actions and outcomes. The first step in using the framework is to identify the set of actors, which may go beyond the boundaries of a resource or ecosystem.

The framework recognizes that action arenas are linked across different levels of analysis, with rules nested within, and influenced by, other sets of rules. McGinnis (2011) refers to the action situation as the 'black box', where inputs, such as information on the physical conditions and the rules-in-use, are used to inform decision-making. The components and processes of the action situation are shown in Figure 3.4.

Actors may be individuals, groups of individuals or organizations. Ostrom (2009: 12) provides an illustrative set of questions that could be posed to investigate an action situation where resources are being harvested, as shown in Table 3.4.

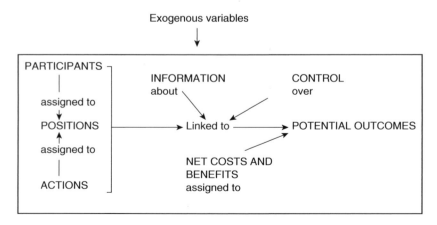

Figure 3.4 The action situation.

Source: Adapted from Ostrom, 2005: 33.

Table 3.4 Investigating an action situation

Component	Questions
Set of actors	Who and how many individuals withdraw resource units (e.g. fish, water, fodder) from this resource system?
Positions	What positions exist (e.g. members of an irrigation association, water distributors and a chair)?
Set of allowable actions	Which types of harvesting technologies are used? (e.g. are chainsaws used to harvest timber? Are there open and closed seasons? Do fishers return fish smaller than some limit to the water?)
Potential outcomes	What geographic region and what events in that region are affected by participants in these positions? What chain of events links actions to outcomes?
Level of control over choice	The level of control over choice: do appropriators take the above actions on their own initiative, or do they confer with others? (E.g. before entering the forest to cut fodder, does an appropriator obtain a permit?)
Information available	How much information do appropriators have about the condition of the resource itself, about other appropriators' cost and benefit functions, and about how their actions cumulate into joint outcomes?
Costs and benefits of actions and outcomes	How costly are various actions to each type of appropriator, and what kinds of benefits can be achieved as a result of various group outcomes?

Source: Ostrom (2011: 12).

Rules-in-use

Rules are a type of exogenous variable according to the framework, which influence what goes on in the action situation and the subsequent outcomes. Ostrom (2011: 17) defines rules as 'shared understandings among those involved that refer to enforced prescriptions about what actions (or states of the world) are required, prohibited, or permitted'. These rules are the institutions that inform and influence behaviour and decision-making at multiple levels. Rules may be made at three levels: the 'operational' level through day-to-day activities of actors; the 'collective' action level, setting the context for operational rules; or the 'constitutional' level where bigger decisions are made about inclusion and how rules are made at the other levels.

The IAD framework is closely associated with the set of 'rules' identified for successful common property management by Elinor Ostrom and these are listed in Box 3.3. These were subsequently translated into a set of 'design principles', also listed in Box 3.3, seen as less prescriptive than the original rules. That is, rather than putting forward a list of factors that are essential for sustainable and effective common property governance, with any system not having these seen as ineffective, the 'design principles' instead offer a set of questions that enable those involved in common property governance or research to know what to ask or look for.

***Box 3.3* Rules and design principles for lasting common property institutions**

1 Clearly defined boundaries;
2 rules governing use or provision of the resource must be appropriate to local conditions;
3 collective-choice arrangements;
4 monitoring of rules and use: by users or accountable to the users;
5 graduated sanctions;
6 conflict resolution mechanisms;
7 recognition of legitimacy;
8 nested enterprises (for common property resources that are part of larger systems).

(Adapted from Ostrom, 1990: 90)

Ostrom subsequently translated these design principles into a set of questions which should be asked when designing and adapting institutional arrangements for a resource system:

- 'Who is allowed to harvest which kinds of resource units?
- What will be the timing, quantity, location and technology used for harvesting?
- Who is obligated to contribute resources to maintain the resource system itself?
- How are harvesting and maintenance activities to be monitored and enforced?
- How are conflicts over harvesting and maintenance to be resolved?
- How will cross-scale linkages be dealt with on a regular basis?
- How will risks of the unknown be taken into consideration?
- How will the rules affecting the above be changed over time with changes in the performance of the resource system, the strategies of participants and external opportunities and constraints?'

(Ostrom, 2008: 28–29)

The 'design principles' are less prescriptive than the rules shown in Box 3.3 but still direct an investigation towards certain directions in a more structured way than a Critical Institutionalism approach would. They also encourage a more interventionist approach to management than a Critical Institutionalism approach, putting forward rules and institutional arrangements that could be adopted to achieve certain predicted outcomes.

Multiple levels and sites of analysis

The IAD framework recognizes that common property resource management spans across levels of governance and enables analysis to take place at multiple levels. Ostrom (2007a) identifies four levels at which analysis is needed and inter-actions between the levels traced. These are:

- metaconstitutional situations;
- constitutional situations;
- collective choice situations;
- operational situations.

Rules pass down from the metaconstitutional level through the other levels to the operational situations, being influenced at each level by the characteristics of the physical world and the relevant community. Rules and structures are therefore 'nested' within another set of rules and structures, which provide the boundaries and direction for sub-levels.

In addition to there being multiple levels of analysis, there can be multiple authorities influencing common property governance, referred to as a 'polycentric' system of governance. McGinnis defines polycentricity as

> a system of governance in which authorities from overlapping jurisdictions (or centers of authority) interact to determine the conditions under which these authorities, as well as the citizens subject to these jurisdictional units, are authorized to act as well as the constraints put upon their activities for public purposes.

> (McGinnis, 2011: 171)

In a further definition, Pahl-Wostl (2009: 357) explains polycentric governance systems as being 'complex, modular systems where differently sized govern-ance units with different purpose, organization, spatial location interact to form together a largely self-organized governance regime'. Integration and coordi-nation between different units of governance therefore characterize polycentric systems. McGinnis (2011) sets out key characteristics of polycentric systems of governance as being:

- *Multi-level:* authorities at different levels, for example, local, district, provin-cial, national, regional and international.
- *Multi-type:* authorities that have a role in the governance of a natural resource may include general purpose authorities such as village councils and district authorities, and more specific structures such as water user committees and the ministry responsible for water.
- *Multi-sectoral:* structures involved in common property governance may come from different sectors, including public, private, voluntary, commu-nity-based and hybrid kinds of organizations. For example, private sector fish-processing factories may be involved in governance as well as commu-nity-based structures and government departments.
- *Multi-functional:* the structures concerned may have multiple functions that interact or go beyond common property governance, for example, planning, financing, coordination, monitoring and dispute resolution.

The characteristics of polycentric governance should be taken into consideration in applying the IAD framework, recognizing that the multiple levels within a governance system may involve multiple structures and functions. The concept of polycentricity is helpful in common property research as it reflects that, very often, governance of commons will involve multi-level, multi-type, multi-sectoral and multi-functional authorities and structures.

Using the IAD framework

The IAD framework is not static, but has evolved over time and continues to be modified and further developed, as shown in the example below from Clement (2010) and by Ostrom herself who further developed the framework to be applied in a social-ecological system context. Di Gregorio *et al.* (2008) adapt the IAD for use in an institutional analysis of poverty and discuss how institutions of property rights and collective action may mediate against the poverty outcomes.

Imperial (1999: 452–453) sets out several attributes of the IAD framework that makes it so useful:

1   It recognizes the full range of transaction costs associated with implementing policies.
2   It draws attention to the contextual conditions (physical, biological, social, economic, cultural, etc.) that can influence institutional design and performance.
3   There is no normative bias, i.e. it does not presume a particular institutional arrangement to be better than another.
4   It suggests using a variety of criteria to evaluate different institutional arrangements that could be adopted.
5   It focuses on rules rather than policies.

As there is no normative bias within the IAD framework, Ostrom (2008) urges that an experimental approach is taken to the design of institutions. Rather than a top-down approach which dictates which forms of institutional arrangements should be in place, she stresses that changes should be made in response to how the system is working. Different entry points can be taken to the framework, depending on the question being asked, with the variables mapped and modified to reflect complexity and diversity within systems and to test the implications of different policy responses.

The IAD framework is, then, fairly flexible and designed for use in complex, multi-level situations. With regard to enabling better understanding of poverty–environment relations, it can explain how and why outcomes are reached in collective action situations. This may include an analysis of the position and role of poor people in defining those outcomes and how rules, the biophysical conditions and community attributes influence how people interact and with what outcomes.

The Social-Ecological System framework

The IAD framework has been further developed by scholars at the Workshop in Political Theory and Policy Analysis to give greater attention to the ecology of a system, rather than seeing the natural resource as an external force, outside of the control of actors. The Social-Ecological System (SES) framework was subsequently developed and continues to be tested and modified. Ostrom explains the purpose of framework as being able to

> examine the nested attributes of a resource system and the resource units generated by that system that jointly affects the incentives of users within a set of rules crafted by local, distal, or nested governance systems to affect interactions and outcomes over time.
>
> (2007b: 15181)

The framework is designed to enable investigation into the complexity of relationships between components of a social-ecological system. It does this by encouraging the decomposition of variables. Each of the four subsystems (resource systems, resource units, governance systems, actors) is composed of a number of variables, referred to as second-level, or tier, variables, which are further composed of variables themselves, creating multiple tiers of explanation. Ostrom (2007b, 2009) describes the components and variables of the framework, setting out a detailed table of second-tier variables. These were further modified by McGinnis and Ostrom (2014), together with several other changes made to the

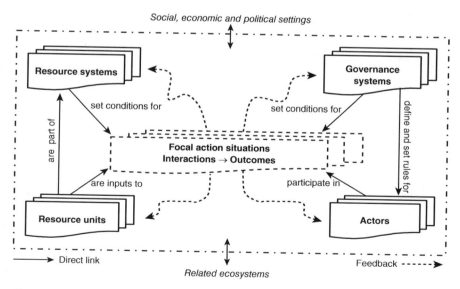

Figure 3.5 The Social-Ecological System framework.

Source: McGinnis and Ostrom, 2014.

framework. The version of the framework from McGinnis and Ostrom (2014) is shown in Figure 3.5.

Application of IAD to an analysis of state afforestation policies in Vietnam

Clement (2008, 2010) used the IAD framework in an assessment of the achievements of two major policies in Vietnam: the Five Million Hectares Reforestation Programme (5MHRP) and Forest Land Allocation (FLA). Her use of the framework is interesting in several respects. First, Clement uses the framework in conjunction with a political ecology perspective, to inform the analysis of discourses and power. Second, she uses the framework to inform the analysis of several 'action situations', reflecting the complexity of the forest policy context, from individual land users to the Ministry of Agriculture and Rural Development. Third, Clement built on Ostrom's IAD framework by adding a political analysis element to the framework. She does this because she observes that the IAD has an 'inadequate consideration of the role of power and interests in the crafting of institutions' (2010: 135). Clement argues that the distribution of power will shape and influence institutional arrangements at multiple levels and so used an adapted version of the IAD, in which political context and discourses were added to the box of exogenous variables.

The analysis is presented at central, provincial and village levels, enabling the interactions between the levels to be displayed, with the IAD framework used at multiple levels and within multiple action situations. Figure 3.6 shows one of Clement's portrayals of the IAD framework in relation to the desired outcomes of the 5MHRP. The framework is used at the central level of government, the provincial level and the operational, farmer, level, with the external variables identified and investigated at each level.

Clement concludes that the wide range of actors involved in forest management in Vietnam have supported afforestation, but for different, and sometimes conflicting, reasons. The overarching objective of increasing forest cover masked the complexity and diversity of forest ecosystems, resulting in the development of tree plantations in inappropriate locations and the use of fast-growing species to feed the paper and pulp industry, in line with arguments that all tree species are useful and beneficial for the environment. Despite evidence of increasing forest cover, there was little evidence of increased benefits to people or the environment. Clement and Amezaga (2009) suggest that there was a lack of incentives for households to become involved in the forestry sector and that the prevalent discourse encouraged forest cover increase at any cost, with inadequate consideration to suitability and livelihoods.

Clement's use of the IAD at multiple levels and in multiple settings illustrates how it can be used in different types of collective action situations, from village level to national policies. Figure 3.6 is rather complex and Clement (2008) produces several of these, reflecting the different policies and settings within forest policy in Vietnam. Figure 3.6 clearly shows how interconnected the levels of governance are and how complex a governance situation may be.

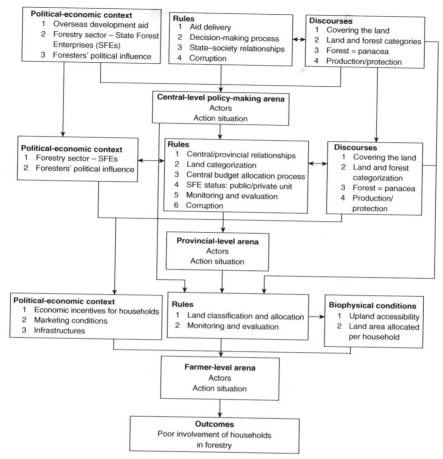

Figure 3.6 Clement's summary IAD for the 5MHRP in Vietnam.

Source: Clement, 2008: 209.

Comparing the approaches

The approaches reviewed in this chapter have different purposes, starting points and disciplinary roots. Which approach to use in a given situation would depend on many factors, including the theory on which you are drawing, the context of the natural resource use situation and the questions being asked. From the perspective of Critical Institutionalism, there are many socially embedded and bureaucratic institutions that have a bearing on how people access and benefit from natural resources, many of which may not appear to be related to natural resources at all. A Critical Institutionalism approach would investigate local social and political life and how these are connected to power and authority. This is far from easy. As Cleaver notes, 'it is far more difficult to capture the invisible workings of power, the informal bargaining and bending of rules in practice, the worldviews which shape participation and the uneven ways that institutions work for different people' (2012: 16–17). Perhaps just as challenging is to identify how different institutions are drawn on to gain and maintain access and benefits through processes of 'institutional bricolage'.

This emphasis on the range of bureaucratic and socially embedded institutions mediating access to and benefits from natural resources is also apparent in the Environmental Entitlements approach, with recognition that how people are able to use their endowments is mediated by these institutions at different levels. The approach can be used to analyse the situation of individuals, organizations and groups of people. The approach has not, however, been widely used since its development in the 1990s, with few examples available to learn from how it can be used and what it may reveal. This may reflect the complexity of the framework and the difficulty involved in identifying the diversity of institutions that mediate access to and control over natural resources. The limited number of examples of its use also reflects the emergence and widespread application of the Sustainable Livelihoods framework, which is described in Chapter 5, the development of which involved one of the proponents of the Environmental Entitlements approach. The framework is closely linked to Critical Institutionalism and provides a structure for using such an approach.

A Mainstream Institutionalism perspective is more closely associated with problems of collective decision-making and is therefore used to analyse collective action situations. It can be used in a predictive, experimental way, to identify the conditions under which sustainability of resource use might best be achieved. Within the IAD and SES frameworks, there is, though, scope for investigating 'rules in use', including socially embedded institutions, and so the two 'categories' of institutionalism, critical and mainstream, are not mutually exclusive.

Key strengths of the IAD and SES frameworks are their link to common property theory and the opportunity to use these alongside other theories and models, such as game theory and rational choice theory, deepening analysis of behaviour and decision-making. The frameworks enable analysis of common property regimes despite the complexity involved by bringing a structure and logic to the analysis. In addition, analysis using the frameworks can focus on one or a few parts rather than on all of the components together. In terms of their use in enabling investigation of poverty–environment relations, the IAD and SES are more concerned with natural resource governance than people's livelihoods and so do not have a clear livelihood or poverty focus.

Critical Institutionalism and the Environmental Entitlements framework are more concerned, then, with investigating the range and nature of institutions that mediate access to and benefits from natural resources, thereby influencing livelihood strategies and outcomes. The approaches can clearly be used to investigate poverty–environment linkages, with a focus on micro-level interactions whilst in a broader and historical political-economic context. The IAD and SES frameworks are more concerned with explaining or predicting outcomes of common property regime governance associated with certain institutional arrangements.

The different objectives, disciplinary backgrounds and assumptions are reflected in the differing applications and outcomes, suggesting different purposes and questions pursued.

Summary of key points

1 Institutions matter for whether and how people can access environmental and natural resources. They mediate such access through regularized 'rules of the game', from formal government policies to gender relations and kinship.
2 There are different approaches to investigating institutions in natural resource settings, with one categorization being between Mainstream and Critical Institutionalism. Mainstream Institutionalism is associated with the work of common property scholars, such as Elinor Ostrom, with focus being on design principles for effective natural resource governance. In contrast, Critical Institutionalism emphasizes the messy, complex and diverse range of institutions that influences access to environmental and natural resources, many, or perhaps most, of which were not designed for the purpose of natural resource governance. Such institutions may include marriage, kinship, power and gender.
3 Processes of institutional bricolage reflect on the way that people use components of different institutions – whether formal or socially embedded – in governing and benefiting from natural resources.
4 The Environmental Entitlements approach takes people as the starting point and provides a framework to enable analysis of how people gain access and claim entitlements from environmental resources. This approach is more akin to Critical Institutionalism, recognizing the diversity and complexity of institutional arrangements mediating access to, and control over, natural resources.
5 The Institutional Analysis and Development (IAD) framework was developed to enable the analysis of institutions involved with governing common property and is associated with the eight design principles of Elinor Ostrom's common property scholarship.
6 Critiques of the IAD in terms of the lack of emphasis on the ecology of natural resources led to the development of the Social-Ecological System framework, which aims to reflect the complexity of social-ecological systems through multiple tiers of variables.

Further reading

Cleaver, F. (2012) *Development Through Bricolage: Rethinking Institutions for Natural Resource Management*, London: Routledge.
How institutions influence people's access, use and management of natural resources is at the heart of this book, which challenges prescriptive approaches to there being ideal institutional arrangements for effective common property governance. Instead, Cleaver argues that institutions that influence access to and control over natural resources are not

necessarily directly concerned with natural resources but reflect the social location of people. For example, kinship, marriage and gender relations may influence such access and decision-making. Institutional analysis is complex and context specific and needs to consider the broader governance context in which the natural resources are situated. Cleaver draws on a range of empirical examples in discussions of why many community-based natural resource management initiatives fail to deliver on their objectives of improved natural resource management and livelihoods.

Ostrom, E. (1990) *Governing the Commons*, New York: Cambridge University Press.
This is *the* classic book on common property resource management. It sets out by critiquing three influential models used to explain natural resource dilemmas: Garrett Hardin's tragedy of the commons; Mancur Olson's logic of collective action; and the Prisoner's Dilemma. Each of these assumes that there is a problem of free riding and has contributed to the attention given to market and state-based solutions to natural resource problems. Ostrom challenges the assumptions made by these models about the lack of cooperation between actors and presents empirical data and case studies to identify a set of conditions under which common property may be successfully governed. Ostrom goes on to demonstrate that when common-pool resource users communicate with each other and establish agreed-upon rules and strategies, the resource can be managed sustainably and equitably. She presents the eight design principles that should contribute to a greater chance of effective and sustainable management of common-pool resources. This is one of the most frequently referred-to books in literature on common property regimes.

Ostrom, E., Gardner, R. and Valker, J. (1994) *Rules, Games, and Common-Pool Resources*, Ann Arbor: University of Michigan Press.
An essential text for understanding the components and application of IAD. The book focuses on three questions (p. 19):

> 1. In finitely repeated CPR dilemmas, to what degree are the predictions about behaviour and outcomes derived from noncooperative game theory supported by empirical evidence? 2. In CPR dilemmas where behaviour and outcomes are substantially different from that predicted, are there behavioural regularities that can be drawn upon in the development of improved theories? 3. What types of institutional and physical variables affect the likelihood of successful resolution of CPR dilemmas?'

The book is an essential guide to the IAD framework, with several chapters exploring the nature and role of rules in common property regimes.

Leach, M., Mearns, R. and Scoones, I. (1997) Environmental entitlements: A framework for understanding the institutional dynamics of environmental change. *IDS Discussion Paper*, no. 359, Brighton: Institute of Development Studies.
The original source for the Environmental Entitlements approach, setting out and explaining why and how the Environmental Entitlements approach was developed, with examples of its application. The development of the approach as a response to the failure of community-based natural resource management is explained, particularly in terms of challenging notions of 'community' and 'resource degradation'.

References

Agrawal, A. (2005) *Environmentality: Technologies of Government and the Making of Subjects*, London: Duke University Press.

Cleaver, F. (2002) 'Reinventing institutions: Bricolage and the social embeddedness of natural resource management', *European Journal of Development Research*, 14(2): 11–30.

Cleaver, F. (2012) *Development Through Bricolage: Rethinking Institutions for Natural Resource Management*, London: Earthscan.

Cleaver, F., Franks, T., Maganga, F. and Hall, K. (2013) 'Institutions, security, and pastoralism: Exploring the limits of hybridity', *African Studies Review*, 56(3): 165–189.

Clement, F. (2008) 'A multi-level analysis of forest policies in northern Vietnam: Uplands, people, institutions and discourses', Thesis submitted for the degree of Doctor of Philosophy, Newcastle: Newcastle University.

Clement, F. (2010) 'Analysing decentralised natural resource governance: Proposition for a "politicised" institutional analysis and development framework', *Policy Science*, 43: 129–156.

Clement, F. and Amezaga, J.M. (2009) 'Afforestation and forestry land allocation in Northern Vietnam: Analysing the gap between policy intentions and outcomes', *Land Use Policy*, 26(2): 458–470.

de Koning, J. (2011) 'Reshaping institutions: Bricolage processes in smallholder forestry in the Amazon', PhD Thesis, Wageningen: Wageningen University.

de Koning, J. and Cleaver, F. (2012) 'Institutional bricolage in community forestry: An agenda for future research', in Arts, B., van Bommel, S., Ros-Tonen, M. and Verschoor, G. (eds), *Forest-People Interfaces*, Wageningen: Wageningen Academic Publishers, pp. 277–290.

Di Gregorio, M., Hagedorn, K., Kirk, M., Korf, B., McCarthy, N., Meinzen-Dick, R. and Swallow, B. (2008) 'Property rights, collective action, and poverty: The role of institutions for poverty reduction', *CAPRi Working Paper No. 81*, Washington, DC: International Food Policy Research Institute.

Hall, K. Cleaver, F., Franks, T. and Maganga, F. (2014) 'Capturing critical institutionalism: A synthesis of key themes and debates', *European Journal of Development Research*, 26(1): 71–86.

Imperial, M.T. (1999) 'Institutional analysis and ecosystem-based management: The institutional analysis and development framework', *Environmental Management*, 24(4): 449–465.

Johnson, C. (2004) 'Uncommon ground: The "poverty of history" in common property discourse', *Development and Change*, 35(3): 407–433.

Kjær, A.M., Muhumuza, F., Mwebaze, T. and Katusiimeh, M. (2012) 'The political economy of the fisheries sector in Uganda: Ruling elites, implementation costs and industry interests', *DIIS Working Paper 2012:04*, Copenhagen: Danish Institute for International Studies.

Leach, M., Mearns, R. and Scoones, I. (1997) 'Environmental entitlements: A framework for understanding the institutional dynamics of environmental change', *IDS Discussion Paper*, no. 359, Brighton: Institute of Development Studies.

Leach, M., Mearns, R. and Scoones, I. (1999) 'Environmental entitlements: Dynamics and institutions in community-based natural resource management', *World Development*, 27(2): 225–247.

Lewins, R. (2007) 'Acknowledging the informal institutional setting of natural resource management: Consequences for policy-makers and practitioners', *Progress in Development Studies*, 7(3): 201–215.

McGinnis, M.D. (2011) 'An introduction to IAD and the language of the Ostrom Workshop: A simple guide to a complex framework', *Policy Studies Journal*, 39(1): 169–183.

McGinnis, M. and Ostrom, E. (2014) 'SES framework: Initial changes and continuing challenges', *Ecology and Society*, 19(2): 30.

Nunan, F. (2006) 'Empowerment and institutions: Managing fisheries in Uganda', *World Development*, 34(7): 1316–1332.

Ostrom, E. (1990) *Governing the Commons: The Evolution of Institutions for Collective Action*, Cambridge: Cambridge University Press.

Ostrom, E. (2005) *Understanding Institutional Diversity*, Princeton, NJ: Princeton University Press.

Ostrom, E. (2007a) 'Institutional rational choice. An assessment of the institutional analysis and development framework', in Sabatier, P.A. (ed.), *Theories of the Policy Process*, 2nd edition, Boulder, CO: Westview Press, pp. 21–64.

Ostrom, E. (2007b) 'A diagnostic approach for going beyond panaceas', *Proceedings of the National Academy of Sciences*, 104: 15181–15187.

Ostrom, E. (2008) 'Institutions and the environment', *Economic Affairs*, 28(3): 24–31.

Ostrom, E. (2009) 'A general framework for analyzing sustainability of social-ecological systems', *Science*, 325: 419–422.

Ostrom, E. (2011) 'Background on the institutional analysis and development framework', *Policy Studies Journal*, 39(1): 7–27.

Pahl-Wostl, C. (2009) 'A conceptual framework for analysing adaptive capacity and multi-level learning processes in resource governance regimes', *Global Environmental Change*, 19: 354–365.

Sen, S. and Raakjær Nielsen, J (1996) 'Fisheries co-management: A comparative analysis', *Marine Policy*, 20: 405–418.

4 A gender lens on poverty and the environment

Introduction

The importance of using a gender lens in analysing social and power relations within poverty–environment linkages was highlighted in Chapter 1. The recognition of the nature and place of gender in influencing access to resources and decision-making has evolved over many years of reflection on women, and then gender, and development. This chapter sets out the evolution of thinking on gender and development, from the Women in Development perspective of the 1970s to Gender and Development of the 1990s and the 'feminization of poverty', moving on to look specifically at women/gender and environment debates within a development context. The chapter then examines literature on gender perspectives within three natural resource settings: land, forestry and fisheries. These have been chosen as there are distinct literatures and issues concerning gender and these natural resource settings that illustrate the more generic points made in earlier sections. Given the importance of climate change in considering poverty–environment linkages, key analytical issues in literature on gender and climate change are then touched on. The chapter concludes with a summary of key points arising from the diverse and considerable literature within the broad area of gender, environment and poverty.

Unlike many other chapters in this book, this chapter does not include any 'off-the-shelf' frameworks. There are many frameworks that exist within gender and development literature, such as the Harvard Analytical Framework, which focuses on the gendered division of labour, the Moser Framework, focusing on planning and policy, and the Gender Analysis Matrix (GAM), which provides a tool for communities to identify and analyse gender differences (March *et al.*, 1999; Warren, 2007). Such frameworks are particularly useful for initiatives to 'mainstream' gender in policy and practice, that is, ensure that a gender perspective runs through policy and plans rather than is 'added-on' at the end. However, there are no ready-made frameworks to analyse gender, environment and poverty together and so this chapter aims to identify key points to guide analyses of the gendered experience and dynamics of poverty–environment relations.

It should be noted, though, that many of the frameworks and approaches reviewed in other chapters incorporate, or could incorporate, a gendered perspective within them. These include the institutional analysis approaches in Chapter 3, especially

Critical Institutionalism, and the Sustainable Livelihoods framework and Wellbeing in Developing Countries approach in Chapter 5.

Box 4.1 starts off the chapter by drawing on Agarwal's (1994) definition of gender relations, emphasizing that gender relations can refer to relations 'within' genders as well as between. This is followed by Box 4.2 setting out the key message of this chapter: that it is a gender lens approach that should be taken to analysing how men and women interact with the environment, rather than a portrayal of static, universal linkages between men, poverty and the environment and women, poverty and the environment.

Box 4.1 What are 'gender relations'?

Agarwal (1994: 51) explains her use of the term 'gender relations' as referring to

> the relations of power between women and men which are revealed in a range of practices, ideas, and representations, including the division of labour, roles, and resources between women and men, and the ascribing to them of different abilities, attitudes, desires, personality traits, behavioural patterns, and so on.

She goes on to note, however, that 'gender hierarchies also influence and structure relations between individuals of the same sex – e.g. how two women of the same household relate to one another is affected by the gendered character of their relations with the household men' (1994: 52).

More recent literature would go further than this, suggesting that a 'gender lens' approach should investigate relations among as well as between men and women (noting plural categories of men and women), rather than suggesting that gender relations among a sex should only be investigated in relation to gender relations between sexes.

Box 4.2 Why a 'gender lens'?

A key message of this chapter is that a 'gender lens' approach should be taken to the analysis of how people gain and maintain access to, and control over, environmental resources and how they interact more broadly with the environment. This implies that there are no static, given assumptions that should be made about the role of women or men in relation to the environment. An analysis of power relations between and among women and men should be undertaken to investigate the nature and influence of gender alongside other criteria of social difference such as race and class.

Examples of questions that may be addressed through a gender lens:

- In what ways and why is access to land influenced by gender relations within households and wider society?
- How and why do women and men benefit differently in a given context from access to natural resources?

'WID, WAD and GAD': women, gender and development

During the first decades of international development practice, following World War II, it was assumed that development was 'gender-neutral'; that is, the needs and priorities of men and women were the same, and their experience of development was the same. There was no need, then, to think about women and men separately, or differently, in planning for and implementing development interventions. This thinking changed in the 1970s, when there was a growing perception that women were not benefiting as much as men from development policy and practice, and, that in some cases, development interventions were failing because of this gender-neutral approach. Esther Boserup's path-breaking book *Women's Role in Economic Development* (1970) contributed to thinking on 'women in development', responding to the concern that women were not benefiting from development interventions and should therefore be 'factored in'. There was no challenge to the orthodox development approach, but advocacy for women to be included in, and benefit from, development programmes. There was no attempt to ask why women were not favoured by development interventions, but instead the focus was on how they could benefit from being incorporated into development, with interventions specifically targeted at women (Rai, 2002). In a 'women in development' (WID) approach, women were seen as a homogenous group, with no reference made to other aspects of their identity, such as class, race and cultural background.

A critique of WID soon emerged with the 'women and development' (WAD) approach growing out of a Marxist-feminist perspective, closely linked to dependency theory which challenged international structures of inequality between the North and the South. Reflecting its close allegiance with dependency theory, a WAD approach suggests that benefits to women from development would accrue when international structures of inequality are challenged and made more equitable. As with WID, gender is taken as a form of identity rather than a matter of social and power relations, with little reference to forms of patriarchy, but instead more focus on class and capital (Rathgeber, 1990).

There are a number of critiques of WID and WAD, including from those advocating for gender equality. Criticisms include the focus of WID and WAD on the productive roles of women rather than also giving attention to reproductive roles (Rathgeber, 1990). The implication of this was that interventions focused on income-generating activities without consideration given to other roles and responsibilities women might have and therefore often had the unfortunate effect of placing additional burdens on women. Further, feminist critique highlighted the homogenous view of women apparent in WID and WAD and the portrayal of gender relations as being fixed and immutable. Feminist perspectives reject theories and approaches that reduce women to a set of characteristics, with commonalities between women everywhere (Pearson and Jackson, 1998). An important contribution by feminist perspectives to analysis of gender and development has been the recognition of the household as an important unit for analysis rather than only at the levels of the economy and in between. The relevance of bringing about an emphasis on intra-household relations, as well as gender relations within other spheres of life, is explained in Box 4.3.

***Box 4.3* Intra-household relations**

The call for a gendered analysis of, and response to, intra-household relations stems from recognition that there are inequalities and relations of power that influence who has a say and who benefits from decisions and resources within households. This attention to what goes on in a household, recognizing different interests and degrees of power, is in contrast to much economic theory and development policy prior to the 1970s and 80s, which treated households as having one set of interests, where benefits and resources were equitably shared. This is clearly not the case, particularly in households where dynamics and norms within extended families have implications for who takes on which roles and who has access to what resources. In relation to natural resources, access to land and its products especially will be subject to intra-household negotiation and decision-making, with gender relations informing and shaping these.

In response to critiques of WID and WAD, a gender and development (GAD) approach was adopted in the 1980s, influenced by the UN decade for women (1976–85). Within a GAD perspective, attention is given to both the productive and reproductive roles of women, asking why women are often assigned to inferior or secondary roles, with a focus on analysis of forms of patriarchy (Rathgeber, 1990). In adopting a gender-based approach, there was recognition that it is not women *per se* who should be the subject of analysis and intervention, but gender relations in which women are subordinated (Everett and Charlton, 2014). The social construction of gender roles and relations became the subject of analysis, with the state expected to play a role in the emancipation of women. Taking a GAD approach proved to be more difficult than perhaps expected, with 'gender' often reduced to referring to 'women' and the underlying reasons for gender relations that lead to the suppression of women going unchallenged. This at least in part reflects the complexity, diversity and entrenched nature of relations of power that impact on gender relations.

Repoliticizing gender

Gender, then, has become institutionalized within development thinking, policy and action. A gendered approach or perspective is almost always expected, but what has it meant in practice? All too often, gender has been translated as implying that interventions should include women, with gender being understood as meaning men and women. This reflects much more of a 'women in development' perspective, which has, to a large degree, dominated national policy and development projects and programmes. Feminist writers have recognized this situation with concern, inferring that their own advocacy for gendered analysis has lost its politicized, critical edge.

Cornwall (2007: 69), for example, observes that 'gender' has 'retained little of the radical promise that was once vested in its promotion. That which lay at the heart of the "power agenda" – transforming unequal and unjust *power relations* – seems to have fallen by the wayside'. This shift away from a concern with power explains the allure of the concept of 'gender'; it became an 'acceptable euphemism' (Cornwall, 2007: 70), negating the need to address rights and power as earlier advocated by feminist approaches to development. Within this gender terrain, 'mainstreaming' has been seen as a critical way forward, where a gendered perspective aims to inform development thinking and practice in an integrated way rather than as an 'add on'. In such an approach, however, women are often portrayed in what has been referred to as 'gender myths': women are seen as victims, for example as the 'poorest of the poor' or, and sometimes and, as brave heroines who 'battle against all odds for a better life for their children and communities' (Cornwall, 2007: 73). Such myths have no recognition of men, focus attention on some women above others and neglect the interaction between gender and power in the lives of both women and men. Such an approach may also neglect other relations of significance such as relations of seniority, of status or kinship.

In response to concern about the depoliticization of gender, Cornwall (2007) calls for a return to gender as an analytical concept rather than its use as a descriptive concept, dominated by a focus on women. So gender should not be seen as 'the socially constructed relationship between women and men', but as a lens to analyse relations of power among and between men and women, with men and women being seen as plural categories informed by social practices.

And what about poverty?: the 'feminization of poverty'

Where is poverty in this? Concern with the nature and extent of poverty and with poverty reduction pervades development theory, policy and practice. As explained in Chapter 1, poverty is generally accepted as being multi-dimensional, as being experienced in different ways in different spaces, with gender being one dimension that may influence the nature, experience and extent of poverty. The above discussion on gender and development concludes with Cornwall's (2007) call for gender to be used as an analytical concept, without preconceived notions of the role and place of all women and all men at any level. This would imply that analyses of poverty should also proceed in this way, with gender as an analytical lens to investigate poverty, rather than there being sweeping statements about how women and men experience poverty.

This has not always been the case, however. Since the 1970s, there has been a broad concern that there has been a 'feminization of poverty'. What does that mean? It refers to the perceived observation that there is a higher incidence of poverty amongst women than men; that their poverty is more severe; and that poverty is increasing amongst women, particularly associated with rising numbers of female-headed households (BRIDGE, 2001). The term originated in the United States in the 1970s, where it was believed that an increase in the proportion of female-headed households and the increasing entry of women into low-wage informal sector work was fuelling the increase of poverty amongst women in relation to men. In relation to global poverty, the UNDP's 1995 Human Development Report is often referred to for its claim that women constitute 70 per cent of the world's poor, with this figure repeatedly referred to as evidence of the 'feminization of poverty'.

The claim of 'feminization of poverty' has been challenged, the 70 per cent figure questioned in terms of its underlying assumptions (BRIDGE, 2001), for suggesting a static state in which more women than men are poor and for over-emphasizing income as the measure of poverty (Chant, 2010). Whilst attention given to the 'feminization of poverty' has not been entirely unhelpful, in that it has contributed to further resources being targeted at women, there is much concern that the term has encouraged attention to the condition of poor women and targets resources directly to women rather than challenging the position of women and the associated 'rules of the game' (BRIDGE, 2001; Chant, 2010). Jackson (1996) expresses particular concern about how gender and poverty were equated and linked together through the 'gender trap', arguing that gender injustices cannot be solved by poverty reduction policies.

The key lesson from this debate for analysis of gender, environment and poverty is that no general assumptions should be made about who is poor, how poverty is experienced in different spaces and over time and how measures that seek to contribute to poverty reduction should be implemented. The debate over the 'feminization of poverty' confirms the need for a 'gender lens' approach to be taken, with a perspective of 'gendered poverty' suggesting a diversity of meanings, causes and processes associated with the experience of poverty for men and women (Chant, 2010).

Women, environment and development

Following on from the WID movement, in the 1980s a strong view emerged within environmental discourse and practice that women have a special, close relationship to nature and are therefore in a better position to be environmental custodians than men. It was observed that women, particularly in rural areas of developing countries, are deeply reliant on land and trees, just because they are women. Women were seen as 'victims of environmental degradation (walking ever further for that wood) but also environmental carers and key fixers of environmental problems' (Leach, 2007: 68). This was a powerful discourse in the 1980s, contributing to development interventions that targeted women in conservation projects. This had, at times, the unfortunate outcome that women had to take on even more responsibilities and work, not taking into consideration their existing roles and responsibilities.

The WED approach emerged within a context of growing concern about global environmental change, particularly land and soil degradation and deforestation, with women seen as central to the solution to these challenges. The approach, however, tended to portray women as a homogeneous group, and was, in part, a response to mainstream development approaches, with ecofeminists such as Vandana Shiva (1989) arguing that women and nature shared the same history of oppression by patriarchal institutions and dominant western culture. The WED approach came to be seen as a critique of the dominant model of development, which, it was argued, had instead contributed to 'the growth of poverty, to an increase in economic and gender inequalities, and to the degradation of the environment' (Braidotti *et al.*, 1994: 1).

It wasn't long though until a vociferous critique emerged, questioning the notion of women as natural carers of the environment and the implications of WED for women and for the design of environmental policies and programmes. Such critiques (e.g. Agarwal, 1992; Green *et al.*, 1998; Jackson, 1993; Leach, 1992; Leach and Green, 1997) challenged the notion that women intrinsically have a close relationship with the environment and emphasized instead the social context of dynamic gender relations as influencing men and women's relationships with the environment. This gendered approach also highlighted the heterogeneity of women as a group, observing that there will be diverse relationships with the environment, associated with women in different cultures, of different ages, wealth and kinship positions, noting that these differences apply to men also (Leach, 2007).

There is little literature, however, that specifically refers to 'gender, environment and development (GED)', although Neefjes (2000: 26) provides a useful summary of what such a GED approach may highlight, suggesting GED includes:

1   the gendered division of labour and responsibility, influencing how women are affected by environmental change;
2   gendered property rights, influencing the nature of gender–environment relationships;
3   gendered positioning in households, communities and within other spheres of social life;
4   the influence of the wider political economy on gender and gender–environment relations;
5   ecological characteristics that influence the interrelationships between gender and the environment.

In more recent literature, concern has been expressed that environment and development work appears to be 'gender-blind', with 'little evidence of a more politicized, relational perspective on gender and environment taking root' (Leach, 2007: 68). Leach (2007) observes that there is a tendency within development policy and practice to refer more broadly to communities and the poor, with little reference to women or gender. Instead, there is attention given to issues of tenure and property rights and other institutional arrangements that influence whether and how resources can be accessed and who has a say in decision-making.

Recognition of differences in access to and control over environmental resources resulting from gender relations between and amongst men and women is critical in many situations in which poverty–environment relations may be analysed. The experience of, and levels of access to and control over, environmental resources will differ between and amongst men and women, often in turn influenced by other institutions such as traditional rules and taboos, which must be identified and understood if appropriate conclusions are to be drawn about how people interact with the natural world.

Feminist political ecology

A more overtly politicized approach to gender, environment and development can be found within feminist political ecology. In a 1996 seminal book, *Feminist Political Ecology: Global Issues and Local Experience,* Rocheleau *et al.* set out a definition of feminist political ecology that

> treats gender as a critical variable in shaping resource access and control, interacting with class, caste, race, culture, and ethnicity to shape processes of ecological change, the struggle of men and women to sustain ecologically viable livelihoods, and the prospects of any community for "sustainable development".
>
> (1996a: 4)

Drawing on the political ecology tradition as set out in Chapter 2 of this book, feminist political ecology puts power at the centre of analysis and argues that gendered differences in experiences of, responsibilities for and interests in the environment are not rooted in biology per se, but are socially constructed and therefore vary by culture, class, race and location, and are subject to change. Gendered differences are not, then, static and should not be assumed to be the same in all situations and places, and across time.

Their text focused on three key themes of:

1   *Gendered sciences of survival:* 'what is science and who does it' (1996a: 7).
2   *Gendered environmental rights and responsibilities:* 'who controls and determines rights over resources, quality of environment, and the definition of a healthy and desirable environment' (1996a: 10).
3   *Gendered environmental politics and grassroots activism:* 'women at the forefront of emerging grassroots groups, social movements, and local political organizations engaged in environmental, socioeconomic, and political struggles' (1996a: 14).

Elmhirst (2011) suggests that feminist theory has moved on since 1996, challenging the approach taken by Rocheleau *et al.* (1996a) which focused on differentiated access to and control over environmental resources and had fixed notions of men and women. She questions why there hasn't been more explicit adoption of a feminist political ecology analysis since Rocheleau *et al.*'s (1996b) edited volume and observes that whilst there is much literature that could be characterized as 'feminist political ecology' it is not labelled as such. In addition, some approaches take gender as one dimension of social difference in their analysis, alongside other dimensions such as class and race, so that gender is not *the* centre of the analysis. Elmhirst (2011) urges for an adoption of a feminist political ecology approach that reflects Cornwall *et al.*'s (2007) call for gender to be seen as a lens to analyse the power effects resulting from the social constitution of difference. Political ecology is still seen as having much to offer a gendered analysis, but could also incorporate investigation into the manifestations, experiences and implications of social difference.

Hawkins and Ojeda (2011) report on a review of current and past work on gender and the environment, discussed by a panel brought together to identify emerging themes and directions. Through their deliberations, the panel were emphatic in their view that gender should not be considered alone in relation to the environment, but as connected to other dimensions of social difference through a range of power dynamics. They urged that gender should be seen as fluid, rather than strictly in binary terms of 'men and women', though also recognized the practical nature of using these categories as they exist in many spheres. A third key theme emerging from their discussion was the connection between 'scales, sites, and struggles' (2011: 243), with Hawkins and Ojeda arguing for 'a rescaling in the gender and environment literature to acknowledge the multiple ecologies that include habitat, home, household, and the body as much as the city, the region, the nation, and the globe' (2011: 244). The emphasis given to the question of scale reflects other areas of literature and investigation into natural resource governance and management, as discussed in Chapters 7 and 8.

'Feminist political ecology' remains a valid label for a feminist analysis of power relations within environmental settings but competes with other gender, feminist and geography approaches (Elmhirst, 2011). It highlights the potential to take a clear gendered perspective to a political ecology analysis, whilst also investigating other forms of social difference and bringing attention to a broader understanding of scale than might be found within other analytical approaches used to investigate environment and natural resource settings.

Natural resource sector examples

From the above review of literature and debates on women, gender, environment, development and poverty, two key points emerge. First, that sweeping conclusions should be avoided about how women and men engage with the environment and are affected by environmental change. Second, a gendered approach to analysis implies that a 'gender lens' should be employed, taking into consideration not only the nature and implications of gender as a type of power relation, but also other criteria of social difference such as caste, class, race and age. In relation to environment and natural resources, then, there should be no given conclusions that women are more likely to be concerned with conservation than men or that they are more likely to take on certain functions in all situations. Gender relations amongst men and women should be investigated as well as between, and plural categories of men and women should be recognized.

To explore these ideas further, this section reviews literature on gender and the natural resource settings of land, forestry and fisheries to identify important literature in these areas, key points raised and approaches taken.

Gender and land

Having access to land is essential for rural households in developing countries, where agriculture continues to be the main provider of food security, employment and income. Having access to land is also important for investment as it can serve as collateral for loans, for passing wealth on to future generations and for livelihood security. How land can be used, however, will depend on the types of access, or rights, that people have to a piece of land. Given that there is only so much land available, access is inevitably subject to numerous policies and norms, formal and informal. A gendered analysis of who gets access to land, what kind of access that entails and why, has been the subject of much debate. Three key themes within the literature on gender and land are touched on here: the dual systems of accessing land in many developing countries, 'formal' and 'informal'; land reform and implications for women; and, the more recent phenomenon of land grabbing and its gender dimensions.

In many developing countries, two systems of controlling access to land exist: the formal, state, system, where land is registered and title deeds issued, and informal, or customary, systems, where access to land is facilitated through customary norms and procedures. These systems may exist in the same area and be used for different purposes, with countries differing in whether, and to what extent, customary systems are recognized in national law. The two systems may offer different types or degrees of access to land, with consequences for how people gain and maintain access, and what that access entails, i.e. what types of land rights people have. There are also examples where hybrid forms of tenure control exist, drawing on both formal and informal systems, with the two systems becoming enmeshed, making it difficult to identify clear boundaries between the two.

Since the 1950s and 60s, governments in many countries, often encouraged by international donors such as the World Bank, sought to formalize and individualize land ownership, moving away from customary systems through processes of land reform (Deininger and Binswanger, 1999). The appropriateness and success of such reforms have been questioned for many reasons, particularly for often failing to deliver on subsequent economic growth. Literature on gender and land has tended to critique land reform processes that often resulted in women being largely excluded as beneficiaries, particularly where customary rights were ignored by statutory systems (Jacobs, 2009, 2010). However, this is not to say that customary systems necessarily offer equal access to land for women, with other criteria of social difference also influencing access to land through both state and customary systems. Relying on customary systems for securing access to land for women in sub-Saharan Africa, for example, will not guarantee access to land for women in ways, and to the extent, that they may want (Whitehead and Tsikata, 2003). In relation to South Asia, the exclusion of women as direct beneficiaries from many land reform processes contributed to Agarwal's (1994) contention that women should have *direct* access to income and productive assets, including land, rather than only having access that is mediated through her husband or other family members. The appropriateness of arguing for land rights for women in all situations is debated in the literature, with Jackson (2003) concluding that a gendered analysis of land should not necessarily lead to demands for formalized land rights for women.

The effects of land reform can go beyond affecting women's access to land; they may in turn influence kinship, family and internal household relations (Jacobs, 2009, 2010). Those involved with designing land reform, or calling for more formalized land rights, should take into consideration the place of land in household, family and kin dynamics, including land in inheritance rules, accessing credit, decisions over how land is used, labour allocation and who benefits from the products of land. Such concerns about women losing out on access to land through formalization processes have raised questions about the portrayal in this way of women as victims rather than as having agency, being able to negotiate access to land. This critique reflects the contention in gender and development literature that the specific context of a situation must be investigated to generate an understanding of the gender dimensions of gaining access to, and control over, land.

With access to land often being contentious and fought over, a gender lens has been advocated for use in relation to examining the processes and implications of 'land grabbing' (Behrman *et al.*, 2012). Large-scale acquisitions of land have been made by foreign and domestic investors in developing countries, the scale and nature of which have led to concerns about local food and energy security, equity and transparency. A gender lens can contribute to an understanding of who is involved in negotiating such deals and with what implications for whom.

Within literature, policy and practice on land in developing countries, questions of the nature and security of access, who has what access and how best to provide access and security are key concerns. Such issues are intricately linked to other spheres of life, including politics, the economy and cultural norms, with examples of diversity across time and space yet also continuity over time. A gender lens offers a perspective that can burrow down into questions of who has access, what types of access, why and how they gain and maintain access. Such a view is critical for understanding both women and men's access to, and use of, land and for informing more appropriate policy and practice that can challenge positions and processes of power that may constrain people's access to, and control over, land.

Gender and forestry

It has been estimated that around 1.6 billion people living in rural areas of developing countries directly depend on forest resources, with 300–350 million being highly dependent (Chao, 2012). Forest resources include timber for construction, fodder for livestock, firewood and other non-timber forest products (NTFPs), such as medicinal plants and fruits. Questions of who has access, what that access is and who makes decisions over forest use, and imposes sanctions, are foremost in analyses of gender, poverty and forest management. Much of the literature on gender and forestry has focused more specifically on women, and particularly on the nature and implications of women's participation in forest management, and on the nature and effectiveness of forest use rules, sanctions and governance, whereas men have not received the same analytical attention.

Participatory, or community-based, approaches to forest management have been widely adopted in the developing world since the 1990s, moving away from centralized control over forest resources. Whilst recognition and promotion of community involvement in forest management has become more formalized, common property type arrangements widely existed before more donor/NGO community-based natural resource management (CBNRM) initiatives were introduced. Whether community-initiated or externally encouraged, such initiatives generally involve the creation of structures, including a committee or user group, drawn from the wider set of users.

Gendered analyses of the composition, operation and effectiveness of such committees or user groups within participatory forestry structures have found mixed pictures in terms of the extent, nature and implications of the involvement of women (Tole, 2010). Certainly there are examples where women have been excluded from such bodies, reflecting social norms about the use of public space and the division of labour, norms about how women and men should behave and social perceptions of women's abilities (Agarwal, 2001). Even where women are included in decision-making structures, it may be nominal participation to satisfy government or donor requirements that a certain number of places should be set aside for women. There may be a tendency for committees to seek to comply with that minimum and not consider that there could be more women on the committee. Still, social norms and perceptions may limit the space and opportunity for women to speak and for men to listen, so having women on a committee is no guarantee of influence and voice.

It may be hypothesized that having women, providing they have space to speak and be listened to, on a committee may lead to different management approaches and decisions. Agarwal (2009, 2010) investigated this in relation to forest user groups in India and Nepal, statistically testing for correlation between the number of women on the committees of such groups against the 'strictness' of rules. Agarwal found that community forest institutions with more women generally, but not always, made stricter rules, but that other factors influenced this as well, including the age of women, their class, the products extracted from the forest for which the rules applied and the availability of that product. Certainly gender relations influence how people get access to, and benefit from, forests in developing countries, but other influencing factors should be investigated alongside gender for a more complete and accurate understanding of the situation.

Power relations more generally influence whether people have a place or are appropriately represented on executive committees, with poor people consistently found to be less advantaged by forest policies and practices. Poorer people may lack power, connections and resources to influence policy and gain access to executive committees. A consequence of this is that rules and sanctions may be biased against the interests and concerns of poorer people and experience has shown that community-based forest management does not necessarily deliver on outcomes that favour the poor, with poor women at the bottom of the hierarchy of power (Larson and Ribot, 2007; Thoms, 2008).

Gender and fisheries

Gender has not been a significant area of study within, or influence on, management and development approaches and interventions in fisheries. Bennett (2005: 451–452) suggests that this is because fisheries policy and management tends to be dominated by concerns about the state of the fish stock, over-exploitation of fish, overcapacity (too many boats, too much gear), overfishing and illegalities. Such concerns have led to a continued focus on the catching sector, which is male dominated, with boat owners and boat crew usually being male. Though women do own boats, in many parts of the world they would not fish from boats as it would not be culturally acceptable. The focus on the catching sector reflects the language and assumptions made about who is a 'fisherman' and what counts as 'fishing', which in turn influences the neglect of women and gender within fisheries. When referring to 'fishing', it is not always apparent that inshore extraction of fisheries resources such as crabs and prawns is fully taken into consideration, referred to as 'gathering' rather than fishing. Narrow definitions of fishers and fishing overlook certain areas of activities and groups of fishers (Kleiber *et al.*, 2014). This neglect contributes to 'a substantial under-estimate of fishing pressure in coastal areas and an under-valuation of the economic and societal benefits that women in fisheries provide' (Harper *et al.*, 2013: 56).

The lack of attention given to gender in fisheries has also been ascribed to the portrayal of fisheries research and policy as gender-neutral, whereas it is really 'gender blind' (Bennett, 2005; Kleiber *et al.*, 2014), not investigating and reflecting complex gender relations that influence occupations, access to fish and marketing, for example. The aggregation of fisheries data with data from other sectors, principally agriculture, with little, or no, segregation of data along gender lines adds to the seemingly 'gender neutrality' of fisheries. The lack of appreciation of gender within fisheries reflects, and is in turn affected by, an often sectoral approach taken to fisheries, without taking into consideration the many other dimensions of individuals and households' livelihoods.

There is very often a clear gendered division of labour within fisheries, though this varies between fisheries. Gender relations also influence how the fish is sold along the value chain and how women get access to fish to process and/or market. Fish may be sold to the boat owner's wife or to women who have given credit to fishers, on the agreement that they will receive the fish, or to the woman from whom they rent a room. Along with the transaction of fish, sex may also be part of the exchange, securing access to fish for the women, but exposing both men and women to greater vulnerability to sexually transmitted diseases, including HIV/AIDS (Béné and Merten, 2008; Nunan, 2010).

A gendered approach to fisheries recognizes not just the different roles and occupations that men and women often have, but that the relationships between and amongst men and women influence how the fisheries are accessed, how fish is traded and by whom, how women and men get income from the fisheries and how this source of income is part of a wider gender-influenced livelihood. Gender relations influence governance at the beach level, as within any other realm of governance. In many parts of the developing world, fisheries are managed through a co-managed approach, where resource users are empowered to manage the fisheries with government (Sen and Nielsen, 1996). The introduction of co-management often involves the creation of new governance structures, which are inevitably influenced by social and power relations within a community and society, including gender relations. Women may not then necessarily be well represented or have voices in management structures created by the introduction of co-management, though there is very little literature that specifically takes a gendered perspective to the analysis of co-management structures and processes. Given the significant role of women in inshore fisheries and post-harvesting activities, their knowledge and experience could be better utilized in fisheries management, including co-management, yet women are far less likely than men to be involved in fisheries management structures and processes.

Taking a gendered approach to investigating fisheries involves asking how men and women get access to the fisheries, who makes decisions at the beach level and how women and men are involved in beach-level governance and beyond, and what the gender norms and relations from wider society are that may influence life within fisheries. This suggests that other frameworks and approaches to analysing people–environment relations should be drawn on to inform gender–fisheries research and take it beyond the focus on a gendered division of labour. Weeratunge *et al.* (2010) suggest that a deeper analysis of gender within the fisheries sector should draw on the following concepts and frameworks: livelihoods, markets and migration, capabilities and livelihoods, networks and identities, and governance and rights. Informed by a review of these conceptual applications, Weeratunge *et al.* (2010) set out an agenda for research on gender and fisheries, including questions such as: how is wellbeing perceived by men and women in fisheries, how do formal networks affect the nature of informal networks and how do men and women participate in fisheries' governance structures and processes?

Box 4.4 identifies a few common themes from the review of literature on gender and land, forests and fisheries.

Box 4.4 Common themes in gender and natural resources analysis

1 The nature and degree of access to, and control over, natural resources and their products are key themes in a gendered analysis of land, forestry and fisheries.
2 Gender relations influence roles within, and benefits from, different parts of the value chain resulting from the natural resource.
3 Context-specific analysis is always needed, as sweeping conclusions such as women are not able to own land in certain parts of the world or engage in fishing would lead a researcher to miss out on the nuances of what access, ownership and rights may mean.
4 There is much scope to draw on a wider range of concepts and frameworks to contribute to a deeper analysis of gender–natural resource relations.

A word on gender and climate change

It was explained above that early commentary about women, and then gender, and the environment tended to portray women as either victims of environmental degradation or, and sometimes 'and', as heroes, more likely to protect the environment and support conservation than men. Approaching gender and the environment in this way has been seen by others as unhelpful and inaccurate, having led, in some cases, to interventions that increased women's work burden, by, for example, enrolling them as 'protectors of the environment' in conservation programmes. You are reminded of this key theme in earlier writing on women/gender and the environment in this note on climate change as it has often been seen to re-emerge within gender and climate-change writing. In such literature, women are often portrayed as making up the majority of the world's poor and as being particularly vulnerable to climate change, partly because women are seen as being more likely to be poor but also because of the roles they have, making them more vulnerable to natural hazards and to the affects of climate change on, for example, water availability, crop productivity and fodder availability (Demetriades and Esplen, 2008).

This focus within literature on gender and climate change is unhelpful as well as being inaccurate. Such a portrayal fits within the broader narrative of the 'feminization of poverty', which has been widely critiqued. With reference to climate change literature, Arora-Jonsson (2011) challenges the stereotypical portrayal of women and environment, arguing that 'the relegation of gender mainly to vulnerability and partly to virtuousness detracts attention from the problem that afflicts both the North and the South, that is gender and power inequalities in decision-making in environmental management' (Arora-Jonsson, 2011: 749). In 1996 Jackson argued that the term 'feminization of poverty' is unhelpful as it was interpreted as the poor are mostly women rather than that poverty is a gendered experience. So too has much gender and climate change literature focused on how women are more likely to be poor and vulnerable and how women will be more adversely affected than men. This could be detrimental to an effective response to climate change, where focus should really be on gender and power inequalities and on multiple and diverse experiences that men and women have, and will have, of a changed climate (Arora-Jonsson, 2011; Resurrección, 2013).

Given the approach taken in this chapter, caution is urged in reading literature on gender and climate change; gender roles and relations should not be viewed as static and a given, but situation-specific and enmeshed in other criteria of social difference, such as class and race. However, at least now gender is more on the climate change agenda as part of a wider shift away from seeing climate change purely as a scientific, technical phenomenon, requiring purely technical, scientific responses (Denton, 2004). Yes, such understanding and responses are needed, but science and technology operate in a world of social difference, political strife and contention, and where the more powerful prevent significant challenges to their interests.

A gendered approach to climate change should promote the analysis of any sector, policy or situation through a 'gender lens', so that whether analysing poverty, water availability or agricultural productivity, there are multiple gendered experiences that mean that many men and women must be consulted and involved in developing responses, reflecting a great diversity and complexity of experiences, concerns and views.

Summary of key points

1   Perspectives towards analysing and portraying gender and environment relations have changed significantly over time, reflecting broader shifts in feminist and gender thinking, within development and beyond.
2   Whether an analytical approach focuses on gender or women depends on the research questions being asked and the specific context of the research problem.
3   Power relations are at the heart of a gendered analysis, reflecting on how gendered relations interact with other axes of social difference.
4   Gendered analysis may include investigation of other forms of social differentiation, for example class, ethnicity and culture, and should always be context specific.
5   The shift in feminist and gendered thinking has more recently attempted to re-emphasize the central focus that there should be on power in relations among and between men and women, with gender as an 'analytical lens' rather than referring to fixed roles and responsibilities.
6   The analysis of gender in relation to specific natural resource sectors, such as land, forestry and fisheries, has, however, paid particular attention to perceived gendered divisions of roles, access and benefits. Sweeping conclusions about these should be avoided, with a gender lens used to investigate the nature and influence of power relations amongst and between men and women, alongside considerations of other dimensions of social difference.

7   The utilization of other analytical concepts and frameworks in a gendered analysis of poverty–environment relations could generate deeper understanding of gender and the environment interactions. Such concepts and frameworks may draw on livelihoods, wellbeing, rights and network approaches.

8   Sweeping generalizations such as women make up most of the world's poor and that women will be more adversely affected than men by climate change are misleading and unhelpful. They can lead to additional burdens being placed on women as 'protectors of the environment'. A 'gender lens' approach should be taken that recognizes multiple gendered experiences of men and women, engages with other dimensions of social difference and seeks an examination of the nature and experience of power relations.

Further reading

Agarwal, B. (1994) *A Field of One's Own: Gender and Land Rights in South Asia*, Cambridge: Cambridge University Press.

Agarwal's groundbreaking monograph provides a rich account of barriers to women having ownership of, and control over, land in South Asia and how these barriers might be overcome. Drawing on evidence from five countries, she emphasizes the importance of arable land as a source of economic wellbeing and how women need to have their own, direct, access to such land rather than only being able to access land through their husbands or other family members. She argues that legal rights are not enough on their own as they have to be socially recognized as acceptable and legally enforced, and that ownership is not sufficient, as it does not necessarily imply control over land, where control refers to making decisions over its use, investment and disposal, for example. Agarwal sets out a clear conceptual framework for her analysis and makes use of an effective gender lens to investigate why women were so often unable to secure sufficient access to productive land.

Agarwal, B. (2010) *Gender and Green Governance: The Political Economy of Women's Presence Within and Beyond Community Forestry*, Oxford: Oxford University Press.

In this text, Agarwal builds on findings from research on gender and local forest governance that has shown that women are too often absent from governance institutions to ask what difference it would make if women were present in these institutions. Drawing on data from research on community forest institutions in India and Nepal, she investigates the nature, extent and impact of women's participation on the nature of rules, how the institutions operate and on the impact of participation and institutions on women themselves. She asks whether women are more conservationist than men, whether women are more cooperative and how much freedom, or space, women have to participate. This analysis of gender and forest governance is undertaken with reflection on the influence of class, caste and economic status, all of which influence the extent and nature of forest dependency of men and women, as well as their access to other resources, including to power and voice in decision-making. The text offers an engaging, comprehensive and rich analysis of gender and forest governance, and makes a significant contribution to gender and environment literature.

Jacobs, S. (2010) *Gender and Agrarian Reforms*, London: Routledge.
Access to and control over land is critical for agrarian societies, and a gendered perspective is essential for an analysis of how agrarian reforms have affected men and women and why. Jacobs provides a rich analysis of the gendered dimensions and implications of agrarian and land reforms, examining reform based on collective and household models. Examples are taken from Eastern Europe, China, Vietnam, Latin America and sub-Saharan Africa, illustrating the relevance of, and insight from, a gendered perspective of land reform.

References

Agarwal, B. (1992) 'The gender and environment debate: Lessons from India', *Feminist Studies*, 18(1): 119–158.

Agarwal, B. (1994) *A Field of One's Own: Gender and Land Rights in South Asia*, Cambridge: Cambridge University Press.

Agarwal, B. (2001) 'Participatory exclusions, community forestry, and gender: An analysis for South Asia and a conceptual framework', *World Development*, 29(10): 1623–1648.

Agarwal, B. (2009) 'Rule making in community forestry institutions: The difference women make', *Ecological Economics*, 68: 2296–2308.

Agarwal, B. (2010) *Gender and Green Governance: The Political Economy of Women's Presence Within and Beyond Community Forestry*, Oxford: Oxford University Press.

Arora-Jonsson, S. (2011) 'Virtue and vulnerability: Discourses on women, gender and climate change', *Global Environmental Change*, 21: 744–751.

Behrman, J., Meinzen-Dick, R. and Quisumbing, A. (2012) 'The gender implications of large-scale land deals', *The Journal of Peasant Studies*, 39(1): 49–79.

Béné, C. and Merten, S. (2008) 'Women and fish-for-sex: Transactional sex, HIV/AIDS and gender in African fisheries', *World Development*, 36(5): 875–899.

Bennett, E. (2005) 'Gender, fisheries and development', *Marine Policy*, 29: 451–459.

Boserup, E. (1970) *Women's Role in Economic Development*, London: George Allen and Unwin.

Braidotti, R., Charkiewicz, E., Häusler, S. and Wieringa, S. (1994) *Women, the Environment and Sustainable Development: Towards a Theoretical Synthesis*, London: Zed Books with INSTRAW.

BRIDGE (2001) *Briefing paper on the 'feminisation of poverty'*, prepared by BRIDGE for the Swedish International Development Cooperation Agency (Sida), Brighton: Institute of Development Studies.

Chant, S. (2010) 'Gendered poverty across space and time: introduction and overview', in Chant, S. (ed.), *The International Handbook of Gender and Poverty: Concepts, Research, Policy*, Cheltenham: Edward Elgar, pp. 1–26.

Chao, S. (2012) *Forest Peoples: Numbers Across the World*, Moreton-in-Marsh: Forest Peoples Programme.

Cornwall, A. (2007) 'Revisiting the "Gender Agenda"', *IDS Bulletin*, 38(2): 69–78.

Cornwall, A., Harrison, E. and Whitehead, A. (2007) 'Gender myths and feminist fables: The struggle for interpretive power in gender and development', *Development and Change*, 38(1): 1–20.

Deininger, K. and Binswanger, H. (1999) 'The evolusion of the World Bank's land policy: Principle, experience and future challenges', *The World Bank Research Observer*, 14(2): 247–276.

Demetriades, J. and Esplen, E. (2008) 'The gender dimensions of poverty and climate change adaptation', *IDS Bulletin*, 39(4): 24–31.

Denton, F. (2004) 'Gender and climate change: Giving the "latecomer" a head start', *IDS Bulletin*, 35(3): 42–49.

Elmhirst, R. (2011) 'Introducing new feminist political ecologies', *Geoforum*, 42: 129–132.

Everett, J. and Charlton, S.E.M. (2014) *Women Navigating Globalization: Feminist Approaches to Development*, Lanham, MD: Rowman & Littlefield.

Green, C., Joekes, S. and Leach, M. (1998) 'Questionable links: Approaches to gender in environmental research and policy', in Jackson, C. and Pearson, R. (eds), *Feminist Visions of Development*, London: Routledge, pp. 259–283.

Harper, S., Zeller, D., Hauzer, M., Pauly, D. and Sumaila, U.R. (2013) 'Women and fisheries: Contribution to food security and local economies', *Marine Policy*, 39: 56–63.

Hawkins, R. and Ojeda D. (2011) 'Gender and environment: Critical tradition and new challenges', *Environment and Planning D: Society and Space*, 29: 237–253.

Jackson, C. (1993) 'Doing what comes naturally? Women and environment in development', *World Development*, 21(12): 1947–1963.

Jackson, C. (1996) 'Rescuing gender from the poverty trap', *World Development*, 24(3): 489–504.

Jackson, C. (2003) 'Gender analysis of land: Beyond land rights for women?', *Journal of Agrarian Change*, 3(4): 453–480.

Jacobs, S. (2009) 'Gender and land reforms: Comparative perspectives', *Geography Compass*, 3(5): 1675–1687.

Jacobs, S. (2010) *Gender and Agrarian Reforms*, London: Routledge.

Kleiber, D., Harris, L.M. and Vincent, A.C.J. (2014) 'Gender and small-scale fisheries: A case for counting women and beyond', *Fish and Fisheries*, in press.

Larson, A.M. and Ribot, J.C. (2007) 'The poverty of forestry policy: Double standards on an uneven playing field', *Sustainability Science*, 2(2): 189–204.

Leach, M. (1992) 'Gender and the environment: Traps and opportunities', *Development in Practice,* 2(1): 12–22.

Leach, M. (2007) 'Earth mother myths and other ecofeminist fables: How a strategic notion rose and fell', *Development and Change,* 38(1): 67–85.

Leach, M. and Green, C. (1997) 'Gender and environmental history: From representations of women and nature to gender analysis of ecology and politics', *Environment and History*, 3(3): 343–370.

March, C., Smyth, I. and Mukhopadhyay, M. (1999) *A Guide to Gender-Analysis Frameworks*, Oxford: Oxfam.

Neefjes, K. (2000) *Environments and Livelihoods: Strategies for Sustainability*, Oxford: Oxfam.

Nunan, F. (2010) 'Mobility and fisherfolk livelihoods on Lake Victoria: Implications for vulnerability and risk', *Geoforum*, 41: 776–785.

Pearson, R. and Jackson, C. (1998) 'Introduction: Interrogating development: feminism, gender and policy', in Jackson, C. and Pearson, R. (eds), *Feminist Visions of Development: Gender Analysis and Policy*, London: Routledge, pp. 1–16.

Rai, S.M. (2002) *Gender and the Political Economy of Development*, Cambridge: Polity Press.

Rathgeber, E. (1990) 'WID, WAD, GAD: Trends in research and practice', *Journal of Developing Areas*, 24: 489–502.

Resurrección, B.P. (2013) 'Persistent women and environment linkages in climate change and sustainable development agendas', *Women's Studies International Forum*, 40: 33–43.

Rocheleau, D., Thomas-Slayter, B. and Wangari, E. (1996a) 'Gender and environment: A feminist political ecology perspective', in Rocheleau, D., Thomas-Slayter, B. and

Wangari, E. (eds), *Feminist Political Ecology: Global Issues and Local Experience*, London: Routledge.

Rocheleau, D., Thomas-Slayter, B. and Wangari, E. (eds) (1996b) *Feminist Political Ecology: Global Issues and Local Experience*, London: Routledge.

Sen, S. and Raakjær Nielsen, J. (1996) 'Fisheries co-management: A comparative analysis', *Marine Policy*, 20: 405–418.

Shiva, V. (1989) *Staying Alive: Women, Ecology and Development*, London: Zed Books.

Thoms, C.A. (2008) 'Community control of resources and the challenge of improving local livelihoods: A critical examination of community forestry in Nepal', *Geoforum*, 39: 1452–1465.

Tole, L. (2010) 'Reforms from the ground up: A review of community-based forest management in tropical developing countries', *Environmental Management*, 45: 1312–1331.

UNDP (1995) *Human Development Report 1995*, New York: UNDP.

Warren, H. (2007) 'Using gender-analysis frameworks: Theoretical and practical reflections', *Gender and Development*, 15(2): 187–198.

Weeratunge, N., Snyder, K.A. and Sze, C.P. (2010) 'Gleaner, fisher, trader, processor: Understanding gendered employment in fisheries and aquaculture', *Fish and Fisheries*, 11: 405–420.

Whitehead, A. and Tsikata, D. (2003) 'Policy discourses on women's land rights in sub-Saharan Africa: The implications of the re-turn to the customary', *Journal of Agrarian Change*, 3(1&2): 67–112.

5 Livelihoods and wellbeing

Introduction

In Chapter 1, it was noted that a shift in thinking occurred in the 1990s away from seeing poverty as purely an economic phenomenon to viewing poverty as multi-dimensional and complex, with wide-ranging perceptions and experiences. As part of this shift, other concepts have come to the fore. The concept of capability is one of these. Capability underlies the key concepts that are the focus of this chapter: livelihoods and wellbeing. Capability in this application draws on the capabilities approach of Amartya Sen (1984). This approach challenged reliance on economic indicators, such as level of income, to reflect people's wellbeing and sought a deeper understanding of what people are able to do and be – their capability. The approach recognizes diversity in what individuals may be able to achieve, even given the same resources, to contribute to a more nuanced understanding of people's wellbeing and potential for improvements in this.

In drawing on the concept of capability and responding to changes in the way that poverty is understood, the concepts of livelihoods and wellbeing respond to the complexity and diversity of people's lives. Multiple frameworks and approaches have been developed that incorporate these concepts, seeking to generate a deeper understanding of how poor people live their lives and of the assets and capabilities they have access to and use. The livelihoods concept has been operationalized through livelihoods approaches and frameworks, with the UK Department for International Development's (DFID) Sustainable Livelihoods framework being widely applied in development research and practice. The wellbeing concept has been operationalized through many approaches and frameworks, but two are given particular attention in this chapter: the Millennium Ecosystem Assessment and the Wellbeing in Developing Countries approach.

The Sustainable Livelihoods framework (SLF) is part of the broader approach to international development, the 'Sustainable Livelihoods approach' (SLA). This refers to programmes and projects that encompass sustainable livelihood principles, objectives and the use of the SLF. The Wellbeing in Developing Countries (WeD) approach takes wellbeing rather than poverty as the core of its focus, being concerned with what people have and could be, rather than what they do not have. Both approaches were developed to put people at the centre of analysis to inform efforts to reduce poverty. The Millennium Ecosystem Assessment (MA) provides two frameworks that facilitate an analysis of the interlinkages between ecosystem services and components of human wellbeing, encouraging analysis of direct and indirect drivers of change. Box 5.1 provides examples of the kinds of questions that can be asked in using these frameworks.

Box 5.1 Examples of livelihood and wellbeing analysis research questions

Sustainable Livelihoods framework

- How are household livelihood strategies constructed?
- Which policies, institutions and processes constrain and enable livelihood strategies?

Millennium Ecosystem Assessment

- How do coastal ecosystem services underpin coastal community wellbeing?
- What are the key drivers of change affecting ecosystem services and wellbeing?
- What trade-offs should be considered in examining options for management measures?

Wellbeing in Developing Countries

- What would people consider to be important for their wellbeing and what challenges do they experience in securing their wellbeing?

The chapter begins with a review of how livelihoods are defined, before going through the components of the SLF in detail. A review of the application of the SLF in a research context within the forestry and fisheries sectors shows how the framework has been used and what kinds of insights can be revealed. The concept of wellbeing is then introduced, followed by a discussion of the two frameworks developed by the MA. The use of the MA frameworks in identifying potential trade-offs between ecosystem services and effects on human wellbeing is emphasized. The WeD approach is then explained, with reflection on how the approach has been applied in the fisheries sector. The chapter concludes with a comparison of livelihoods and wellbeing frameworks and approaches.

Livelihoods

There are many livelihoods approaches, perspectives and frameworks within development literature and practice. A livelihoods perspective recognizes the diversity of survival strategies that people utilize and acknowledges that these strategies do not only have economic dimensions. Economic activities that people employ are interconnected with social interactions, such as within kinship networks and communities. These are critical for enabling people to access support, information, services and resources. Such a perspective implies that a holistic approach is needed for the analysis of how people make a living, requiring the identification and investigation of a wide range of relations, institutions and assets, to understand both opportunities and constraints that people face. Box 5.2 sets out definitions of what a livelihood is understood to be.

Box 5.2 **Definition of a livelihood**

'A livelihood comprises the capabilities, assets (stores, resources, claims and access) and activities required for a means of living' (Chambers and Conway, 1992: 6).

'A livelihood comprises the assets (natural, physical, human, financial and social capital), the activities, and the access to these (mediated by institutions and social relations) that together determine the living gained by the individual or household' (Ellis, 2000: 10).

The definition of a livelihood by Chambers and Conway (1992) in Box 5.2 draws on their development of the concept of *sustainable livelihoods* and it is this definition that has prevailed. In this seminal paper, Robert Chambers and Gordon Conway brought together thinking on livelihoods from development theory and practice with the concept of sustainability to develop a rationale and definition for sustainable livelihoods. Their rationale for the utility of such a concept was their concern arising from predictions of population increases in the developing world and how larger numbers of people could live in rural areas with 'decent livelihoods in a manner which can be sustained' (Chambers and Conway, 1992: 2). In addressing this question, Chambers and Conway drew on three concepts to develop their thinking about sustainable rural livelihoods: capability, equity and sustainability. Ellis (2000) modified the Chambers and Conway definition to bring out the issue of 'access' more strongly, with access being influenced by institutional arrangements and social relations.

Drawing on the work of Chambers and Conway and others, and with reference to *sustainable* livelihoods, Scoones subsequently defined a livelihood as comprising

the capabilities, assets (including both material and social resources) and activities required for a means of living. A livelihood is sustainable when it can cope with and recover from stresses and shocks, maintain or enhance its capabilities and assets, while not undermining the natural resource base.

(Scoones, 1998: 5)

Ian Scoones' 1998 working paper on 'Sustainable Rural Livelihoods' drew on a range of writing and thinking on livelihoods and developed a framework for the analysis of rural livelihoods. This framework formed the basis for the subsequent development of one of the most often cited and used livelihoods framework which is the UK Government's Department for International Development (DFID) Sustainable Livelihoods framework. Other livelihoods frameworks that have been developed include the modification of Scoones and DFID's frameworks by Ellis (2000) and frameworks developed by a number of non-governmental organizations (see Carney, 1999, for a review).

This emphasis on the natural resource base came about from the recognition of the close dependency of many rural livelihoods on natural resources and from the concern with livelihoods being sustainable in the long term, with environmental sustainability being part of that. In their guidance sheets on SLA, DFID (2001) advise that livelihoods are sustainable when they:

- are resilient in the face of external shocks and stresses;
- are not dependent upon external support (or if they are, this support itself should be economically and institutionally sustainable);
- maintain the long-term productivity of natural resources; and
- do not undermine the livelihoods of, or compromise the livelihood options open to, others.

(DFID, 2001: sheet 1.4)

The question of sustainability of livelihoods has not always received attention in the application of SLA or SLF, particularly in research, where the framework may be used for investigation into a range of issues and questions that may not focus on sustainability. This illustrates the wider potential for application than perhaps initially envisaged, but also reflects the challenge of many livelihoods of achieving sustainability as set out in the DFID definition. Certainly many livelihoods in the developed world would be viewed as being far from sustainable.

Sustainable Livelihoods framework

Livelihoods frameworks are often used by non-governmental organizations and in projects to identify opportunities for, and constraints on, improvements in livelihoods, whether at an individual, household, community or occupational level. As noted earlier, DFID's Sustainable Livelihoods framework has been particularly widely used, in both development practice and research settings and so forms the focus of consideration here. The framework is set out in Figure 5.1.

The DFID framework initially referred to rural livelihoods and specifically referred to natural resource-based and non-natural resource-based livelihood strategies, as well as to migration, but later left 'livelihood strategies' open, with no pre-determined categories, as shown in Figure 5.1. The framework since has

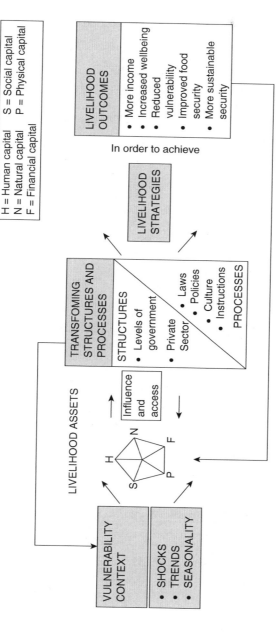

Figure 5.1 DFID's Sustainable Livelihoods framework.

Source: Ashley and Carney, 1999: 47.

been used in urban and peri-urban settings (see Rakodi and Lloyd-Jones, 2002, for example), as well as within specific natural resource sectors.

Livelihood frameworks, or approaches, have been used in both a research context as a way of ordering and informing data collection and analysis, and in a development context, to inform the design and approach of development interventions, where interventions are encouraged to take a 'holistic' approach. This requires recognition that many livelihoods have multiple dimensions to them, and that they are complex and unique, making a sectoral or one-dimensional approach to an intervention potentially ill-informed and counterproductive. The framework is designed to encourage the identification of multiple entry points, so that interventions could be targeted at any point in the framework, whilst recognizing the interconnections between the components. Emphasis is given in the framework to the importance of 'transforming structures and processes', which refers to the breadth of policies, legislation, organizations and institutions that can both enable or constrain the use of assets in livelihood strategies.

Scoones usefully summarizes the components of the livelihoods framework by setting out the questions being asked at each point in the framework, as follows:

> Given a particular context (of policy setting, politics, history, agroecology and socio-economic conditions), what combination of livelihood resources (different types of 'capital') result in the ability to follow what combination of livelihood strategies (agricultural intensification/extensification, livelihood diversification and migration) with what outcomes? Of particular interest in this framework are the institutional processes (embedded in a matrix of formal and informal institutions and organisations) which mediate the ability to carry out such strategies and achieve (or not) such outcomes.
>
> (Scoones, 1998: 3)

The framework was developed to be applied at different scales, that is, from individual to household or village levels, occupational group or even nation, with analysis of the interactions between the levels being important. Whichever level the SLF is applied, social disaggregation is critical, recognizing dimensions of difference such as age, gender, ethnicity and wealth. Different livelihood analyses can be undertaken for different 'groups' of people, depending on the manifestation of social differences and the questions being asked in the research. Dimensions of social difference also form part of the 'transforming structures and processes' box, through social norms, power relations and formal legislation, and form a lens for the investigation of the nature of assets people have access to and to what extent they are able to use those in their livelihood strategies.

As can be seen in Figure 5.1, DFID's framework has five components: the vulnerability context, livelihood assets, transforming structures and processes, livelihood strategies and livelihood outcomes. Each of the components is explained below. Whilst it is useful to examine each part of the framework in turn, the components are strongly interlinked, with multiple relationships between parts of the framework.

Vulnerability context

The concept of vulnerability was reviewed in Chapter 1, referring to Adger's definition of vulnerability as 'being constituted by components that include exposure and sensitivity to perturbations or external stresses, and the capacity to adapt' (2006: 270). Sources of vulnerability are many and may include social factors as well as environmental and economic, such as social obligations within a community. According to the framework, sources of vulnerability include shocks, trends and seasonality. These have been further broken down into:

- *Shocks:* climate (such as rainfall variability) and conflict (such as conflict over resources).
- *Trends:* in the stock of natural resources (e.g. exploitation levels, quality), population density, existence of beneficial technologies, political representation and in the economy, such as price fluctuations and access to markets.
- *Seasonality:* variations in prices, access to resources, availability of products and opportunities during the course of a year, and associated uncertainty.

Whilst these sources of vulnerability can create and deepen vulnerability of individuals, households and communities, they can also reduce or prevent vulnerability, through, for example seasonality providing opportunities for farm labouring work. Sources of vulnerability will affect the nature and extent of assets that people have access to and how those assets can be utilized as part of livelihood strategies. This explains why it is important to have an understanding of the vulnerability context.

Livelihood assets

Livelihood assets in Figure 5.1 are disaggregated into five types of capital, together constituting the 'asset pentagon'. As DFID (2001) notes, not all of the assets are capital stocks in a strict economic sense, but this terminology is widely used in the literature. DFID (2001) suggests that the capitals can be thought of as 'building blocks' (2001: Section 2.3) and Scoones (1998) refers to assets as livelihood resources. The terminology can then be slightly confusing, with capitals and assets used interchangeably. The use of such terms enables the approach to link to economic analysis and thinking.

Definitions of the five types of capitals are given in Box 5.3, though it should be noted that the types of capitals are interconnected. For example, if an individual or household has good access to natural capital and/or a good level of human capital, their economic capital may be more substantial than if they had poor access and provisions of such assets. As noted above, the types, nature and amount of assets will be influenced by the vulnerability context but also by the institutional context, as suggested in the 'transforming structures and processes' component. The endowment of assets is likely to change over time, an important consideration in undertaking an analysis of livelihoods at a given point.

Box 5.3 **The five capitals**

- *Natural:* the stocks of natural resources that the people whose livelihoods are the subject of the analysis have access to and make use of, e.g. fisheries, water, forests.
- *Social:* social resources, such as families, networks and associations, which people can, and do, draw on in pursuing their livelihood strategies.
- *Financial:* the capital base, including cash, credit/debit, savings and other economic assets, such as equipment.
- *Human:* the skills, knowledge, health and physical ability to undertake livelihood strategies.
- *Physical:* includes the basic infrastructure available, such as transport, shelter, water, energy and communication, and other equipment through which people pursue their livelihoods.

(Adapted from Scoones, 1998)

Some commentators have suggested that other forms of capital can be identified and should be included in the analysis, such as political capital, given the importance of politics in accessing resources. This is discussed further in the section 'Issues and debates in the SLA'. Bebbington (1999: 2022) puts forward an alternative way of conceiving a set of capital assets to the one used in the SLF, consisting of: produced, human, natural, social and cultural capitals. He argues for recognition of culture as a capital asset from his research in the Andes, where he observed that culture enables forms of 'action and resistance' to take place that the other forms of capital could not deliver on their own (1999: 2034). Culture as a capital cannot be quantified, which is perhaps why it is not generally included in the assets pentagon. Bebbington (1999) makes several observations about assets that are particularly informative for thinking about the nature and potential of assets:

- Assets are not just the means through which people make a living, or secure their livelihoods, they give meaning to people's lives.
- Assets are not just used but give people capability to be and to act. Assets can be a source of power.
- The distinction between access and resources is blurred – access can be seen as *the* most critical asset people have – without access to resources, people will not have the capability to secure their livelihoods and desired meaning in their lives. Access to resources is very often dependent on social capital; relationships with other actors are critical to accessing resources.

Bebbington's (1999) observations suggest that the SLF should be used with care and not used too rigidly, as some dimensions could be placed in more than one component of the framework. His observation concerning access and resources shows the close interlinkages between the asset pentagon and the 'transforming structures and processes' box of the SLF in particular. The nature and degree of access to resources can be considered a type of resource as well as referring to a range of institutions that mediate the ability to use and benefit from resources, or assets.

The form of each type of capital and how they are manifested and accessed are subject to many issues, as seen in other chapters of this book. What access people have to natural capital, for example, will be influenced by institutional arrangements and can be analysed through one of the frameworks or approaches to institutional analysis discussed in Chapter 3. The concept of 'social capital' is quite controversial, with different views on what exactly it is and how it can be measured, as discussed in Chapter 1.

The endowment of assets an individual or household has will influence the composition of their livelihood strategies and the subsequent outcomes. The extent of access to assets can be shown in the asset pentagon. This can be illustrated through the shape of the pentagon, with different length of lines showing how much access a person has to one type of capital compared with others or through a 'spider diagram', setting out scores for each type of asset and how these change over time or compare with others. An example of such a pentagon is provided in the section 'Applications of the SLF in research'.

Developing an understanding of the assets can be a challenge. The nature of assets and the capability to use and benefit from assets are closely related to the next component of the framework.

Transforming structures and processes

The 'transforming structures and processes' box in the framework shown in Figure 5.1 reflects the importance of structures and processes in mediating how assets are used, or are constrained in their use, with consequences for livelihood strategies and outcomes. This component of the framework requires an analysis of the organizations, institutions, policies and legislation that influence the livelihoods under investigation. These 'structures and processes' influence whether, or how, people can access resources and how they may use and benefit from the assets they have in pursuing different livelihood strategies. Gender, power and social relations are all examples of institutions that may influence the types and amounts of different types of capital assets and how these can be utilized, and the types of livelihood strategies pursued. They are formed through social negotiation and may be open to multiple interpretations. Formal structures, policies and legislation can also influence the scope to utilize assets within livelihood strategies. This section of the framework is sometimes referred to by different terms, such as 'policies, institutions and processes' (PIPs for short).

Livelihood strategies

Livelihood strategies that are pursued make up a portfolio, with different livelihood 'pathways' over time, perhaps with seasonal variations. Income and subsistence are derived from multiple sources, such as casual employment, crops, livestock, remittances and access to common pool resources for fuelwood, non-timber forest products and grazing, for example. The combination of activities may change over time and differ between members of a household. There are strong connections between the strategies adopted and the assets and structures and processes that influence the 'options' available; there may in fact be very few options open to people, with livelihood strategies adopted through necessity rather than choice. The term 'livelihood strategy' also reflects the *process* characteristic of livelihoods, in that livelihoods evolve and change over time. The nature of livelihood strategies in turn has implications for livelihood outcomes.

Livelihood outcomes

The livelihood outcomes refer to what happens as a result of those strategies. How much income or subsistence has resulted? Is poverty reduced or deepened? Are assets strengthened or run down? Is vulnerability reduced, deepened or about the same? Is food security improved or reduced? Is wellbeing increased or reduced? Whichever strategies are employed, the objective is to survive and improve wellbeing and hopefully reduce poverty. Livelihoods are 'sustained' over time.

Scoones' checklist for the SLF

The framework is intended as an analytical tool, in which the context, nature and dynamics are interrogated. Scoones (1998: 8) puts forward a checklist of questions that can be asked in using the framework:

1 *Sequencing* – what is the starting point for a particular livelihood strategy? Is it necessary, for example, to have a particular asset already in order to gain access to others?
2 *Substitution* – can different types of capital be substituted for others or are there some forms of capital that cannot be substituted? Are there some capital assets that are essential for certain livelihood strategies?
3 *Clustering* – are certain combinations of assets associated with particular groups or livelihood strategies?
4 *Access* – what kinds of access do people have to different types of resources and how is access facilitated or constrained? What kinds of institutional arrangements exist?
5 *Trade-offs* – what kinds of trade-offs are being made in making decisions about livelihood strategies?
6 *Trends* – a dynamic approach to the application of SLF should be pursued. Understanding trends over time in the availability of resources, access to resources, policies and institutional arrangements is important for understanding the environment in which strategies are pursued, as well as for explaining change and assessing how strategies may change into the future, or as a result of different scenarios.

This checklist is useful in that it illustrates the interconnections between different components of the framework and encourages a dynamic approach to be taken to the analysis, examining changes over time. Whilst it may be necessary to consider each component on their own, it is also essential to look for and investigate interlinkages. The checklist summarizes the livelihoods framework and provides a useful tool for planning research and undertaking analysis of findings.

Issues and debates in the SLA

There are many issues and debates that have arisen within the course of the development, application and review of the SLA. The perceived lack of explicit inclusion of politics and power has been one particularly contentious issue (Baumann, 2000; Carney, 2003), with Baumann (2000) arguing that the category of 'political capital' should be included as a type of asset, rather than politics and power being left to the 'transforming structures and processes' analysis. Such an approach, Baumann argues, would give recognition to the need for people to have and use power and political connections in mobilizing their other assets and securing livelihood strategies and outcomes.

This critique is acknowledged by Scoones (2009) in his review of livelihood approaches, where he identifies four areas of failings since the inception of livelihood approaches in the 1990s:

1   lack of engagement with processes of economic globalization, with limited means of responding to major shifts in global markets and politics;
2   lack of attention given to power and politics, with limited linkage made between livelihoods and governance debates within the development community;
3   lack of acknowledgement of the bigger environmental picture, particularly in relation to climate change, despite the use of the word 'sustainable';
4   failure of livelihood approaches to engage with long-term changes in rural economies and with agrarian change.

In responding to these four perceived failings of livelihoods perspectives, Scoones (2009) identifies four areas of challenges for the SLA: knowledge, politics, scale and dynamics. In terms of knowledge, Scoones (2009) urges that the framings, assumptions and values underlying the application of a livelihoods perspective are made explicit, rather than portraying the analysis as purely rational and objective. In relation to politics and power, Scoones argues that these 'must be central to livelihoods perspectives' (2009: 185). An analysis of power and politics should not just focus on the local level but at the wider context and over time. He does not, however, support Baumann's (2000) contention that a category of political power should be included in the set of assets. Scoones also states that in relation to politics, attention should be given 'to how livelihoods are structured by relations of class, caste, gender, ethnicity, religion and cultural identity' (2009: 186). In terms of scale, Scoones argues that whilst livelihoods analyses have often focused on the micro-level, they should be able to 'examine networks, linkages, connections, flows and chains across scales' whilst also remaining 'firmly rooted in place and context' (2009: 188). Finally, a dynamic perspective is needed, examining livelihoods over time, including looking into the future through examining the directions and potential impacts of long-term change.

A further set of critiques of the SLA are identified by Morse *et al.* (2009). The limitations of SLA for them include the lack of explicit presence of people in the framework, the difficulties experienced in analysing and measuring the five types of capital, the inevitable unpredictability of the vulnerability context and the complexity of livelihoods not being adequately captured by the SLF.

Critiques of the SLA will, at least to some extent, reflect the approach taken and purpose of the analysis. Perceived limitations of the SLA and SLF can be addressed through drawing on other frameworks and analytical approaches, as well as through adapting the framework.

Applications of the SLF in research

Whilst livelihoods analysis can be used to generate an holistic view of an individual's or household's livelihood strategies and outcomes, the approach has also been used in relation to specific natural resources, investigating and highlighting key issues that relate to those resources. The following sections review how the SLA has been used within research in the forestry and fisheries sectors.

Livelihoods analysis in the forestry sector

Two key issues have received particular attention through the application of the SLF within forestry: how decentralization of forest management has affected livelihood and environmental outcomes and to what extent non-timber forest products make a real difference to peoples' livelihoods.

Decentralization of the management of forests has taken place internationally, taking different forms, dependent on how, and to what extent, power is shared (in theory and in practice). Such forms include Joint Forest Management in India, Community-Based Forest Management (CBFM) and Community-Based Co-Management (CBCM). As suggested by these terms, some forms of decentralization involve local user groups having control over an area of forest, whilst in other arrangements there is cooperation between users and government. The scope for decision-making and enforcement of rules will vary depending on the legal and institutional context. The application of the SLF to an analysis of how decentralization has impacted on local and community livelihoods can therefore enable an investigation of how livelihood assets have been affected and how changes in structures and processes have contributed to these changes in assets and livelihood outcomes. An example of such analysis is given by Larson *et al.* (2007), where a modified form of the SLF focuses on the interactions between assets, 'policies, institutions and processes' and outcomes. The framework emphasizes the context within which decentralization of forest management responsibilities to local government and users takes place. It identifies five areas of policies, institutions and processes of relevance: markets, public policy (including land, forest and economic), increased local government authority, key governance institutions/access mechanisms (formal and informal) and organizations/ social movements' demands. A key finding of the analysis was that the vulnerability of forest-dependent people is increased when decentralization is not accompanied by policy that secures access rights. Decentralization of management functions is not of itself necessarily good for livelihoods and conservation – the broader social, economic and political context matters. This example shows two things: first, how the SLF can be adapted to focus on a particular part of the framework in depth and second, how the framework can be used to investigate the inter-relationships between components of the PIP box.

A further example of using a component of the SLF to investigate decentralization and livelihoods in relation to forests is given by Chen *et al.* (2013). In this example, the focus is on how assets have altered as a result of the change in management approach and on a comparison of assets between people participating in community-based management and those not. Chen *et al.* (2013) report on a system of indicators and variables associated with livelihood and environmental outcomes and how these were applied in research in Baishuijiang National Nature Reserve, northwest China. The indicators include 'forest protection activities' and 'perception of the state of forest health' for natural capital and 'household energy structure' and 'household durable goods' as indicators of the level of physical capital. Having collected data through household interviews in a number of villages, the indicators and capitals were weighted in terms of whether they were in a 'poor, average or good' condition or level of availability. These scores were then plotted in spider diagrams of asset pentagons, comparing livelihood capitals between 2006 and 2010 and comparing livelihood capitals between participating and non-participating households. One of the asset pentagons is shown in Figure 5.2. The diagram shows how natural capital had increased over the four years and whilst physical capital had also increased, it was still only scored within the 'average' category.

Studies that have used the SLA and SLF in relation to the use of non-timber forest products (NTFP) have used the approach to investigate the place of NTFP in the livelihoods of different types of households. Kusters *et al.* report on research that asked 'to what extent and under what conditions NTFP trade leads to both livelihood improvement and forest conservation' (2006: 1), taking evidence from 55 cases from across Africa, Asia and Latin America. The research involved the development of assessment tools using livelihood and environmental indicators. The livelihood indicators addressed each of the five capitals of the asset pentagon and were applied at household and community level. Examples of indicators used include legal access to the target resource and control over the target resource as indicators of natural capital, and health and nutritional status and access to information as examples of indicators of human capital. Environmental indicators included impacts on species in terms of population size and distribution, developed to assess the sustainability of extraction. From the findings, different groups of households were identified and it was concluded that although there are positive impacts on

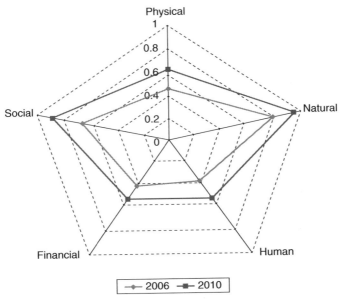

Figure 5.2 Livelihood asset pentagon showing assets in 2006 and 2010 of forest-using households in the Baishuijiang National Nature Reserve.

Source: Chen *et al.*, 2013: 911.

local livelihoods from the trade, this is not always the case for natural assets, challenging the view that extraction of NTFPs does not damage a forest.

These examples show how parts of the SLF can be used to investigate a particular question about impacts on livelihoods resulting from livelihood strategies or changes in policies, institutions and processes. The examples also show that the SLF can be adapted and modified, bringing in insights from theory and literature to guide data collection and analysis, and that there is a need to identify context specific indicators to operationalize the different asset categories.

Livelihoods analysis in small-scale fisheries

Millions of people with dependence on fisheries for their livelihoods live in the developing world and operate within 'small-scale' or 'artisanal', or non-industrialized, fisheries. This implies that people go out to fish in their own boats or hire a few labourers (or boat crew), with locally made boats, using engines, paddles or sails. Many people who work within artisanal fisheries have many strands to their livelihood strategies. These may include having a piece of land for growing crops for household consumption, working as an agricultural labourer for some of the year or migrating to other parts of the fishery or to other water bodies in search of better fish catches and higher prices. Despite there being multiple strands to many fisherfolk livelihoods, there are certain key sources of vulnerability that affect fisherfolk assets and decisions about livelihood strategies. In addition, there are numerous structures, institutions and policies that mediate how their assets can be utilized in livelihood strategies.

The SLF can be used not only to enable a better understanding of the complexity and dynamics of fisherfolk livelihoods but also to inform fisheries management approaches. Allison and Ellis (2001) argue that using SLF to investigate fisheries highlights a number of characteristics of small-scale fisheries that suggest that traditional, top-down management approaches cannot be sufficiently responsive to change. These include the diversity of livelihood sources that many fisherfolk have, the range of responses that fishers undertake to adapt to shocks and trends and the need for a more integrated approach to enable fishers to move out of poverty that goes beyond the fisheries sector.

The SLA was used in the early 2000s to inform a multi-country development programme in West African fisheries, the Sustainable Fisheries Livelihoods Programme. The purpose of using the SLA was to encourage the sector to make linkages with wider development programmes, reflecting the diversity of fisheries stakeholders' livelihoods, the complex institutional environment in which their livelihoods are situated and the nature of poverty experienced by fisherfolk (Allison and Horemans, 2006; Neiland and Béné, 2004). Taking an SLA informed the design and implementation of poverty-profiling amongst fisherfolk communities, leading to the implementation of small projects to address specific constraints and opportunities. These included training in adult literacy and post-harvesting techniques, initiatives to address HIV/AIDS and improving access to saving and credit schemes. The programme encouraged fisheries stakeholders, including the government departments responsible for fisheries, to look beyond the sector to identify constraints and opportunities for development for those operating within the sector.

An example of the use of the SLF to investigate fisherfolk livelihoods is given in the author's own research on livelihoods and migration within the fisheries of Lake Victoria, East Africa. Nunan (2010) reports on how the vulnerability context changes as fisherfolk, primarily boat crew, move between landing sites in search of better catches and higher prices for their catch. Figure 5.3 sets out the generic vulnerability context, examples of assets, structures and processes mediating the use of those assets for livelihood strategies and the subsequent livelihood outcomes for boat crew. This provides a general overview of the kinds of livelihoods found amongst boat crew and illustrates how migration around the lake both reduces sources of vulnerability and brings in new sources of vulnerability. Table 5.1 complements the figure by setting out in detail the types of assets boat crew may have and how the assets affect and are affected by movement between landing sites. The table also includes an analysis of how the vulnerability context of boat crew is affected by the changes in assets resulting from migration. In Figure 5.3, it can be seen that a wide range of policies, institutions and processes affect assets and how those assets may or may not be used in livelihood strategies. These range from government policies on fisheries, such as those setting out what types of gear can and cannot be used in fisheries, to institutions such as the relationships between boat crew and boat owners, where boat owners have greater power and resources than crew, who depend on owners for employment. The analysis in this case study suggests that whilst moving from one landing site to another to access better fishing grounds and higher fish prices reduces some sources of vulnerability (low catches and low income, with the possibility of no employment when fish catches are low), these are exchanged for other sources of vulnerability, particularly those arising from risky sexual behaviour and increased fishing pressure. 'Risky sexual behaviour' arises from practices within some fishing communities with sex being exchanged for access to fish (i.e. for the right to buy fish) and from people having multiple partners as they move from one landing site to another, in part attributed to daily cash income associated with fisheries, access to alcohol and a culture of risk (Béné and Merten, 2008).

The analyses arising from the application of the SLF within fisheries highlight the benefits of taking a more holistic overview, identifying interdependencies between types of captials, the breadth of sources of vulnerability and how vulnerability can be affected by as well as affect livelihood strategies. The framework is useful for enabling a better understanding of fisherfolk decision-making, of the constraints on their livelihoods and opportunities that exist for improving livelihoods and fisheries management.

Wellbeing analysis

An alternative approach to investigating livelihoods is a focus on wellbeing. Interest in understanding wellbeing and why it matters in a development context has grown during the last couple of decades, and approaches have been developed to enable analyses of wellbeing. These include the wellbeing analysis framework developed through work of the Wellbeing in Developing Countries Research Group (WeD) at the University of Bath, UK, in the 2000s and the Ecosystem Services and Wellbeing frameworks of the Millennium Ecosystem Assessment in the early 2000s. The concept of 'wellbeing' has been around for far longer, particularly associated with social psychology, welfare economics and anthropology. Within development studies, an economics approach to understanding wellbeing dominated until the 1990s, when the capabilities approach influenced conceptual developments. Different disciplinary understandings of wellbeing share the recognition of both objective and subjective components of wellbeing, making people's perception of their own, or collective, wellbeing important. Other terms are sometimes used almost interchangeably with wellbeing, such as quality of life, living standards and happiness, but within different approaches to analysing wellbeing, definitions are given that make this concept distinct from others.

The adoption of the concept of wellbeing is not seen as abandoning poverty, but rather offering a way of recognizing that no-one is defined by their poverty or wealth alone and that where poverty is experienced, there are many ways of portraying, understanding and investigating poverty, from income poverty to social exclusion. The concept of wellbeing is seen as providing a more encompassing term than poverty, embracing all of the dimensions and experiences of poverty.

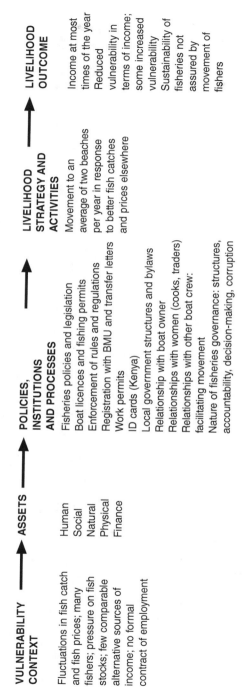

VULNERABILITY CONTEXT

Fluctuations in fish catch and fish prices; many fishers; pressure on fish stocks; few comparable alternative sources of income; no formal contract of employment

ASSETS

Human
Social
Natural
Physical
Finance

POLICIES, INSTITUTIONS AND PROCESSES

Fisheries policies and legislation
Boat licences and fishing permits
Enforcement of rules and regulations
Registration with BMU and transfer letters
Work permits
ID cards (Kenya)
Local government structures and bylaws
Relationship with boat owner
Relationships with women (cooks, traders)
Relationships with other boat crew:
facilitating movement
Nature of fisheries governance: structures, accountability, decision-making, corruption

LIVELIHOOD STRATEGY AND ACTIVITIES

Movement to an average of two beaches per year in response to better fish catches and prices elsewhere

LIVELIHOOD OUTCOME

Income at most times of the year
Reduced vulnerability in terms of income; some increased vulnerability
Sustainability of fisheries not assured by movement of fishers

Figure 5.3 Sustainable Livelihoods framework: analysis of boat crew livelihood strategies.

Source: Nunan, 2010: 780.

Table 5.1 Asset definition and role in movement of fisherfolk, Lake Victoria

Capital asset	Role and impact on assets from moving	Impacts on vulnerability
Human	Fishing skills and knowledge of the fisheries are said to increase as a result of movement. No adverse impacts on access to health services due to moving between landing sites reported	Vulnerability reduced by gaining skills and knowledge
	Greater exposure to risky sexual behaviour reflected by relatively high levels of HIV prevalence in fishing communities	Vulnerability increased due to health and income implications
Social	Social capital is essential in facilitating the movement of fisherfolk through the use of contacts and networks to identify better fishing grounds and in enabling conflict-free residence at landing sites	Vulnerability is reduced as social capital is built up through interaction at a number of landing sites, but could also increase through marriage breakdown
	Social networks at home may be damaged through movement, with marriage breakdown reported as a disadvantage of moving in some cases	
Natural	Access to fisheries requires a boat licence and fishing permit, and registration with a Beach Management Unit. No limit on the number of boat licences and fishing permits issued. The movement of fish influences the movement of boat crew. Many fishers also farm land, growing both food and cash crops	Access to natural resources reduces vulnerability through income generated through fish catch and food security through subsistence farming. Concern over Nile perch stocks and the number of fishers, boats and gear on the lake suggest that vulnerability is increasing due to smaller catches and reduced income
	Movement could increase pressure on fish stocks by more fishers moving to areas of higher productivity, but could also relieve pressure and could be less destructive than increasing numbers of boats with engines	
Physical	Boat crews require access to boats and gear, mediated through boat owners. Some reported moving to landing sites with better facilities and services, and being driven to moving because of the theft of fishing gear. Increasing motorization of boats led some fishers to migrate so that they were not competing with motorized boats. At some landing sites, there was too much demand for services, particularly public toilets and housing at certain times because of an influx of fishers	Boat crews are vulnerable because of their inability to afford boats and gear. Most landing sites are poorly served with basic services, such as clean drinking water, sanitation, electricity, all weather roads and health facilities, increasing the vulnerability of all members of fishing communities. Movement may reduce vulnerability by enabling fishers to move to better sites, but also fluctuating populations make it difficult for local governments to plan and gives them an excuse for inadequate provision
Financial	Income is largely from daily catch/processing/ trading. No differences in daily pay between migrant and local fishers; payment depends on skill, experience and catch. Few boat crews belong to savings schemes and about half of all women belong to local schemes, most run by the members themselves. Money is sent home on a regular basis in many cases through friends and family. Access to credit said to be easier if people remain at one location	Movement increases chances of income throughout most of the year, though there are always times in a year when catches are low everywhere. Money is not always remitted home, with implications for women and children left behind, increasing their vulnerability. Membership of effective savings and credit schemes could reduce vulnerability

Gough *et al.* (2010: 3–4) suggest that wellbeing can 'encompass and connect these debates over different types of poverty'.

Key characteristics of 'wellbeing' are identified as its positive perspective, the holistic outlook of the concept and the focus on people and their own priorities and perspectives. The positive perspective of 'wellbeing' is in contrast to more negative connotations associated with poverty and social exclusion, for example, focusing more on what people have rather than what they do not. Taking a wellbeing perspective implies that the person or group of people would be viewed as a whole rather than on a sectoral basis, reflecting the complexity of people's lives.

Wellbeing is, then, an attractive concept. However, it is also difficult to define, with different understandings of its meaning and implications. White conceptualizes wellbeing as 'doing well – feeling good' and 'doing good – feeling well' (2010: 160), whilst McGregor offers the following definition: 'Wellbeing is a state of being with others, where human needs are met, where one can act meaningfully to pursue one's goals, and where one enjoys a satisfactory quality of life' (McGregor, 2008: 1).

Two approaches to the investigation of wellbeing that have quite different underlying assumptions and perspectives are now reviewed.

Millennium Ecosystem Assessment framework

The Millennium Ecosystem Assessment was carried out in the early 2000s, with the assessment informed by the ecosystem and wellbeing framework set out in Figure 5.4. It was initiated by the United Nations and brought together scientists, governments, non-governmental organizations and the private sector to collate and review evidence on the state of ecosystems, with a view to influencing policy and action the world over (MA, 2005). The review process was informed by an assessment of linkages between ecosystem services and human wellbeing, as set out in Figure 5.4. This is the micro level of analysis, which was complemented by a more macro framework, set out in Figure 5.5.

As can be seen in Figure 5.4, ecosystem services are categorized as supporting, provisioning, regulating and cultural, with different levels of effects on different parts or manifestations of well-being. In the framework, wellbeing is composed of security, basic materials for a good life, health and good social relations, underlain by freedom of choice and action. Linkages between specific ecosystem services and constituents of human wellbeing are multiple, varying in importance and intensity.

The macro-level framework enables:

1   identification of options that can deliver on both human development and sustainability goals;
2   an understanding of trade-offs that would result from certain decisions and where, and by whom, those trade-offs would be felt adversely;
3   decisions to be made on which levels of governance policies would be most effective.

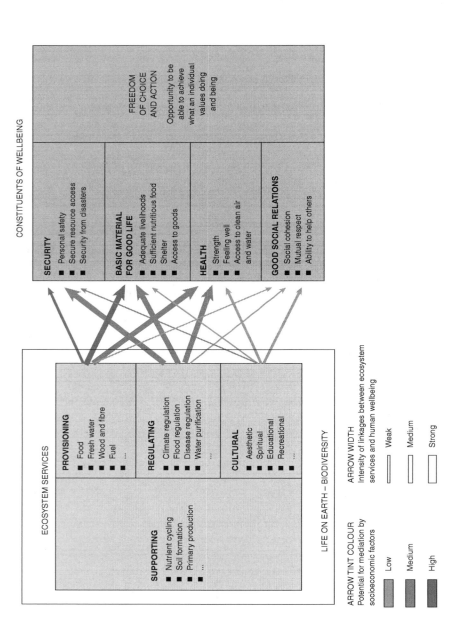

Figure 5.4 Millennium Ecosystem Assessment: linkages between ecosystem services and human wellbeing.

Source: MA, 2003: 78.

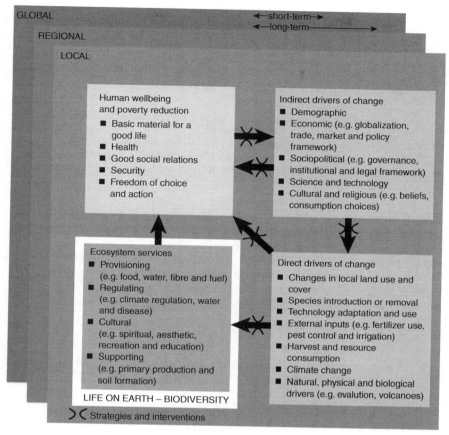

Figure 5.5 Millennium Ecosystem Assessment: conceptual framework.
Source: MA, 2003: 37.

The frameworks guided the analysis of numerous ecosystems in the assessment and have since been drawn on and further developed in seeking to understand human–ecosystem interactions.

One area of analysis noted above concerns the capacity of the frameworks to enable the identification and analysis of trade-offs between ecosystem services and their associated effects on human wellbeing. An understanding of how ecosystem management decisions impact on different types of ecosystem services is critical for understanding the implications for human wellbeing. Trade-offs cannot, however, always be predicted or fully known. Rodríguez *et al.* (2006) classify trade-offs according to their spatial scale, temporal scale (whether trade-offs are rapid or appear slowly) and reversibility, that is, an assessment of the likelihood of the ecosystem service that has been disturbed returning to its original state once the disturbance has stopped. They further suggest that supporting services are more likely to be taken for granted in any analysis of ecosystem services, as the other types of services are more apparent, and that decision-making should take into account how decisions have cumulative effects on ecosystem services and interact with other decisions. An analysis of trade-offs is deemed essential in the face of evidence that 'win–win' situations of conservation and increasing human wellbeing appear elusive (McShane *et al.*, 2011).

The frameworks developed for the MA go some way towards enabling the identification and understanding of human–environment relations, but have been criticized for failing to acknowledge social differentiation. The frameworks continue to be adapted, drawing on other concepts and frameworks, such as the development of a framework which has greater emphasis on poverty alleviation by Fisher *et al.* (2014), with 'access to and control over' ecosystem services at the centre of their framework.

The Wellbeing in Developing Countries approach

This approach was developed by a group of researchers at the University of Bath, UK, in the early to mid-2000s, who formed a Wellbeing in Developing Countries (WeD) group and secured funding to develop and test an approach to researching wellbeing. Wellbeing in this approach is viewed as bringing together the following strands:

1   The resources that a person is able to command;

2   What they are able to achieve with those resources, and in particular what needs and goals they are able to meet; and

3   The meaning that they give to the goals they achieve and the processes in which they engage.

(McGregor, 2010: 317)

The framework has three dimensions: the material, the relational and the subjective. These are explained as:

- *Material:* consisting of assets, welfare and standards of living.
- *Relational:* these are divided into two areas: social and human. 'Social' refers to social relations and access to public goods. 'Human' refers to capabilities, attitudes to life and personal relationships.
- *Subjective:* this dimension also has two aspects: people's perceptions of their positions with respect to material, social and human positions, and cultural values, ideologies and beliefs (White, 2010: 161).

These dimensions are presented as being linked together in a pyramid, with subjective feelings of wellbeing dependant on the material, social and human dimensions. Each of the material, social and human dimensions have objective and subjective aspects. For example, in the material dimension, subjective aspects might include the level of satisfaction with income and wealth or an assessment of standard of living compared with others'. Box 5.4 sets out dimensions of wellbeing from White (2010), which provides examples of the types of variables of relevance.

Box 5.4 Dimensions of wellbeing

- *The material* concerns practical welfare and standards of living.
  - Objective aspects include:
    - income, wealth, and assets;
    - employment and livelihood activities;
    - levels of consumption.
  - Subjective aspects include:
    - satisfaction with income and wealth;
    - assessment of one's standard of living compared with others';
    - assessment of present standard of living compared with past.

- *The social* concerns social relations and access to public goods.
  - Objective aspects include:
    - social, political, and cultural identities;
    - violence, conflict, and (in)security;
    - relations with the state: law, politics, welfare;
    - access to services and amenities;
    - networks of support and obligation;
    - environmental resources.
  - Subjective aspects include:
    - perceptions of safety, respect, and discrimination;
    - (dis)satisfaction with access to services;
    - assessment of treatment/support given or received;
    - perceptions of environmental quality.

- *The human* concerns capabilities, attitudes to life, and personal relationships.
  - Objective aspects include:
    - household structure and composition;
    - education, information, and skills;
    - physical health and (dis)ability;
    - relations of love and care.
  - Subjective aspects include:
    - (dis)satisfaction with levels of health, information, skills, education;
    - self-concept and personality;
    - trust and confidence;
    - religious faith.

(White, 2010: 163)

The framework draws on the Theory of Human Need (THN) of Doyal and Gough (1991), which sets out eleven 'need satisfiers', such as adequate nutritional food and water, adequate protective housing and significant primary relationships with others. These can be seen within the material, social and human dimensions set out in Box 5.4.

In the initial research to investigate how people seek to construct their wellbeing, the WeD team developed a methodology with six components (McGregor, 2010). The purpose of setting out the components and methods of the research project here is to illustrate how the multi-faceted nature of the fieldwork reflected the multiple dimensions of wellbeing and how essential a multi-method approach is to wellbeing research. The six components of the methodology were:

1 *A Resources and Needs Questionnaire (RANQ):* A household survey seeking information in relation to five categories of resources (material, human, social, cultural and natural) and categories of need satisfaction, taken from the Theory of Human Need, including health, education, food and housing. The questionnaire was used to generate data on all members of a household rather than the household as a whole and the results of the survey then fed into subsequent phases of the fieldwork.

2 *Quality of life:* A three-phased research strategy was developed to study quality of life as the outcomes experienced and processes that generate outcomes, leading to the generation of data through interviews.

3 *Community profiling:* Secondary data, key informant interviews and participatory methods were used to develop a profile of a community that describes the relevant demographic, social and physical characteristics. Additional insights were added as the subsequent phases of the research progressed.

4 *Structures research and welfare regimes:* Secondary quantitative and qualitative data were gathered to 'locate the research sites within national and global structures of power, exchange and information' and to investigate how 'actors within the research sites mediate between the households and outside organisations and institutions, including government, business and civil society' (McGregor, 2010: 343).

5 *Process research:* The purpose of this part of the fieldwork was to identify key relationships that people engage with as part of their striving for a desired level of wellbeing. Two components to this research were developed. The first involved the identification of themes to be investigated in relation to processes that individuals and households engage in. The second component involved a sample of individuals and households keeping a diary and being interviewed at intervals to record in detail how they engage with various processes.

6 *Income and expenditure research:* Different methods were used to collect information on how the resources of individuals and households generate income or other means by which wellbeing is sought. Surveys and monthly diaries were used to collect data at different sites.

As a relatively new approach to investigating how people experience their lives and how they feel about their experiences and situation, wellbeing analysis is very much still under development, with modifications underway. For example, a 'wellbeing pathways' approach is being presented as having seven domains, including competence and self-worth, and social connections, with subjective and objective perspectives layered and interconnected (White, 2013). There is as yet little critique on the WeD approach, though McGillivray and Clarke (2006) observe that much of the work on wellbeing does not explicitly mention gender.

Wellbeing in fisheries: application of WeD approach

The application of the concept of wellbeing within research on human–environment, or poverty–environment, interactions is limited to date, reflecting the recent development of the analytical approach. One example of application within the natural resource field is within fisheries research. Coulthard *et al.* (2011) and Coulthard (2012) set out a rationale for the application of a wellbeing approach within fisheries, arguing that such an approach could provide better evidence of the social impacts of changes in fisheries on people and the societies in which they live, particularly changes associated with declining stocks and catches. Coulthard (2012) argues that wellbeing analysis recognizes that fisher behaviour is not always economically motivated, but there may be other motivating factors that would fall within a 'wellbeing' umbrella. The identification and understanding of motivating factors could inform the design of more effective approaches within fisheries management. Coulthard suggests that the emphasis of the WeD approach on relations reflects well the reality of operating within fisheries, where 'a diversity of relationships such as dependency, obligation, support, reciprocity, exploitation, and collective action in fishing communities can determine both a persons' wellbeing outcomes and fisher behaviour' (2012: 361).

Coulthard *et al.* (2014) report on the application of the WeD approach in a Sri Lankan fishing village, observing that the concept of wellbeing was well understood and appreciated during the research, generating much debate, particularly due to the research approach used, which encouraged people to generate their own criteria of assessment. The importance of relationships was brought out using the approach, with both positive and negative connotations, including relying on family relationships in times of difficulty to being dependent on middlemen for the sale of catch. Coulthard *et al.* (2014) also note challenges in using the WeD approach, as subjective responses may be influenced by people's limited knowledge of alternative opportunities or states of being, or by people's unwillingness to say anything negative about relationships pertaining to family and friends, for example.

Weeratunge *et al.* (2014) review the potential benefit from the application of the concept of social wellbeing within fisheries, situating the WeD approach in the context of related frameworks and approaches, including economics of happiness, sustainable livelihoods and capabilities. Related frameworks and approaches include the 'economics of happiness', with Weeratunge *et al.* (2014) highlighting the contributions of Pollnac and Poggie (2008) and Pollnac *et al.* (2001), who emphasize the level of job satisfaction and happiness that comes from fishing, attributed to the perceived risky nature of the occupation. In relation to social wellbeing, Weeratunge *et al.* (2014) highlight the importance of identity, both in relational and subjective terms, observing the breadth of work on identity within fisheries and reflecting the importance of identity with their occupation for many of those working in fisheries.

This initial application of wellbeing type thinking within research on small-scale fisheries suggests scope for application and contribution, particularly in terms of understanding motivations, relationships and identity, with implications for the nature and processes of fisheries governance. Such application would build on existing work that has been undertaken on these issues, from different conceptual perspectives, suggesting that wellbeing analysis can establish links with other perspectives and concepts whilst also providing a new lens through which to view people–environment relationships.

Livelihoods and wellbeing approaches compared

Both livelihoods and wellbeing approaches aim to encourage holistic analysis, viewing livelihoods and wellbeing within a broad context, reflecting the complexity of people's lives and relationships. Both are more concerned with what people have rather than what they do not, though both also seek to understand how people's lives may be improved. The two approaches can be contrasted in terms of their methodological approach, with the SLF being associated with rapid assessment of people's livelihoods, looking for generalizations and key trends in livelihoods, whilst the WeD is more associated with undertaking a deeper investigation of people's lives, particularly in relation to how they feel or view their own wellbeing and what affects their wellbeing (Dawson, 2013). In addition, the WeD approach is viewed as requiring a more multidisciplinary approach, drawing on psychology, economics and sociology, for example, though both can, and often do, require both quantitative and qualitative data and hence a mixed-methods approach to data collection and analysis.

As examples of the application of the SLF and WeD were taken from the fisheries sector, a comparison of their areas of application and findings may be illustrative. The applications had different areas of interest – with the SLF literature examining fisheries within the broader social-economic context, paying particular attention to the vulnerability context, and the WeD literature examining motivations, relationships and job satisfaction – there are areas of overlap and similar ultimate aims of informing fisheries management. However, it is not possible to draw strong conclusions from their application, as in all cases, specific questions and angles were investigated and application to other issues is not precluded. Ultimately, the approaches have similar roots, but the frameworks are constructed with different concepts and variables and have different perspectives. Which framework a researcher should use would depend on the questions being asked, their own academic interests and the context of the empirical situation.

The MA conceptual framework offers a much more ecologically based approach that could complement both the SLF and the WeD approach. By having a more detailed focus on ecosystems in terms of the nature of services provided and how these operate, are maintained and interact, the framework enables a deeper understanding of the ecological situation, constraints and opportunities than the SLF and WeD. For some research situations, it may be useful to draw on the MA frameworks in conjunction with the SLF or WeD approach to deepen understanding of the ecosystem in relation to livelihoods and wellbeing.

Summary of key points

- Attention to livelihoods and wellbeing reflects recognition of the multifaceted nature and diverse experiences of poverty, as more widely accepted from the 1990s.
- Both have roots in the concept of capability – what people are able to do and be.
- DFID's Sustainable Livelihoods Approach, with its associated framework, is one example of a livelihoods approach, with the framework enabling an analysis of the opportunities and constraints on livelihood strategies and outcomes.
- Wellbeing analysis is an emerging lens for the analysis of people–environment relationships, with the Millennium Ecosystem Assessment providing two frameworks that facilitate an analysis of the interactions and trade-offs between ecosystem services and human wellbeing and the Wellbeing in Developing Countries approach providing a three-dimensional framework, with material, relational and subjective dimensions.
- The frameworks enable an analysis of what people have rather than focusing on what they do not, though also recognize constraints on livelihoods and wellbeing. They encourage a more holistic analysis of people's lives, responding to the complexity of how resources may be accessed and benefited from, the diversity of relationships and the range of perspectives and attitudes that people have about their own lives and aspirations.

Further reading

Ellis, F. (2000) *Rural Livelihoods and Diversity in Developing Countries*, Oxford: Oxford University Press.
This book does not focus on poverty or livelihoods in relation to the environment, although it does have a chapter on this subject, but provides an excellent insight into issues concerning rural livelihoods through the application of an adapted form of DFID's Sustainable Livelihoods framework. The book is primarily concerned with an investigation into the livelihood diversity of rural households in the developing world. In examining this, Ellis uses the framework to examine key factors that influence diversity within livelihoods, such as seasonality, opportunities for migration and access to credit, and agricultural productivity. He examines the context of the environment for rural livelihoods, looking, for example, at resource management institutions, how gender relations are relevant to rural livelihoods and at macro-level policies of relevance to rural livelihoods. In relation to using a livelihoods approach to investigate poverty–environment relations, this book is useful for in-depth reflections on the components of the livelihoods framework, enabling insightful application of these in a research context.

Gough, I. and J.A. McGregor (eds) (2010) *Wellbeing in Developing Countries: From Theory to Research*, Cambridge: Cambridge University Press.
This edited collection brings together chapters that explore the components of the Wellbeing in Developing Countries framework, with sections on human needs and human wellbeing, resources, agency and meaning, quality of life and subjective wellbeing, and researching wellbeing. The authors come from a range of disciplinary backgrounds to explore the potential of a wellbeing-centred approach to development, rather than one that focuses on poverty and economic growth.

References

Adger, W.N. (2006) 'Vulnerability', *Global Environmental Change*, 16: 268–281.

Allison, E.H. and Ellis, F. (2001) 'The livelihoods approach and management of smallscale fisheries', *Marine Policy*, 25: 377–388.

Allison, E.H. and Horemans, B. (2006) 'Putting the principles of the Sustainable Livelihoods Approach into fisheries development policy and practice', *Marine Policy*, 30: 757–766.

Ashley, C. and Carney, D. (1999) *Sustainable Livelihoods: Lessons from Early Experience*, London: Department for International Development.

Baumann, P. (2000) 'Sustainable livelihoods and political capital: Arguments and evidence from decentralisation and natural resource management in India', *Working Paper 136*, London: Overseas Development Institute.

Bebbington, A. (1999) 'Capitals and capabilities: A framework for analyzing peasant viability, rural livelihoods and poverty', *World Development*, 27(12): 2021–2044.

Béné, C. and Merten, S. (2008) 'Women and fish-for-sex: Transactional sex, HIV/AIDS and gender in African fisheries', *World Development*, 36(5): 875–899.

Carney, D. (1999) *Livelihood Approaches Compared: A Brief Comparison of the Livelihoods Approaches of the UK Department for International Development (DFID), CARE, Oxfam and the United Nations Development Programme (UNDP)*, London: Department for International Development.

Carney, D. (2003) *Sustainable Livelihoods Approaches: Progress and Possibilities for Change*, London: Department for International Development.

Chambers, R. and Conway, G. (1992) 'Sustainable rural livelihoods: Practical concepts for the 21st century', *IDS Discussion Paper 296*, Brighton: Institute of Development Studies.

Chen, H., Zhu, T., Krott, M., Calvo, J.F., Ganesh, S.P. and Makoto, I. (2013) 'Measurement and evaluation of livelihood assets in sustainable forest commons governance', *Land Use Policy*, 30: 908–914.

Coulthard, S. (2012) 'What does the debate around social wellbeing have to offer sustainable fisheries?', *Current Opinion in Environmental Sustainability*, 4: 358–363.

Coulthard, S., Johnson, D. and McGregor, J.A. (2011) 'Poverty, sustainability and human wellbeing: A social wellbeing approach to the global fisheries crisis', *Global Environmental Change*, 21: 453–463.

Coulthard, S., Sandaruwan, K.L., Paranamana, N. and Koralgama, D. (2014) 'Taking a wellbeing approach to fisheries research: Insights from a Sri Lankan fishing village and relevance for sustainable fisheries', in Camfield, L. (ed.), *Methodological Challenges and New Approaches to Research in International Development*, Basingstoke: Palgrave-McMillan, pp. 76–100.

Dawson, N.M. (2013) 'An assessment of multidimensional wellbeing in rural Rwanda: Impacts of and implications for rural development and natural resource conservation', PhD Thesis, Norwich: University of East Anglia.

DFID (2001) *Sustainable Livelihood Guidance Sheets*, London: Department for International Development.

Doyal, L. and Gough, I. (1991) *A Theory of Human Need*, Basingstoke: Macmillan.

Ellis, F. (2000) *Rural Livelihoods and Diversity in Developing Countries*, Oxford: Oxford University Press.

Fisher, J.A., Patenaude, G., Giri, K., Lewis, K., Meir, P., Pinho, P., Rounsevell, M.D.A. and Williams, M. (2014) 'Understanding the relationships between ecosystem services and poverty alleviation: A conceptual framework', *Ecosystem Services*, 7: 34–45.

Gough, I. and McGregor, J.A. (eds) (2010) *Wellbeing in Developing Countries: From Theory to Research*, Cambridge: Cambridge University Press.

Gough, I., McGregor, J.A. and Camfield, L. (2010) 'Theorising wellbeing in international development', in Gough, I. and McGregor, J.A. (eds), *Wellbeing in Developing Countries: From Theory to Research*, Cambridge: Cambridge University Press, pp. 3–43.

Kusters, K., Achdiawan, R., Belcher, B., and Pérez, M.R. (2006) 'Balancing Development and conservation? An assessment of livelihood and environmental outcomes of nontimber forest product trade in Asia, Africa, and Latin America', *Ecology & Society*, 11(2): 20.

Larson, A.M., Pacheco, P., Toni, F. and Vallejo, M. (2007) 'The effects of forestry decentralization on access to livelihood assets', *The Journal of Environment & Development*, 16(3): 251–268.

MA (2003) *Millennium Ecosystem Assessment, Ecosystems and Human Wellbeing: A Framework for Assessment*, Washington, DC: Island Press.

MA (2005) *Ecosystems and Human Wellbeing: Synthesis Report (Millennium Ecosystem Assessment)*, Washington, DC: Island Press.

McGillivray, M. and Clarke, M. (2006) 'Human well-being: Concepts and measures', in McGillivray, M. and Clarke, M. (eds), *Understanding Human Well-being*, New York: United Nations University Press.

McGregor, J.A. (2008) 'Wellbeing, poverty and conflict', *WeD Briefing Paper 01/08*, WeD Research Group, Bath: University of Bath.

McGregor, J.A. (2010) 'Researching wellbeing: Concepts to methodology', in Gough, I. and McGregor, J.A. (eds), *Wellbeing in Developing Countries: From Theory to Research*, Cambridge: Cambridge University Press, pp. 316–350.

McShane, T.O., Hirsch, P.D., Trung, T.C., Songorwa, A.N., Kinzig, A., Monteferri, B., Mutekanga, D., Van Thang, H., Dammert, J.L., Pulgar-Vidal, M., Welch-Devine, M., Brosius, J.P., Coppolillo, P. and O'Connor, S. (2011) 'Hard choices: Making trade-offs between biodiversity conservation and human well-being', *Biological Conservation*, 144: 966–972.

Morse, S., McNamara, N. and Acholo, M. (2009) 'Sustainable livelihood approach: A critical analysis of theory and practice', *Geographical Paper No. 189*, Department of Geography, Reading: University of Reading.

Neiland, A.E. and Béné, C. (eds) (2004) *Poverty and Small-Scale Fisheries in West Africa*, Dordrecht: Food and Agricultural Organization of the United Nations and Kluwer Academic Publishers.

Nunan, F. (2010) 'Mobility and fisherfolk livelihoods on Lake Victoria: Implications for vulnerability and risk', *Geoforum*, 41: 776–785.

Pollnac, R.B. and Poggie, J.J. (2008) 'Happiness, well-being and psychocultural adaptation to the stresses associated with marine fishing', *Human Ecology Review*, 15: 194–200.

Pollnac, R.B., Pomeroy, R.S. and Harkes, I.H.T. (2001) 'Fishery policy and job satisfaction in three Southeast Asian fisheries', *Ocean and Coastal Management*, 44: 531–544.

Rakodi, C. and Lloyd-Jones T. (eds) (2002) *Urban Livelihoods: A People-Centred Approach to Reducing Poverty*, London: Routledge.

Rodríguez, J.P., Beard Jr., T.D., Bennett, E.M., Cumming, G.S., Cork, S.J., Agard, J., Dobson, A. P. and Peterson G.D. (2006) 'Trade-offs across space, time, and ecosystem services', *Ecology and Society*, 11(1): 28.

Scoones, I. (1998) 'Sustainable rural livelihoods: A framework for analysis', *IDS Working Paper, 72*, Brighton: Institute of Development Studies.

Scoones, I. (2009) 'Livelihoods perspectives and rural development', *Journal of Peasant Studies*, 36: 1.

Sen, A. (1984) *Resources, Values and Development*, Chapter 13,'Rights and capabilities', Oxford: Basil Blackwell.

Weeratunge, N., Béné, C., Siriwardane, R., Charles, A., Johnson, D., Allison, E.H., Nayak, P.K. and Badjeck, M-C. (2014) 'Small-scale fisheries through the wellbeing lens', *Fish and Fisheries*, 15(2): 255–279.

White, S. (2010) 'Analysing wellbeing: A framework for development practice', *Development in Practice*, 20(2): 158–172.

White, S. (2013) 'An integrated approach to assessing wellbeing', *Wellbeing and Poverty Pathways Briefing 1*, Centre for Development Studies, Bath: University of Bath.

6   Social network analysis

Introduction

In previous chapters, we have seen that relations between people matter for how individuals and groups of people can access and benefit in different ways from natural resources. One way of looking at relations is to view them as institutions, or 'rules of the game', as discussed in Chapters 1 and 3. Social network analysis provides an alternative approach to examining relations between people within particular settings. This chapter provides an introduction to social network analysis and examines case studies of the application of the approach to natural resource settings in developing countries to provide illustrations of how it can be used and the types of questions that can be answered. The chapter introduces some of the key terms, approaches and measures within social network analysis, but specialist textbooks should be consulted if readers wish to use this methodology. There are many available, some of which are listed in the references for this chapter. In addition, specific software, such as UCINET, is available to facilitate social network analysis.

The chapter begins by explaining what characterizes social network analysis, identifying key properties and concerns and providing examples of research questions that may be asked. A section on planning a social network analysis study follows, beginning with the need to decide on whether the study takes a whole-network approach or will investigate the personal networks of actors, whether individuals, organizations or groups. Sections follow on these two key approaches to social network analysis, focusing on individuals and their personal networks, or on whole social networks. Finally, examples of the application of social network analysis in natural resource settings are reviewed.

What are social networks and social network analysis?

A social network refers to a set of actors, either individuals or organizations, and the ties between the actors. Social networks are not the equivalent of groups or communities, but are seen by network analysts as primary building blocks of the social world. In contrast to much social science survey work, the focus of data collection and analysis is not on the attributes or characteristics of actors and how these influence how people behave or the choices they make (for example, investigating gender to explain job promotion opportunities and outcomes), but on how structured relations between people can explain behaviour and decisions. It is the relations between people and the patterns of those relations within networks that are the focus of investigation. Peer pressure or access to powerful people, for example, could influence how people behave, the decisions they make and their access to resources. Definitions of social networks and key properties of social network analysis are set out in Box 6.1.

Box 6.1 Definitions of social networks and properties of SNA

A social network has been defined as:

- 'a set of relations that apply to a set of actors, as well as any additional information on those actors and relations' (Prell, 2012: 9);
- 'a way of thinking about social systems that focus our attention on the relationships among the entities that make up the system, which we call actors or nodes' (Borgatti *et al.*, 2013: 1–2).

Freeman (2011: 26) identifies four characteristics of social network analysis, as follows:

1   It involves the intuition that links among social actors are important;
2   It is based on the collection and analysis of data that record social relations that link actors;
3   It draws heavily on graphic imagery to reveal and display the patterning of those links; and,
4   It develops mathematical and computational models to describe and explain those patterns.

The four characteristics or defining properties of social network analysis, or SNA as it is often referred to, given by Freeman (2011) provide a useful summary of what it is all about – social relations, how they link actors and what those links, and the patterns of links, tell us about how social networks function and result in certain outcomes. SNA provides a way of identifying and analysing relations between people. It seeks to understand how these relations become structured and influence how people behave, what access they have to resources, ideas or support, for example, and what constraints and opportunities they face. You would not, then, necessarily ask people about their 'networks' or the 'network' in which they operate, but about who they turn to or know in relation to a particular question, whether it is concerned with kinship, access to credit or seeking advice. Examples of the types of questions that might be asked in employing SNA are given in Box 6.2.

Box 6.2 Examples of questions that may be addressed using SNA

- Who has influence within a forest users' network and with what implications for governance outcomes?
- How does a person's personal network affect their access to irrigation water?

A useful set of questions that could be asked by taking a social network approach is provided by Prell (2012: 64):

- 'How does an individual's personal network affect that person's ability to access certain kinds of resources?
- How do individuals gain access to social support through their personal networks?
- How does the structure of a given social network affect the formation (or maintenance) of collective norms?
- To what extent are particular behaviours, such as smoking or academic performance, influenced by one's friendships ties to others?'

SNA draws on multiple models, theories, methods and concepts and is best viewed as an approach or perspective taken for analysis. It is necessarily multidisciplinary, drawing on ideas and concepts from several disciplines, and is, in turn, used within many disciplines and applied to many spheres of life. In addition, in many studies using SNA, other data collection and analysis tools are used as well, so that attribute and other data, for example on attitudes, are also collected. This use of multiple methods and perspectives enriches the data available and the nature of the analysis, as well as providing opportunities for triangulating (or checking) data generated from one source against data from other sources. Multiple methods can also be used to feed into each other in a staged approach, rather than necessarily in a complementary way. For example, to be able to design appropriate questions for the data collection related to SNA, greater understanding of the network and relations may be needed. Attribute data may be collected to help define network boundaries. There could be, then, a process where attribute data feeds into the SNA stage of a piece of research, rather than being purely complementary. Qualitative data on people's experiences and views can also enrich the analysis associated with social networks, providing a richer and deeper picture of the situation being researched.

SNA was developed in the 1960s and 70s, although built on existing theory and methodological approaches developed prior to that, particularly in the 1930s and 40s, and is rooted especially in the disciplines of psychology, sociology and social anthropology (see Scott, 2012, for example, for a review of the development of SNA). SNA is descended from multiple disciplines, due to interest in social networks arising and being pursued from different perspectives. This has given rise to a range of terminology, sometimes with more than one term referring to one aspect. For example, within SNA, people listed in a social network are referred to as *actors*, stemming from sociology, but are also referred to as *nodes* or *vertices*, terms used within graph theory, the study of graphs within mathematics and computer science. The term 'network' is used in many more contexts and disciplines, but SNA is concerned only with social networks.

SNA enables researchers to investigate how characteristics of networks, for example how big they are or how dense the connections are, affect how people behave and the decisions they make. Using a network perspective, indirect as well as direct connections can be traced; for example, someone may not have direct access to another person or organization, but may be able to access them through another connection. This kind of analysis can be particularly useful in analysing how people gain access to natural resources or to other resources connected to how they use or benefit from natural resources, for example access to credit or markets.

The application of SNA to natural resource settings is quite recent. Bodin *et al.* (2011) observe that a lot of work on natural resource governance, including on common pool resources, focuses on institutional analysis, but does not investigate the social relations that are connected to and support the institutional arrangements. They suggest that SNA could be particularly helpful in investigating communication, collaboration and coordination, for example to understand how natural resource governance works, or fails, to produce sustainable or equitable outcomes.

One challenge facing SNA is the question of time: can SNA provide a picture of how a situation may change over time, how, why and with what implications? Certainly SNA can do more than give a snapshot picture of a situation as the dynamics of a situation could be considered in many analyses. This can be done, for example, by creating a series of matrix cross-sections, showing how a network changes over time, but this requires collecting data over a period of time, which is not always feasible. Relying on memory and other data sources can also contribute to creating a more dynamic picture of a research situation.

Planning a social network analysis study

There are two overarching approaches taken within SNA. An analyst may focus on one individual and be interested in identifying the people they interact with for a certain purpose, for example friendship, seeking advice within a work environment or recreation. The person focused on is referred to as the *ego* and so their network is known as an *ego network*. Alternatively, analysts may be interested in the entire social network and so take a *complete, or whole, social network approach*. Analysis of a whole network can, however, be undertaken at smaller levels, focusing on subgroups and even pairs (known as dyads), or groups of three people (triads). The approach taken depends on the questions being asked and the context within which the data collection takes place. Whether investigating an ego or complete network, a boundary must be set for the network which sets limits on the types of people of interest for the research. For example, a boundary could be a family or place of work. It is not always easy though to distinguish between ego and complete social networks, as there may be unclear boundaries between them in terms of where an ego network finishes and a complete network emerges.

In undertaking an SNA study, a range of data collection methods can be used, collecting both quantitative and qualitative data. Although SNA requires quantitative data, qualitative data can be very helpful in providing depth of explanation and experience. The data being collected is largely 'relational', that is, information about relations, or 'ties', is being sought. Primary data collection often commences with 'name-generator' questions, where the interviewee is asked to name a given number of, or perhaps all, the people they interact with for a certain purpose. Name-generator questions could, for example, include questions such as: 'Who do you turn to for advice on fishing methods?' In addition, very often actor attribute data is also collected, which may include questions on age, sex and occupation. Data is often collected that has a value connected to it, i.e. information on the strength, frequency or duration of a tie may be sought.

Social networks can be presented as either graphs or matrices. In a graph, the actors are represented as nodes or vertices, with ties drawn as lines between nodes where a relation has been reported. Ties can be drawn as lines with or without arrows, with arrows depicting the direction of the relation, which could be two-way as well as one-way. A graph in which there are directed lines is referred to as a digraph. In large networks, visual representation can be too complex and chaotic and so social networks may also be displayed in matrix form, with each row representing a specific case and the columns either being cases (people) or events.

A simple example of a matrix is shown in Figure 6.1 for a fictitious friendship network in a class of students.

A few points to note about this matrix:

1   This is an example of a binary matrix, where only 1s and 0s are used. 1 denotes the presence of a tie, whereas a 0 is the absence of a tie.
2   The above is an example of an asymmetric matrix, where the direction of the tie is given, with 'senders' of the tie in the rows and 'receivers' in the column. So, for example, Anna named Tom as one of her friends, but Tom did not mention Anna. In a symmetric matrix the data would form an undirected network, where a tie is noted only and is assumed to be reciprocal.
3   The diagonal of the matrix represents the ties of the senders with themselves and so is ignored in SNA.

	1 Anna	2 Tom	3 Mary	4 Joshua	5 Peter	6 John	7 James	8 Sarah	9 Hannah
1 Anna	0	1	0	0	0	1	0	0	1
2 Tom	0	0	1	1	1	0	0	0	1
3 Mary	0	1	0	0	0	1	0	0	0
4 Joshua	0	1	0	0	1	0	1	0	0
5 Peter	0	0	0	1	0	0	1	1	0
6 John	1	0	1	0	0	0	0	0	0
7 James	0	0	0	1	1	1	0	0	0
8 Sarah	0	0	0	0	1	0	1	0	1
9 Hannah	1	0	1	0	0	1	1	1	0

Figure 6.1 Binary matrix showing friendship network in student class.

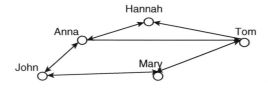

Figure 6.2 A digraph of who is friends with whom in a class setting.

Instead of a binary matrix, where the tie either exists or does not, the tie can be represented by a number to indicate the strength of that tie, generating a 'valued matrix' or 'valued network'.

A subgroup of the above matrix is shown in Figure 6.2 as an illustration of a digraph or graph of a social network, showing how nodes and ties are depicted.

A much more complicated depiction of a social network in a graphical form is shown later in the chapter in Figure 6.3, taken from Ramirez-Sanchez and Pinkerton (2009).

Types of ties or relations

The questions being asked in an SNA study will be related to the nature of the relation being examined. Borgatti *et al.* (2009, 2013) identify four broad categories of relations or ties that are studied within SNA. These are shown in Table 6.1.

In examining relations within SNA, data on both the quantity and quality of ties is collected. The quantity refers to the number of ties, whether from an actor or within a subgroup or entire network. The quality of a tie refers to how it is ranked or scored. For example, a tie can be scored according to how frequently

Table 6.1 Types of ties in social networks

Type of tie	Examples of questions and issues
Similarities	Similar location, membership of the same or similar group(s) or having similar attributes
Social relations	Kinship, knowing people, naming people they socialize with or work with, naming people they like or dislike
Interactions	Who do people turn to for advice on a particular subject or for certain kinds of help, who do they talk to?
Flows	From whom do people get access to information or resources? Who influences an actor's beliefs or ideas?

Source: Adapted from Borgatti *et al.* (2009: 894).

there is interaction between actors or how important that tie is for a certain actor. A higher value would indicate a stronger tie. The strength or weakness of ties can be shown in network diagrams through the thickness of the lines or by showing two plots; one with all the ties and one with just strong ties, for example.

Some studies focus on one kind of relationship among actors, for example who they turn to for a certain kind of advice or to borrow money from, but social relations are usually more complicated than that, with actors being connected in multiple ways at the same time. This creates multiplex data that can be analysed by taking 'slices' or a series of matrices describing each tie separately. Whilst the various tools of SNA can then be applied to each matrix, the information on the multiple relations can also be combined, creating a single index based on the quantity of ties (a reduction approach) or the quality of ties (a combination approach).

Specifying boundaries

Setting out what the boundaries of a network are is essential so that key actors are not missed in either an ego or whole network. If the boundaries are not adequately or appropriately specified, the network could be misrepresented, leading to meaningless, or even misleading, analysis and inappropriate conclusions drawn. Social networks do not necessarily correspond to observable social systems and so a common measure of relevance of actors must be specified.

Laumann *et al.* (1983) identify two main approaches to determining network boundaries: the nominalist and realist approaches. In a nominalist approach, the analyst imposes the network boundary on the basis of the conceptual framework and questions being asked in the research. Therefore, the boundaries exist to serve the purposes of the research. Reality does not necessarily conform to the network imposed by the analyst, but in this approach, the network forms a structure or framework to enable the identification and analysis of certain relations. In a realist approach, the investigator defines the boundaries of the network themselves, taking into consideration what they know about the situation and the actors involved. The social network in this perspective exists 'as a social fact only in that it is consciously experienced as such by the actors composing it' (Laumann *et al.* 1983: 20–21). Boundaries of social networks, however they are constructed or identified, may be 'fuzzy'; that is, unclear in terms of where they are and how they are interpreted.

Part of the process of specifying the network boundaries is deciding on the focus of the enquiry. This is not only concerned with what questions are being asked, but also whether the initial focus is on the actors, the relations or the activities. For example, is the analyst more interested in who, or what type of actor, is in the network, or are they more interested in how people are connected and what those ties are used for, that is, how do they enable or constrain decisions and actions?

- *Actors:* In taking an actor approach to specifying the network boundaries, the criterion could either focus on the *position* of actors or on their *reputation*. The position refers to whether an actor possesses a defined attribute, for example have a position in a formally defined group. In taking a reputational approach, knowledgeable informants specify the actors within the network. These two approaches can be combined to specify the boundaries of a network.
- *Relations:* A relational approach seeks to specify boundaries on the basis of including those actors who participate in a social relationship of a certain type. Snowball sampling may be used to identify actors using this approach, where actors named by an interviewee are traced and the people they name are then also traced, until the criterion for determining that the boundaries of the network have been reached are fulfilled.
- *Activity or event:* Participation in a specific activity or event determines the membership of a network and the social relationships that structure the network.

These approaches can, however, be used in combination, thereby strengthening the specification of the network boundaries and the potential for appropriate and meaningful data collection and analysis.

Related to the question of boundaries is the question of scale. Scale is particularly relevant to natural resource governance, as explained in Chapters 7 and 8, referring particularly to the dimensions of time and space. Levels may refer to individual, village, district, national and regional levels, for example when investigating the management of a watershed or transboundary lake. Bodin and Prell (2011b: 358) suggest that SNA is particularly suited to investigating cross-scale interactions, where there are interactions across levels, in addition to within a level. Interactions within and between levels may be investigated through analysis of ego networks, subgroups or complete networks, recognizing that relations may transcend boundaries and levels.

Ego networks

Ego networks refer to personal networks, and SNA investigates ego networks to ask questions such as how does an ego use or make use of their connections. The collection of data on multiple ego networks enables comparisons between ego networks to explain certain phenomena. The network of an ego is defined by the people, referred to as alters, identified by the ego as being people they interact with in response to the question, with the respondent (ego) being at the centre of their network. In investigating ego networks, the size and density of the network are studied, together with the strength of the ties. With the vast global uptake of electronic communication and social media, an individual's network, or community, can be widespread and diverse.

Personal network analysis is useful for an investigation into the relative effects of ties and networks on people's behaviour. In carrying out an analysis of personal networks, analysts would collect data on the types of people in an ego's network and what kinds of resources flow through different networks (Wellman, 2007). In undertaking an ego network study, name- or position-generator and interpreter questions are put to the ego, where the position-generator approach asks whether the ego has links to a specific location in a social structure. Interpreter questions are asked to generate information about the alters, such as their occupation, gender or age. Questions on the ties between alters are also posed to the ego. As it can be a long exercise to identify all of the alters in an ego's network and their ties, Hogan *et al.* (2007) used a more visual and practical approach with paper, pencils and removable tags, with respondents placing their contacts within a given concentric circle. Questions about the alters can then be asked in a more interactive and engaging way, with questions posed about the attributes of each alter in turn.

The types of analyses that are undertaken for ego networks include:

1   The size of an ego's network, measured as the number of nodes that are one step away from the ego, plus the ego themselves.
2   Measuring the density of the ego network by counting the number of ties present that do not involve the ego and dividing that number by the number of pairs of alters in the network. Alters can have direct ties that do not involve the ego.
3   Investigating the presence and number of structural holes, that is, where there are empty spaces, or no ties, between certain actors. Where an alter does not have a direct link to another alter, the ego may act as a 'broker', enabling the flow of information or other resources. If an ego has lots of structural holes in their network, they may have access to diverse information and be able to play off alters against each other. Where there are no, or few, structural holes, the actor's contacts are able to communicate with each other and coordinate, perhaps even against the ego.
4   Homophily, where actors have social relations with others who are similar to themselves, either through choice or through necessity. This is measured by counting all the ties where the ego and their alters share the same attribute and divide this by the total number of ties in the network. The attribute could be age, education level or occupation, for example.

Hogan *et al.* (2007) identify four criticisms of using name-generator questions, as associated with the investigation of ego networks. These are reliability, generalizability, specificity and cost. In terms of reliability, in using name-generator questions the analyst is relying on the respondent to remember accurately who they interacted with in relation to the topic of the question and being honest and unbiased in that recall. The sample of egos may also raise questions in terms of how generalizable the findings are; it would be difficult to draw conclusions about the entire social network from a small sample of egos. Specificity refers to the name-generator questions seeking the names of a limited number of alters and so other networks of the ego may be neglected with implications for the network of study. This specificity of the ego network of interest may also reduce the ability to draw wider conclusions. Finally, whilst it does not take too long to generate a list of alters, it can take hours to investigate the ties between alters, the charac-teristics of alters and the nature of the ties between the ego and their alters. The design of the research can seek to mitigate these challenges, as can the conduct of the research and the interpretation of findings.

Complete social networks

Within a complete social network approach, actors are asked who they have a tie with in a given boundary, with the aim of collecting information on all of the people in the network. The analysis can, however, also be carried out at actor level and on dyads and triads or subgroups. In analysing a complete network, the roles and positions of actors can be investigated. There are many different types of analysis that can be undertaken with data on social networks, depending on the data collected and the questions being asked of the data. Key analytical measures include the following.

Position

Fundamental to SNA is the belief that the position of an actor in a network deter-mines in part what opportunities the actor has, including what access to resources there is, as well as what constraints an actor will face. Role analysis may flow from positional analysis, interpreting the positions and attribute data to ascertain what kinds of roles actors play in a network. The position of an actor is defined within a social network by the group or 'block' in which analysis suggests it is located. Roles are defined by the relations between these blocks, such as being active connectors and therefore communicators.

Centrality

There are multiple measures of centrality which identify important actors within a social network. Whilst centrality can be measured in part by the number of ties an actor has, having the most ties does not necessarily imply centrality. There are many measures of centrality; an actor's degree, betweenness and closeness being key. Degree centrality refers to the number of immediate contacts an actor has in a given network, regardless of the direction of the tie and whether it has a value and what that value is. Degree centrality measures how involved an actor is in a network rather than whether they are popular or influential. The measure does not, however, take into consideration the entire network, but focuses on the immediate contacts of an actor. Betweenness centrality takes a different perspective and reflects the assumption that if an actor is between two other unconnected actors, they have certain advantages, for example over the flow of information. In the measure of closeness centrality, a node with a lower total distance to all other nodes will be able to share information quickly. There are other measures of centrality that can be used to investigate from where an actor derives their power within a network – from their immediate contacts or from the wider social network. The measure of centrality is particularly useful for determining who the more powerful and influential actors are in a social network, but care should be taken with interpretation and multiple measures would be needed to lead to conclusions regarding who the powerful are and what makes them powerful.

Density

Density in a social network refers to the percentage of all possible ties that could exist that do actually exist. It is concerned with recording the extent of linkages between individual actors. Social networks with a high level of density may be conducive for information flow, but could have less diversity and more homogenous views and knowledge than less dense networks. It is not, though, straightforward to link the level of density and the cohesiveness of a network. There are three main issues to consider when assessing the potential of the measure of density to reflect cohesiveness: centralization, network size and cohesive subgroups (Prell, 2012). In terms of centralization, there could just be one or two well-connected actors who raise the density score, meaning that the network is not as cohesive as the high density score may have suggested. Size of the network should also be taken into consideration, as it is easier for a small network to have a high density score than a larger network. An implication of this is that it is important to consider the size of networks when comparing the density scores of networks. Finally, with regard to there being a number of cohesive subgroups and therefore many ties, leading to a relatively high density score, the whole network could actually be fragmented and so a conclusion that the entire network is highly cohesive would be inaccurate. Care needs to be taken, then, in drawing conclusions from the measure of density.

Connectivity

Investigating the nature and extent of connections between actors is another avenue of analysis and connectivity can be assessed in multiple ways. For example, the 'reachability' of an actor by another can be determined by investigating whether there is a set of connections through which they can be 'reached', perhaps going through many other actors to get there. If some actors are not reachable by others, there could be the potential for division in the network as communication including all members will not be enabled and some in the network may miss information flows.

Being able to reach an actor is an indicator of connectivity, but the extent of the connection may be weak, with perhaps only one route for one actor to reach another. If there are multiple pathways that connect two actors, the level of connectivity is high. 'Connectivity' can be measured by counting the number of nodes that would have to be removed to make one actor reachable by another, which can indicate the level of dependency and vulnerability of a particular actor in relation to the focus of the network.

Distance

The distance between actors tells the analyst how embedded actors are in a network. The greater the distances, the longer it will take for information to be shared across a network. There may be some actors who are not aware of certain other members in the network and the level of influence may be less than it would be in a network with shorter distances between actors. Network analysis generally refers to the *geodesic* distance, which is the number of relations in the shortest possible pathway from one actor to another.

Examples of the use of social network analysis in natural resource management

Table 6.2 provides a summary of a sample of studies undertaken within natural resource settings in developing countries using SNA. The number of studies available using SNA in natural resource settings is not huge, but these examples provide an indication of the kinds of questions that can be asked and approaches taken in carrying out these kinds of studies. The studies reported in the reviewed papers did not focus on poverty–environment relations directly, but it can be seen how questions of relevance to understanding poverty–environment relations can be asked.

Most of the case studies included in the table map entire social networks, with only the Chilean example investigating only ego networks. The Ghanaian cocoa-farming study employed both ego and whole SNA. The dominance of taking a whole-social-network approach reflects the common concern of relating network structures to the process and performance of natural resource management. This can be seen particularly in the Kenyan and Mexican case studies, where the implications of the structure of networks for natural resource management outcomes were investigated. In both these cases, the actors are individual fishers, with a range of ties building a social network through which fisheries are utilized and decisions relating to behaviour and practice made.

In contrast, the actors in both the Chilean fisheries management and Tanzanian water governance examples are organizations. The organizations are fisher organizations involved in fisheries management in Chile, with a range of organizations involved in water governance in Tanzania, such as state agencies, community-based

Table 6.2 Social network analysis natural resource management case studies

Authors; year of publication; study location and context	Whole or ego network approach; who are the actors	Questions asked	Key findings
Marín et al. (2012) Chile Fisheries management	Ego network with egos being fisher organizations in the co-management system and their alters other co-management counterparts	Assesses 'to what extent social capital, measured by means of egocentric networks, make a difference in the performance of co-management' (Marín et al., 2012: 1). Interviewees asked to characterize a relationship as facilitating, hindering or non-existent for co-management and the relationship strength in terms of 'trustworthiness'	• Fisher organizations have different levels of social capital • Connections with external agencies (linking social capital) are associated with better performance of fisher organizations, more so than connections between groups and organizations who may not have the same objectives (bridging social capital) • Fisher organizations that have more and better connections are more likely to show enhanced performance in terms of co-management capacity and livelihood diversification
Stein et al. (2011) Tanzania Water governance	Whole network approach. Actors are organizations, including community-based organizations, state agencies, private companies and relevant NGOs. Village leaders also considered as actors	Used SNA as an analytical tool to systematically describe certain aspects of social complexity of water resources governance. Asked respondents to mark their relations with other organizations on a recall list in relation to funding, information and knowledge exchange and collaboration. Also recorded organizational attributes. Focused only on reciprocated ties (i.e. not one-way ties)	• Village leadership plays a key role in the governance of water resources in the catchment, linking internally and between villages • Their inclusion increased the overall connectivity in the social network considerably • Few bridging ties between villages. Neither the Catchment Forestry Office nor the River Basin Office is well connected to the community level, though are well connected with other parts of the network

(Continued)

Table 6.2 (Continued)

Authors; year of publication; study location and context	Whole or ego network approach; who are the actors	Questions asked	Key findings
Crona and Bodin (2006) Kenya Fisheries	Mapped the whole social network used for communication of knowledge and information to natural resources	Can a lack of collective action to regulate inshore fishery be attributed to the structures of the social networks in the community? Two hypotheses were tested: '1. Occupation, and more specifically the gear-defined fishing technique among fishermen, is important in defining group membership in the community in relation to communication of resource-related information. 2. Social network structure can explain the distribution of common and group specific ecological knowledge among user groups. More specifically, groups with strong links between each other tend to have similar knowledge, in this case local ecological knowledge (LEK).' (Crona and Bodin, 2006: 2)	• Gear-defined occupation plays an important role in defining communication of resource-related knowledge and information in the community • The fishermens's groups have strong links among each other and have similar knowledge • Deep-sea fishermen are most centrally positioned in the network and most knowledgeable, many of whom are migrant fishermen returning to Tanzania during seasons of low fishing activity. They do not perceive the target stocks to be overfished. Less likely to instigate action to regulate fishing activity
Ramirez-Sanchez and Pinkerton (2009); Ramirez-Sanchez (2011a, 2011b) Mexico Fisheries	Whole network mapped, with fishers as actors, from seven coastal communities in Loreto	Tested five hypotheses through posing two key questions: 'Who do you consult to obtain trustworthy information regarding abundant fishing areas in (1) your community, and (2) six other rural fishing communities in Loreto municipality?' (Ramirez-Sanchez and Pinkerton, 2009: 3) The hypotheses were concerned with examining the relationship between the structure of the social networks associated with information-sharing within a community and the level of resource scarcity, investigating: • The level of bonding in the community • The dominance of different types of ties, whether kinship, friendship or acquaintance • The form of social capital	Findings include: 1 The level of resource scarcity impacts the activity of fishers' social networks within and between communities, but resource scarcity does not always reflect how much fishers share information on fisheries 2 Information sharing is strongly related to trust, which is influenced by kinship, friendship and acquaintance ties 3 Friendship ties are more important than kinship ties within and across communities 4 The effect of resource scarcity on fishers' social networks is mediated by the nature of social ties and internal conflict and the history of the community

Isaac et al. (2007);
Isaac and Dawoe
(2011);
Isaac (2012)
Ghana
Cocoa farming

Both whole and ego
network approaches
were used to study
the flow of agrarian
information. Cocoa
farmers as actors in
Sefwi Wiawso
District in four
farming communities
of 60 villages in the
area, interviewing
one adult from each
farming household,
giving a total of 89
interviews

'Do informal advice networks within these farming
communities have comparable structures, and can some
general statements be made about farming advice
networks?' (Isaac et al., 2007: 3)

Findings include:

1 A core of farmers exists within the social
network who provide and seek advice from
other core members more often than from
farmers outside of the core ('peripheral'
farmers), resulting in a high level of
communication within a small group

2 A relatively small, dense group of farmers is
regularly sought by the larger farming
community for advice on farming practices

3 Information from formal external sources is
sought by the core members of the advice
networks. The connections between the
members and the external agencies function
as possible bridging links. Peripheral farmers
sought advice from external sources less
frequently

4 The formation of ties between farmers was
assisted by the involvement of highly sought
farmers in community activities

organizations and private companies. Village leaders are included as an organization in this case as their inclusion relates to the structure they represent rather than the individual themselves.

The exchange of knowledge is a focus of three of the cases – Kenyan and Mexican fisheries and Ghanaian cocoa – illustrating an important theme in natural resource governance of the sharing of knowledge and how that might take place, or be constrained, and the implications of such knowledge sharing. In these cases, the actors are individuals, with knowledge exchange investigated within the context of whole networks, although the Ghanaian study also analysed ego networks. This enabled the generation of a richer picture of the importance of social relations in the transfer of knowledge amongst the farmers as well as triangulation of the data.

The Crona and Bodin (2006) article is one of several published by Crona and Bodin from research carried out in Gazi Bay, Kenya, using SNA, asking a number of research questions. The research is largely concerned with fisheries, though also concerns the use of the mangrove forests in the bay. A whole-network approach was undertaken, interviewing as many of the household heads as possible in Gazi village, using the criterion that the head of household should have been resident in the village for at least the previous six months. Of the research population of 206 households, heads of 171 households were interviewed, representing 83 per cent of the population, generating around 1,500 reported relations (Crona and Bodin, 2006). In addition, interviews were carried out with individual fishers and 13 groups, with between four and six participants. An overview of the questions used to collect network data from the individual fishers is given in Table 6.3. This provides a useful example of the kinds of questions that should be asked and provides guidance on how responses might be recorded. The nature of the questions and the size of the network studied suggest that a significant amount of data was generated and so has been reported on in a number of articles and book chapters. For example, Crona and Bodin (2006) report on their mapping of the social network for communication of knowledge and information related to natural resources, whereas Bodin and Crona (2008) report on a combined social support and knowledge network, assessing the nature of community social capital and leadership and why collective action has not taken place despite declining fisheries and inshore habitat degradation. In a 2010 paper, they explore informal power structures and knowledge-sharing networks (Crona and Bodin, 2010).

In the 2006 paper, Crona and Bodin report that they investigated whether occupation (defined by fishing gear) is important in structuring communication networks related to natural resources through calculating the number of within group ties and ties between members of different groups. Relational groups were also identified from the relations reported by respondents. In assessing community social capital, Bodin and Crona (2008) quantify characteristics of the community's social networks, evaluate mechanisms in use for conflict resolution and villagers' attitudes towards self-monitoring and reporting. In quantifying the characteristics of the community's social networks, they used the network measures of density of relations (to measure cohesiveness), the number of isolated network components to measure fragmentation and the ratio of relations that falls within versus between sub-groups, referring

Table 6.3 Overview of questions in Kenyan fisheries study

Question number	Question	Method	Type of relation
Q1	Personal information regarding age, gender, civil status, etc.	–	–
Q2	Do you have close family outside of #village name# (Y/N)? If yes, fill in the table below for all close family members outside of #village name#	Recall	External social relations
Q3	With whom can you discuss important matters? Anything important to you. List the names in the table below	Recall	Social support
Q4	If you noticed changes in the natural environment, e.g. the number of fish caught, the condition of the mangrove forest or reef, availability of firewood, etc., who would you discuss this with? Name persons in table below	Recall	Information/knowledge exchange
Q5	Do you exchange information with anyone which is useful for you to carry out your common occupation? (Y/N) If yes, name persons in the table below. For example, told you about practices, good fishing spots, equipment, timing and season, etc.?	Recall	Information/knowledge exchange
Q6	Is there any person(s) on whom you depend, or who depend on you, to carry out your/their occupation? (Y/N) If yes, name persons in table below, e.g. do you need someone else's boat, gear, nets, etc. to carry out your occupation?	Recall	Gear dependency
Q7	In your occupation do you buy and/or sell your goods to anyone in particular? (Y/N) If yes, name persons in table below, e.g., do you sell your fish, poles, firewood, makuti, etc. to a particular person? Or, from who do you buy bait, nets, etc. If no, see question below	Recall	Economic exchange
Q8	Do you ever send/receive money or other valuables to/from anyone outside of the village? If yes, name person in table below	Recall	Remittance pathways
Q9	Have you ever encountered a dispute with anyone outside of the village? Specify why and with whom	Recall	Conflict resolution
Q10	If you encounter a dispute with someone, do you turn to someone to settle the conflict? If yes, to whom?	Recall	Conflict resolution
Q11	If you see that someone is breaking the law within the area of your occupation, do you tell someone? If so, who?	Recall	Conflict resolution
Q12	Below is a list of 10 randomly selected individuals from the village. Based on Questions 4 and 5, can you tell us if you know them? If so, do you exchange information with them and how often, on a scale of 1–3?	Recognition	Information/knowledge exchange

Source: Crona and Bodin (2006: 6).

to these relations as bonding and bridging ties, forms of social capital, respectively. A number of centrality measures were used to identify key individuals, feeding into the assessment of leadership within the social network. In the 2010 paper, centrality is also investigated in the knowledge and gear-exchange networks, examining the individuals who rank highly in these networks to identify their perceptions of the status of the fishery (Crona and Bodin, 2010).

In relation to findings on community social capital, Bodin and Crona (2008) report that the level of social capital within the network depends on which aspect is under consideration. In relation to conflict resolution, for example, there is a strong consensus over which mechanisms exist and with regard to reporting rule breaking, there was, in general, reluctance to report. Bodin and Crona (2008) suggest that such reluctance could be supported by the existence of coherent social networks across the entire village. In terms of leadership, the 2008 paper suggests that homogeneity amongst much of the leadership, with many of the leaders being deep sea fishermen (as reported in the 2006 paper and noted in Table 6.2), contributed to the lack of problem internalization of the declining fisheries, as well as there only being one person occupying a very central role within the network, with connections to formal government officials. In the 2010 paper, it is reported that people who are central in the gear-exchange network are also central individuals in the knowledge network, so are referred to as 'opinion leaders' with the capacity to influence fishers' behaviour and knowledge. These 'opinion leaders' are identified largely as deep-sea fishers, but also as seine netters, using illegal gear because of its' destructive nature and therefore unlikely to embrace

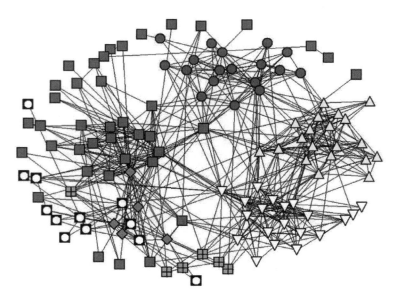

Figure 6.3 An example of a fishers' network.

Source: Ramirez-Sanchez and Pinkerton, 2009: 8.

an approach that seeks more sustainable fisheries management through collective action. Further details of this case study can also be found in Bodin and Crona (2011) and Crona and Bodin (2011).

An illustration of a fishers network taken from Ramirez-Sanchez and Pinkerton (2009) is shown in Figure 6.3 to provide an example of a network diagram. The different shapes refer to different fishing communities included in the study, showing inter- and between-community connections. The diagram shows just how complex a network can be, though there can of course be even more connections than that in other networks.

Summary of key points

1   Social network analysis provides a valuable approach to understanding how relations between people, and the patterns of those relations, influence how people behave, which decisions are made and how people get access to other people and resources, or how that access may be constrained. The focus then is on relations rather than on actor attributes.

2   Social network analysis can be used with other data collection approaches and theory, enabling the creation of a meaningful data collection approach to the social network analysis as well as supporting interpretation of the social network data and the data generated on actor attributes.

3   Within social network analysis, data can be collected to generate a picture of the entire social network (whole social network) or of the personal networks of individual actors (ego network), whether those actors are people or organizations. In both cases, the boundaries of the networks must be carefully specified so that key people and relations are not excluded.

4   There are many, many measures that can be used to analyse social networks and only a few have been touched on here, but hopefully this chapter has provided a flavour of what social network analysis is able to do and how it has been, and could be, applied in environmental and natural resource settings. There is certainly much potential for greater application of social network analysis in environment and natural resource settings, not only focusing on governance and management but also to investigate livelihood options and constraints in terms of how people get access to resources or cope in times of stress.

5   There are a number of associations and journals dedicated to social network analysis and an annual international conference, Sunbelt, organized by the International Network for Social Network Analysis (INSNA). Journals such as *Social Networks* and the *Journal of Social Structure*, produced by INSNA, focus on social network analysis, although articles can be found in many other journals.

Further reading

Prell, C. (2012) *Social Network Analysis*, London: Sage.
An excellent introduction to social network analysis, suitable for those new to the subject. Prell takes the reader through the use of SNA, from the design and planning of a study to

the analysis and interpretation of results. The text also includes a history of SNA and key theoretical approaches drawn on in utilizing SNA as a methodology. The book is written in a very accessible way, taking the reader through the language and process of SNA. After an introductory section, the second part addresses investigation at the actor level in whole and ego networks, and then covers how an analysis at dyad and triad levels, subgroups and network levels would proceed. The final section introduces more advanced application of SNA through statistical models and identifies recent advances and areas of interest.

Bodin, Ö. and Prell, C. (eds) (2011) *Social Network Analysis and Natural Resource Management*, Cambridge: Cambridge University Press.
This book is a must for anyone embarking on the application of SNA in a natural resource setting. It both introduces the potential application of SNA to natural resource management and provides case studies of how this has been done. The book has three sections. Part I provides an introduction, with three chapters explaining why a relational approach is relevant to natural resource governance, what SNA is all about and how social network approaches can be combined with social theories to improve understanding of natural resource governance. Part II has chapters covering case studies of the use of SNA from many parts of the world, including the UK, Canada, Kenya, Ghana and Mexico, in settings such as fisheries, cocoa farming and forest management. The case studies are categorized into sub-parts, focusing on analysis at the individual (node) level, the subgroup level and the network level. Through this approach, the book provides an excellent and informative range of cases drawn from different countries and sectors, using different levels and tools of analysis from SNA. The book concludes in Part III with a summary and outlook.

Hanneman, R.A. and Riddle, M. (2005) *Introduction to Social Network Methods*, Riverside: University of California (available online).
This textbook is worth investigating not just because it's available free, online, but because it provides a methodical and accessible overview of social network analysis. The text starts with an introduction to the approach and goes on to explain many of the measures used to analyse social networks, all written in a clear and well-structured manner.

Borgatti, S.P., Everett, M.G. and Johnson, J.C. (2013) *Analyzing Social Networks*, London: Sage.
A practically oriented book that takes the reader through the research process using social network analysis. The book is written by well-known experts in the field of social network analysis, two of whom, Borgatti and Everett, developed, with Linton Freeman, the UCINET software. The book therefore has a strong connection to the UCINET software. Components of a research process are considered, including research design, data collection, data management, testing hypotheses and interpreting data. Key elements of network methodology are explained, such as visualizing networks, characterizing whole networks, measuring centrality and investigating ego networks. This is an invaluable book for researchers getting to grips with SNA and using UCINET.

References

Bodin, Ö. and Crona, B.I. (2008) 'Management of natural resources at the community level: Exploring the role of social capital and leadership in a rural fishing community', *World Development*, 36(12): 2763–2779.

Bodin, Ö. and Crona, B. (2011) 'Barriers and opportunities in transforming to sustainable governance: The role of key individuals', in Bodin, Ö. and Prell, C. (eds), *Social Network Analysis and Natural Resource Management*, Cambridge: Cambridge University Press, pp. 75–94.

Bodin, Ö. and Prell, C. (eds) (2011a) *Social Network Analysis and Natural Resource Management*, Cambridge: Cambridge University Press.

Bodin, Ö. and Prell, C. (2011b) 'Social network analysis in natural resource governance – summary and outlook', in Bodin, Ö. and Prell, C. (eds) *Social Network Analysis and Natural Resource Management*, Cambridge: Cambridge University Press, pp. 347–373.

Bodin, Ö., Ramirez-Sanchez, S., Ernstson, H. and Prell, C. (2011) 'A social relational approach to natural resource governance', in Bodin, Ö. and Prell, C. (eds), *Social Network Analysis and Natural Resource Management*, Cambridge: Cambridge University Press, pp. 3–28.

Borgatti, S., Mehra, A., Brass, D. and Labianca, G. (2009) 'Network analysis in the social sciences', *Science*, 323(5916): 892–895.

Borgatti, S., Everett, M.G. and Johnson, J.C. (2013) *Analyzing Social Networks*, London: Sage.

Crona, B. and Bodin, Ö. (2006) 'What you know is who you know? Communication patterns among resource users as a prerequisite for co-management', *Ecology and Society*, 11(2): 7.

Crona, B. and Bodin, Ö. (2010) 'Power asymmetries in small-scale fisheries: A barrier to governance transformability?', *Ecology and Society*, 15(4): 32.

Crona, B. and Bodin, Ö. (2011) 'Friends or neighbours? Subgroup heterogeneity and the importance of bonding and bridging ties in natural resource governance', in Bodin, Ö. and Prell, C. (eds), *Social Network Analysis and Natural Resource Management*, Cambridge: Cambridge University Press, pp. 206–233.

Freeman, L.C. (2011) 'The development of social network analysis – with an emphasis on recent events', in J. Scott and P. J. Carrington (eds), *The SAGE Handbook of Social Network Analysis*, London: Sage, pp. 26–39.

Hanneman, R.A. and Riddle, M. (2005) *Introduction to Social Network Methods*, Riverside: University of California. Available online at http://faculty.ucr.edu/~hanneman

Hogan, B., Carrasco, J.A. and Wellman, B. (2007) 'Visualizing personal networks: Working with participant-aided sociograms', *Field Methods*, 19: 116–144.

Isaac, M. (2012) 'Agricultural information exchange and organizational ties: The effect of network topology on managing agrodiversity', *Agricultural Systems*, 109: 9–15.

Isaac, M. and Dawoe, E. (2011) 'Agrarian communication networks: Consequences for agroforestry', in Bodin, Ö. and Prell, C. (eds), *Social Network Analysis and Natural Resource Management*, Cambridge: Cambridge University Press, pp. 322–344.

Isaac, M., Erickson, B.H., James Quashie-Sam, S.J. and Timmer, V.R. (2007) 'Transfer of knowledge on agroforestry management practices: The structure of farmer advice networks', *Ecology and Society*, 12(2): 32.

Laumann, E., Marsden, P. and Prensky, D. (1983) 'The boundary specification problem in network analysis', in Burt, R. and Minor, M. (eds) *Applied Network Analysis,* Beverly Hills, CA: Sage.

Marín, A., Gelcich, S., Castilla, J.C. and Berkes, F. (2012) 'Exploring social capital in Chile's coastal benthic comanagement system using a network approach', *Ecology and Society*, 17(1): 13.

Prell, C. (2012) *Social Network Analysis*, London: Sage.

Ramirez-Sanchez, S. (2011a) '*Who* and *how*: Engaging well-connected fishers in social networks to improve fisheries management and conservation', in Bodin, Ö. and Prell, C.

(eds), *Social Network Analysis and Natural Resource Management*, Cambridge: Cambridge University Press, pp. 119–146.

Ramirez-Sanchez, S. (2011b) 'The role of individual attributes in the practice of information sharing among fishers from Loreto, BCS, Mexico', in Bodin, Ö. and Prell, C. (eds), *Social Network Analysis and Natural Resource Management*, Cambridge: Cambridge University Press, pp. 234–254.

Ramirez-Sanchez, S. and Pinkerton, E. (2009) 'The impact of resource scarcity on bonding and bridging social capital: The case of fishers' information-sharing networks in Loreto, BCS, Mexico', *Ecology and Society*, 14(1): 22.

Scott, J. (2012) *Social Network Analysis*, London: Sage.

Stein, C., Ernstson, H. and Barron, J. (2011) 'A social network approach to analyzing water governance: The case of the Mkindo catchment, Tanzania', *Physics and Chemistry of the Earth Parts A/B/C*, 36(14–15): 1085–1092.

Wellman, B. (2007) 'Challenges in collecting personal network data: The nature of personal network analysis', *Field Methods*, 19(2): 111–115.

7   Analysing governance

Introduction

The importance of governance in facilitating or constraining access to benefits from natural resources and influencing the condition of natural resources is apparent throughout the earlier chapters. The overarching context of who is making decisions, at which levels, why and how, can be wrapped up in the concept and arrangements of 'governance'. But this concept is rather nebulous, with many definitions offered. It is used in many settings and for different purposes, and is used differently between and within academic disciplines and in different sectors. There is no one single way of examining the nature and performance of governance.

Many of the frameworks and approaches reviewed in other chapters of this book can be used to investigate governance arrangements and performance, though are not always discussed directly in relation to governance. Institutions, for example, form part of the governance landscape and the approaches to institutional analysis described in Chapter 3 can be used to investigate governance arrangements. The nature of governance may be part of the 'transforming structures and processes' of the Sustainable Livelihoods framework, mediating how people use, or can use, their assets in forming their livelihood strategies. The structures and processes of governance could be investigated through an analysis of social networks as described in Chapter 6, with governance itself sometimes viewed as networks of actors.

This chapter introduces literature and frameworks that focus on governance more explicitly and on how governance can be analysed for the purpose of understanding relationships between poverty and the environment. It therefore identifies what must be understood about governance to inform an investigation of how people are affected by, or get access to, the environment and natural resources. The term 'governance' suggests that the responsibility for determining how natural resources are used, who has access, who benefits and how includes multiple levels of government and goes beyond government agencies and departments. Governance can involve community-based organizations, the private sector and non-governmental organizations, as well as different parts of government, potentially having different objectives, priorities and levels of power, capability and resources. The question then is, whose interests prevail? Understanding of the nature and performance of governance is essential in seeking explanations for the condition of natural resources and of the livelihoods of resource users.

The chapter begins by drawing on literature on governance and 'good' governance more broadly to identify what is understood by the concept. Principles of governance for natural resources are then set out, followed by reflection on why governance is so important in natural resource settings in order to identify how poverty–environment relationships are shaped. The prevalence of, and constraints on, decentralization of natural resource governance is explained, with a framework for analysing decentralization described, emphasizing the importance of representation and accountability. A section on frameworks for the analysis of governance of natural resources follows, reviewing three frameworks: a framework for the analysis of water governance and poverty by Franks and Cleaver (2007); Kooiman *et al.*'s (2008) interactive governance and governability approach; and Batterbury and Fernando's (2006) components for the analysis of governance. The final section identifies three key issues within the literature on environmental and natural resource governance: power, scale and responding to change, or 'adaptive governance'.

The chapter focuses on concepts, frameworks and literature on governance that draw on the experience of the developing world and on natural resources in a developing country context. It does not, then, draw significantly on literature and theory relating to environmental governance, which mainly (though not exclusively) is concerned with the experience and situation of developed countries (see, for example, Evans, 2012). Few frameworks and approaches on natural resource governance relate the governance context with the experience of the poor, though it is apparent from several that poverty-related concerns can be investigated through the frameworks. Analysing the impact and consequences of governance arrangements and performance on the poor could particularly be undertaken through analysing representation, participation and accountability, as these influence access to and benefits from natural resources. Box 7.1 provides examples of research questions that might be addressed through an analysis of governance.

Box 7.1 Examples of questions asked in the analysis of natural resource governance

- Who makes decisions in relation to how natural resources are used and who benefits?
- Why were certain decisions reached?
- Why is the natural resource system in the condition it is in?
- How effective is the governing system and why?

What is governance?

Whilst it is widely recognized that the concept of governance has many uses and interpretations, drawing on a few definitions provides insight into its key characteristics. Definitions of governance are given in Box 7.2.

> *Box 7.2* **Definitions of governance**
>
> - '[T]he formation and stewardship of the formal and informal rules that regulate the public realm, the arena in which state as well as economic and societal actors interact to make decisions' (Hyden *et al.*, 2004: 16);
> - 'the setting, application and enforcement of the rules of the game' (Kjær, 2004: 12);
> - 'the rules of collective decision-making in settings where there are a plurality of actors or organisations and where no formal control system can dictate the terms of the relationship between these actors and organisations' (Chhotray and Stoker, 2009: 3).

From the definitions given in Box 7.2, it can be seen that governance is something broader than 'government'; it reflects a shift in thinking that the act of governing rests with government alone to the recognition that governing happens at many levels, in many parts of life and concerns many different kinds of actors. Institutions (see Chapter 3) are seen as an important component of governance arrangements and processes, particularly in Kjær's definition. Governance has been particularly associated with 'networking', with governance viewed as a network of relationships between different sectors, actors and organizations, including citizens and civil society organizations. As linkages and relationships form, a network emerges, reflecting the breadth and complexity of a governance system.

Governance should be clearly distinguished from 'management'. There are, of course, linkages between governance and management, but they are different concepts. According to Kooiman *et al.* (2008: 2), 'governance . . . is qualitatively different from the related task of management in directing societal and environmental processes. Governance adds dimensions that are absent in a hands-on management approach'. Jentoft and Chuenpagdee (2009: 555) agree with this, stating that governance is 'broader than management. Management is a technical issue, something that involves a set of tools that can be applied to solve a concrete task, where the goal is clear and the outcome measurable'. Finally, Béné and Neiland (2006: 10) are very clear in their observation of the differences:

> management is about action, governance is about politics. Management is about the implementation – in a technocratic sense – of decisions and actions in accordance with rules . . . Governance is about sharing responsibility and power; it is about setting the policy agenda and objectives and about the processes of implementing management actions.

The reason for emphasizing the difference between governance and management is not only because they are sometimes used synonymously, but also because having an effective governance system does not necessarily imply that a natural resource system is well, or sustainably, managed, or that people benefit equitably.

The concept of governance is sometimes used in a normative way, as well as in a descriptive or analytical manner. The notion of 'good governance' in particular is used in a normative sense, referring to how governance *should* be, rather than necessarily is. The idea of good governance was initiated in the World Bank's (1989) report on why countries in sub-Saharan Africa had 'failed' to develop in the 1980s despite the intervention of structural adjustment programmes (SAPs). In the 1980s, the World Bank and International Monetary Fund imposed neoliberal policies in developing countries through SAP agreements aimed at rolling back the state, cutting state expenditure and opening up the delivery of certain services to the private sector (Mohan *et al.,* 2000). The 1989 report attributed the perceived lack of economic growth to 'bad governance', entailing corruption, nepotism and bad policies. The report pointed to the subsequent need for 'good governance', requiring an increase in transparency and accountability in the public sector. The model promoted by donors and international finance institutions of good governance was built upon Anglo-American liberal-democratic states and good governance conditions and programmes were rolled out in the 1990s.

This approach to promoting good governance led to the development of long lists of characteristics of what good governance entailed. Grindle (2004, 2007) critiqued such lists and requirements for good governance, arguing instead for 'good enough governance' – prioritizing action, recognizing what can realistically be achieved over a given timeframe and in the existing circumstances, and acknowledging that there could be trade-offs that have to be made.

Given that the donor agenda in particular has been concerned with wanting to see an improvement in governance, attempts have been made to measure governance, including the World Bank's 'Worldwide Governance Indicators' and the Mo Ibrahim Foundation's 'Ibrahim Index of African Governance' (IIAG). The Worldwide Governance Indicators project collects data from 215 economies on the following dimensions of governance: voice and accountability, political stability and absence of violence, government effectiveness, regulatory quality, rule of law and control of corruption (World Bank, 2014). The subsequent report ranks countries according to each dimension using data aggregated from a number of sources, so that the ranking of countries can be compared over time and with each other. The IIAG has a similar set of categories within which data are collated for different indicators. These categories are: safety and rule of law, participation and human rights, sustainable economic opportunity and human development (Mo Ibrahim Foundation, 2014). Data collected against sets of indicators are aggregated into a composite index so that countries are ranked according to an overall score, enabling comparison across countries and over time.

Whilst measures of governance can be controversial in terms of reducing the complexities of governance and governance performance to numbers, such indices are useful for investigating poverty–environment relationships by providing information on the broad governance context. Governance of any natural resource situation is influenced by the nature and performance of governance at other levels and within other spheres. It would be unreasonable to expect decentralized forest governance, for example, to fully display features of good governance in a country where there is 'poor' governance at the national level. Measures of governance are also useful in breaking down what is understood by the broad concept, making it more manageable and meaningful to investigate.

Principles of governance

Many approaches to governance and good governance have identified sets of principles that could be used to guide the design of governance arrangements and interventions, and to assess the nature and performance of governance. Such principles offer a way of breaking down the elusive concept of governance into something that can be better understood, addressed and analysed. Gisselquist (2012: 2) reviewed a range of definitions of governance and good governance that donors have generated and identified from these a set of seven core components: 'democracy and representation, human rights, the rule of law, efficient and effective public management, transparency and accountability, developmentalist objectives and a varying range of particular political and economic policies, programmes, and institutions'. A similar set of governance principles was developed by Lockwood *et al.* (2010) specifically for natural resource management in Australia, through a consultative approach, reference to literature and testing through application. The seven principles identified by Lockwood *et al.* (2010) are set out and explained in Table 7.1.

Table 7.1 Governance principles for natural resource management

Principle	Components
Legitimacy	• The source(s) of legitimacy of governance structures should be identified. May come from legislation and/or through acceptance by stakeholders that the structures have authority to govern • Very often power is devolved to the lowest level appropriate for effective governance • Integrity of the governance structures and processes matters for legitimacy
Transparency	• How visible are decision-making processes? • Are reasons for decisions communicated to stakeholders? • Information about the arrangements and performance of governance structures should be available
Accountability	• Allocations of responsibility for decisions and actions should be clear and accepted • Information should be available on how those responsibilities have been met
Inclusiveness	• Are mechanisms available to enable all groups of stakeholders to participate in and influence decision-making processes and outcomes?

(Continued)

Table 7.1 (Continued)

Principle	Components
Fairness	• The interests of all stakeholder groups should be given due attention and respect • There should be no bias towards any particular group/interest in decision-making • Consideration should be given to how the costs and benefits of decisions are distributed
Integration	• Is there coordination between and within levels of governance? • How do information and resources flow? • Do priorities, plans and activities within and across levels of governance fit together?
Capability	• Do those involved in governance have the skills, resources, experience and knowledge needed? • Are there systems in place that enable effective governance?
Adaptability	• How do the governance structures seek and respond to new knowledge? • How is uncertainty coped with? • How are problems and issues anticipated and managed? • Do individuals and structures reflect on and learn from performance?

Source: Adapted from Lockwood *et al.* (2010: 991–996).

The principles provide a framework for understanding what might be expected in natural resource governance, with the questions elaborating on that framework and providing a way into an analysis of the nature and performance of governance.

Why governance?

Governance is seen as a prevalent concern in influencing poverty–environment relationships where natural resources are important for people's livelihoods. Very often, natural resources are not only important for livelihoods, but also for government revenue, through requiring that licenses or permits are purchased for access to forests or fisheries, for example, or through the payment of taxes for the resources extracted. There are, then, very often, multiple stakeholders and interests competing for natural resources and benefits from these, with different levels and arenas of power in which to exert influence and secure benefits. In addition, many natural resources cut across administrative boundaries and are considered to be cross-boundary resources. Cooperation across multiple levels of government administration is essential for such resources, from sub-village level to regional cooperation between countries in some cases, for example large water bodies and national/transfrontier parks.

Governance of natural resources is likely to require collaboration and cooperation between stakeholder groups. Given issues of scale, representation of stakeholder groups is likely to be necessary, bringing in issues of how selection of representatives should be undertaken, how such selection may be affected by power relations and other factors, and whether it is actually effective in practice.

Representation of stakeholder groups, particularly different groups or types of users, occurs within decentralized approaches to natural resource governance. Decentralization of governance has occurred since the mid-1980s within a number of renewable natural resource areas, especially forests and fisheries, but has rarely delivered more sustainable natural resource management or improved livelihoods. The following section describes the nature of decentralization in natural resource settings and identifies some of the challenges experienced in a developing country context.

Decentralization of natural resource governance

Many natural resource governance arrangements have been subject to some form of decentralization since the mid-1980s. Decentralization is generally understood as referring to 'a transfer of powers from central authorities to lower levels in a political-administrative and territorial hierarchy' (Larson and Soto, 2008: 216). The different forms of decentralization are often categorized as:

- *Democratic decentralization:* transfer of power and resources to local representative bodies, whether at municipal, regional, district, village or other levels, which are downwardly accountable to their constituencies (usually through regular elections). Such bodies have the resources and power to make decisions concerning the local area, affecting the lives of local people.
- *Deconcentration (or administrative decentralization):* this refers to where central ministries transfer power to branch offices outside of the capital city.
- *Devolution:* refers to the transfer or delegation of power from central government to a lower level, which may include community-level organizations.

Within natural resources, there are examples of all of these forms of decentralization and of combinations. For example, in some countries forestry governance involves forest offices that have been deconcentrated from the central ministry, where officers report to the central ministry rather than a locally elected body. They may work on their own in forest management or in some countries, and for some types of forests, work with, or support, community-based forest management committees or user groups, which have some degree of devolved power.

Decentralization has generally been seen as a positive development, bringing governance closer to the people who use and depend on the resources. However, decentralization in natural resource governance has rarely led to substantial improvements in the condition of the natural resource and in people's lives, largely due to incomplete devolution of power and resources, limiting the scope for decision-making and enforcement of rules. Research into the effects of decentralized forms of forestry management on users' livelihoods, for example, has generally found little evidence of improvement (Larson *et al.*, 2007; Ribot *et al.*, 2010; Tacconi, 2007; Thoms, 2008). Elite capture of decentralized structures is also identified as a challenge that limits the scope for effectiveness of decentralization and its ability to deliver on equity and poverty reduction. Government officers and other actors have also been seen to prevent real devolution of power. Poteete and Ribot (2011) developed the idea of 'repertoires of domination' to describe 'the myriad tactics government officials and nonstate actors use to limit meaningful shifts of authority associated with decentralization' (2011: 440) from their research into forestry management in Senegal and wildlife management in Botswana. Such tactics may include changing policies, roles or narratives, ensuring that decentralization is a contested process rather than an achieved state.

Within literature examining examples of decentralization of natural resource management, issues of accountability and representation of users have been identified as key areas of concern (see, for example, Agrawal and Ribot, 1999; Béné *et al.*, 2009). Agrawal and Ribot (1999) developed a framework for the analysis of the nature and effectiveness of decentralization that encourages investigation of actors, power and accountability. This framework is set out in Table 7.2, with one of the examples from the 1999 article used to illustrate how the framework was used.

Agrawal and Ribot's (1999) analysis emphasizes the need for *downward* accountability if there are to be genuine benefits to local users from decentralized management. Very often, however, such downward accountability is lacking (Agrawal and Ribot, 1999; Béné *et al.*, 2009; Larson and Ribot, 2004). This is largely because resources and power remain at higher levels within governance systems, encouraging those involved in decentralized governance structures to look upwards and not be as concerned with reporting on their decisions and actions to the people they represent.

Representation within natural resource governance regimes is usually necessary because not everyone can be involved in making and enforcing decisions. Within decentralized governance systems, decisions have to be made about which bodies to devolve power and responsibilities to and how those bodies will be representative of the local users and other stakeholder groups. With respect to decentralization in fisheries, Jentoft *et al.* (2003: 282) suggest four questions that should be considered in deciding who should be involved in collaborative management:

- Who can claim legitimacy as a user or stakeholder? Users and stakeholders should be clearly defined.
- How should users and stakeholders be represented? By geographical area, occupation, gender, age?
- How much involvement should there be? How much is required of the representatives and what kinds of duties and responsibilities are expected? How much time commitment is required?
- How should representation be carried out? How important is consultation with, and accountability to, those being represented? Who does the representative speak for? Themselves or a constituency?

These questions could usefully be applied in any analysis of representation within natural resource governance, recognizing that representation can be a burden for the individual as well as an opportunity.

Table 7.2 Agrawal and Ribot's framework for the analysis of decentralization

Element	Composition	Example of Kumaon, India
Actors	Those in the local arena who exercise powers over the concerned resources. May include appointed or elected officials, NGOs, chiefs, powerful individuals, or corporate bodies such as communities, cooperatives, and committees	Forest councils elected by villagers, with authority mediated by the Forest and Revenue Departments
Power	Power is used for multiple purposes: • To create and modify rules • Make decisions on how resources are used • Ensure compliance with rules • To adjudicate when there are disputes, whether in relation to making rules, ensuring compliance or in how people access and benefit from resources	Forest Councils have powers to make rules and enforce them, with limits set by legislation. Councils meet regularly to reconsider and make rules concerning the extraction of forest products, and develop monitoring and sanctioning mechanisms. Officials of the Forest and Revenue Departments supervise and facilitate decisions and actions of the Forest Councils, but their enforcement powers are limited
Accountability	Accountability is brought about through a range of mechanisms and requires other actors to hold 'counterpower'. This is often through elections, but may also happen through legal redress to court, auditing, political pressure and civil unrest	Between Forest Councils and villagers: elections in which all adult villagers can stand for election and vote. Villagers can attend and speak at Forest Council meetings. Between villagers and Forest Councils: Guards are employed by the Forest Councils to enforce rules. Between Guards and Forest Councils: the performance of Guards in their job is a form of accountability

Source: Adapted from Agrawal and Ribot (1999).

Ratner *et al.* (2013) draw on Agrawal and Ribot's (1999) framework and others in developing a similar analytical framework to investigate the governance of aquatic agricultural systems. The elements of their framework are slightly different to those of Agrawal and Ribot's (1999), being: stakeholder representation, distribution of power and mechanisms of accountability, with formal and informal mechanisms identified within each dimension. This provides a clear, practice-oriented framework for application to any natural resource governance setting.

Governance frameworks

There are many frameworks that have been developed to enable an investigation of governance, not all with application to environment and natural resources or to natural resources and poverty or livelihoods. Two frameworks are explained in this section as examples that have been applied in a natural resource setting in a developing country context. These are a framework for analysing water governance and poverty by Cleaver and Franks (2008), which has a clear poverty focus, and the interactive governance and governability approach of Kooiman *et al.* (2008), developed to address problems and create opportunities through encouraging interaction between civil, public and private actors. In addition, the five dimensions of governance within natural resource decentralization that should be analysed according to Batterbury and Fernando (2006) are explained.

Analysing water governance and poverty

Franks and Cleaver define water governance as 'the system of actors, resources, mechanisms and processes which mediate society's access to water' (2007: 303). This definition is expanded upon through a framework to analyse water governance and poverty. The version of the framework presented in Figure 7.1 is an adapted form of the original, taken from Cleaver and Hamada (2010). The framework differs from many other water governance frameworks in its inclusion of an analysis of how arrangements for water governance impact on the poor, whether positively or negatively. Franks and Cleaver drew on social theory, post-institutionalist thinking, sustainable livelihoods approaches and research on chronic poverty in developing the framework.

According to the framework, actors draw on a range of resources in different ways in organizing access to water – these 'different ways' are referred to as *mechanisms*. These in turn influence the outcomes for the poor and for ecosystems, in terms of trends and changes in poverty and in ecosystem health. Mechanisms are not static but are themselves shaped by processes of governance, with subsequent changes realized in terms of outcomes. Cleaver and Hamada (2010) suggest that the framework can be used for a gendered analysis of water governance as well as for poverty analysis, reflecting gendered dimensions of access to water and participation in governance.

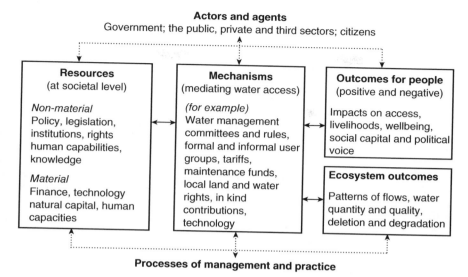

Figure 7.1 A framework for analysing water governance and poverty.

Source: Cleaver and Hamada, 2010: 29.

An example of the application of the framework is given by Franks and Cleaver (2007) in an analysis of water governance in the Kimani catchment in south-western Tanzania, where there is competition for water in the area between certain groups and for different uses. Table 7.3 provides examples of the components of the framework, other than actors and processes. The actors include local people, public officials, political leaders, non-governmental and community-based organizations, traders, technologists and other stakeholders. The example illustrates the complexity of the water governance situation, the way that social inequalities are reproduced through access to resources and the influence of socially embedded institutions that may not immediately appear to have anything to do with water governance in giving people voice and social capital. The analysis reveals how outcomes are realized within different domains (access, livelihoods, social cohesion and political voice), with differentiated outcomes according to status, gender, location and other factors. In addition to the outcomes on people, changes in flows affect the broader ecosystem, particularly wetlands, with implications for wetland and downstream users.

Franks and Cleaver (2007) see the benefit in using this framework as generating understanding of components of governance to identify areas where governance could be more effective in delivering on positive outcomes for the poor. They observe, however, that extensive analysis is needed for each component, for example investigating structures and processes of decision-making and how social relationships interact with management systems, with implications for how people access water. Finally, they also note that this framework could be used in other natural resource settings to investigate similar questions of governance and outcomes for the poor.

Table 7.3 Water governance in the Kimani catchment

Resources	Mechanisms	Outcomes for people
Non-material Mix of customary norms and understandings; modern manifestations of rights *Material* Economic resources vary considerably; limited access to economic resources linked to limited access to technology and irrigated land Provision of education and health services is low Land for productive agriculture is limited Extensive woodlands Reasonably abundant water	• Village governments, water user groups, pastoralist groups • Associational groups (choirs, women's groups) • Family relationships, kinship groups • Customary and modern land and water rights • Turns, queues, rotations • Communal labour for canal maintenance • Payments for water rights • Payments and in-kind contributions for maintenance by user groups • Structures to manage access to water for domestic supply and irrigation • Access sites to seasonal surface flows	Access differentiated according to whether close to piped water system and can pay costs; close to river and can access directly; or access is limited, so more time and effort is needed, impacting women and children especially, as they collect water for domestic use Livelihood outcomes differ: those on the irrigation schemes benefit more than those reliant on rainfed farming Pastoralists excluded from the formal institutions of village government Networks established by irrigated farmers support political representation Pastoralists have political links with regional and central government

Source: Adapted from Franks and Cleaver (2007).

Interactive governance and governability

These two concepts – of interactive governance and governability – were developed by Kooiman *et al.* (2005, 2008) through research on fisheries with the purpose of informing an assessment of the governance of natural resource systems. The idea of 'interactive governance' stems from recognition of there being multiple governing systems in society (Kooiman, 2003) and is defined as: 'The whole of interactions taken to solve societal problems and to create societal opportunities; including the formulation and application of principles guiding those interactions and care for institutions that enable and control them' (Kooiman and Bavinck, 2005: 17).

In this perspective, interactions have a particular understanding, seen as 'specific forms of action, undertaken in order to remove obstacles and to follow new paths' (Kooiman *et al.*, 2008: 2). The interactive governance approach encapsulates the concept of 'governability', which is defined by Kooiman *et al.* (2008: 3) as 'the overall capacity for governance of any societal entity or system'. Governability is seen to be dynamic, subject to change in response to internal and external factors, and is explored within this approach in relation to the 'governance interactions' between a 'system to be governed' and the 'governing system', the two components of a societal system, as shown in Figure 7.2.

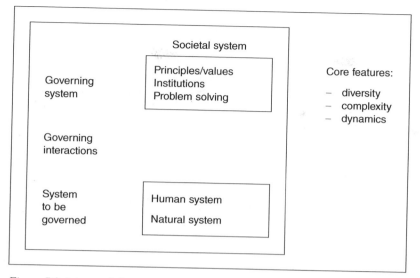

Figure 7.2 Integrated framework for governability of a societal system.

Source: Kooiman *et al.*, 2008: 4.

The interactive governance approach identifies three elements within the concept of governance: images, instruments and actions. Images may refer to visions, facts and narratives, such as the tragedy of the commons. Instruments refer to mechanisms that enable the images to be achieved through action, such as providing information, peer pressure, taxes and licenses. Instruments are operationalized through actions, the last element of governance.

These elements of governance take place over three 'orders' of governance: first-order, second-order, and meta-, or third-order governance, portrayed as three nested concentric circles. First-order governance relates to day-to-day affairs, where 'people and their organizations interact in order to solve societal problems and create new opportunities' (Kooiman *et al.*, 2008: 7); second-order governance relates to the institutional arrangements within which first-order governance takes place, referring to the 'agreements, rules, rights, laws, norms, beliefs, roles, procedures and organizations' (Kooiman *et al.*, 2008: 7); and, meta-governance refers to principles that govern activities in relation to natural systems, such as sustainability and responsibility, often enshrined in international agreements.

A further dimension to the interactive governance approach, is recognition of three types of 'modes' of governance: self-governance, co-governance and hierarchical governance. Self-governance refers to situations where actors take care of themselves, such as in common property regimes, where people agree on how a natural resource will be managed. Co-governance implies that there are organized forms created for governing, such as co-management arrangements in forestry and fisheries. Hierarchical governance implies top-down governance, between state and citizens, characterized by steering and control by government.

An example of how this approach has been operationalized is through the development of a governability assessment matrix. Chuenpagdee and Jentoft (2009) set out examples of the types of questions that would be asked in an assessment of the governability of the natural and social systems within the interactive governance approach. This matrix is shown in Table 7.4.

An example of the application of this governability assessment matrix is given by Song and Chuenpagdee (2010), who use the framework to assess the governability of the fisheries of the Southeast Arm of Lake Malawi. A summary of their assessment is given in Table 7.5.

From their analysis, Song and Chuenpagdee (2010) equate the relatively high levels of dynamics and complexity of the systems-to-be-governed (natural and socio-economic) with low governability of the fisheries. They highlight the highly dynamic nature of the natural system and the complexity of the socio-economic system as requiring particular attention. The governing system has a low level of capacity, accompanied with low to medium governing interactions. The analysis highlights limitations within the system, enabling discussion and reflection amongst those concerned with developing a more robust and effective governance response.

Analysis of governance in decentralized natural resource management

In an editorial to a special issue on decentralization of natural resource management, Batterbury and Fernando (2006) set out an approach to the analysis of governance that has five dimensions. There are similarities to the frameworks above, but there are also different dimensions, providing further variables for an analysis of environmental and natural resource governance. The components of their approach are:

1   *Governance needs to be analysed in a historical context:* an understanding of the context and approach that existed before the focus of analysis is critical. The nature and performance of governance will be influenced by previous governance regimes and by events and circumstances beyond the immediate governance concern.
2   *Framing the political economy of governance:* governance reforms are often political in nature and governance necessarily interacts with the interests of capital, influencing the shape and nature of governance arrangements.
3   *Working between places and across scales:* an appreciation of the 'scale' of governance and of interactions between places and across policies and practices is essential.
4   *Interrogating rules in use:* this reflects back onto the focus of Chapter 3, where institutions as 'rules of the game' may be socially embedded or more formal, state-led institutions. An investigation into the 'rules in use' would identify institutions that people use to engage with governance processes and functions.

Table 7.4 Governability assessment matrix

	Natural system	Socio-economic system	Governing system	Governing interaction
Diversity	What is the level of biodiversity: species, types of ecosystems or habitats, and the relative abundance and health?	Who are the stakeholders: demographics, organization, interests, uses, norms and values, etc., and their quality of life?	What is the governing mode: topdown, co-management or bottom-up, and the formal and informal institutions, mechanisms and measures?	What are the existing forms of interactions: communication, participation, representation, etc.?
Complexity	How are species, habitats and ecosystems inter-linked; the system productivity and external pressure?	How do stakeholders interact: conflicting, collaborating, communicating, integrating, specializing, complying, etc.?	How do the goals/visions of the governing institutions relate: differ, compete or cooperate?	How do the forms of interactions add up and relate: mutually supportive, consistent or incomplete?
Dynamics	What are the biological and physical changes that take place over time: long-term, short-term, seasonal; main internal and external drivers?	What is the change in the stakeholder composition, values and attitudes over time: main drivers and consequences?	Have there been any changes in the governing institutions, mechanisms and measures: main drivers and consequences?	How adaptive are the forms of interactions? Do they actually transmit information, raising demands and exercising influence?
Scale	What is the size and geographical range of the ecosystem: natural boundaries, system uniqueness and functions?	What is the size and geographical range of the social system: social boundary, ethnic and class division, mobility, uniqueness and functions?	What is the size and geographical range of institutions: local, national, regional; political boundaries, history, uniqueness and functions?	How are interactions channelled within and across scales: from national, regional to local – and vice versa?

Source: Chuenpagdee and Jentoft (2009: 114).

Table 7.5 Governability assessment of fisheries of the Southeast Arm of Lake Malawi

	Natural system	Socio-economic system	Governing system	Governing interaction
Diversity	Good diversity of fish species, but compared with tropical coastal fisheries, diversity is considered to be at a medium level	Small-scale, multi-gear and multi-species fisheries; Yao ethnic group dominates; low to medium level of diversity	High level of diversity: Department of Fisheries, Beach Village Committees (BVCs), traditional authorities, area and village development committees, Members of Parliament and others	Governing interactions take place within hierarchical system, given limited success of Participatory Fisheries Management; interactions are haphazard and ad hoc. Low level of diversity
Complexity	Considered to be low to medium, given the climatic and environmental conditions	High level of complexity attributed to factors including diverse livelihood strategies, including remittances, farming and petty trading, poor living conditions and gender disparity	Given the array of actors and institutions, complexity is high. Hierarchical system; difficult relationships between BVCs and others; witchcraft	Low level of complexity due to inconsistent and incomplete governing interactions; very top-down
Dynamics	Considered to be high; seasonal climatic variations lead to environmental fluctuations that affect fish; slow fish recovery from overexploitation	Fishers have modified fishing practices, have additional livelihood sources and there is some movement of fishers. However, style of fishing has not changed over decades; a medium level of dynamics	Low level of dynamics given the long prevailing hierarchical structure of the governing system. The introduction of BVCs has had little impact	Not adaptive or responsive, with limited change over decades, despite introduction of Participatory Fisheries Management. Low level of dynamics
Scale	Clear boundaries and no large-scale fish migration contribute to an assessment of a low issue relating to scale of the natural system	Extensive network of family kinship and social institutions and easy movement between beaches. Medium level of scale issues for the socio-economic system	The scale issue of the governing system is considered to be high. Two dimensions: institutional and ecosystem	Interactions are not effectively channelled across and between levels owing to systems of communications not working well

Source: Adapted from Song and Chuenpagdee (2010).

5   *Framing the political ecology of governance:* Batterbury and Fernando (2006) illustrate how a political ecology perspective can contribute to an analysis of governance through recognition of factors at multiple levels that influence people and the environment and encouraging investigation into how governance reforms affect people in relation to their use of environmental resources.

Key components of governance analysis

Key components of an analysis of governance can be identified through a comparison of the frameworks, together with reflection on definitions of governance, principles of governance and issues emerging from the experience of decentralization of natural resource governance. The three approaches to the analysis of governance reviewed above include quite different components, reflecting different routes to their development and context, despite each having the same aim of analysing the nature and performance of governance to identify where there are issues that may limit effectiveness or positive outcomes for the poor and/or the environment. The existence of such different approaches confirms the need for a researcher to be clear about the questions being asked, which variables and concepts should be included in a framework and what makes sense for the empirical situation. The three approaches are compared in Table 7.6.

The elements of the different approaches broadly reflect definitions and principles of governance in terms of reflecting the 'plurality of actors and organisations' (Chhotray and Stoker, 2009: 3), the existence of formal and informal rules that inform the nature of governance and the performance of governance in terms of accountability, transparency and inclusiveness.

A recent innovation in the field of development practice in relation to analyses of governance is the application of 'political economy analysis'. The analysis of political economy has, of course, been pursued for decades, as noted in Chapter 2,

Table 7.6 Comparison of approaches to the analysis of governance

Decentralization	*Water governance and poverty*	*Interactive governance and governability*	*Analysis of governance*
Actors	Actors and agents	Governing system	Historical context needed
Power	Resources	System to be governed: human/societal and natural systems	
Accountability	Mechanisms		Political economy of governance
Representation	Outcomes for people and ecosystems	Governing interactions	Scale and levels
		Analysis in terms of:	Rules-in-use
	Processes of management and practice	• Diversity • Complexity • Dynamics • Scale	Political ecology of governance

where the subject of 'political economy' was introduced. Political economy analysis (PEA) within international development practice stems in part from analyses of governance, but with more specific recognition of politics and bringing in more concern with economic processes. Collinson (2003) defines PEA as:

> Political economy analysis is therefore essentially concerned with the interaction of political and economic processes in a society. It focuses on the distribution of power and wealth between different groups and individuals, and on the processes that create, sustain and transform these relationships over time.
>
> (Collinson, 2003: 10)

There are a range of tools associated with PEA used by donors (Duncan and Williams, 2012) that share a concern with investigating how power and resources are distributed in a society and with what implications. PEA has less of a normative edge than an analysis of governance within a development context, but shares with governance analysis a concern with identifying actors and formal and informal rules, or institutions, and analysing the nature and exercise of power. PEA is often carried out at country level, informing donor country strategies and programmes, but has also been used to analyse sectors, within and across countries. The adoption of PEA is a reminder of the importance of the political environment which can be downplayed in an analysis of governance, but which is essential for understanding who has access to and control over natural resources.

Governance challenges

There are many challenges that face governance in different contexts. This section focuses on three key areas of particular concern for the governance of environment and natural resources: power, scale and coping with change.

Power

The issue of power has arisen in several of the frameworks and approaches examined in this book, and is discussed in detail in Chapter 8. It does not, however, come out strongly in the frameworks reviewed. Power can be seen as implicit in these frameworks through analyses of the distribution of resources, mechanisms used in governing processes and in the distribution and experience of outcomes. The nature and exercise of power matters in many ways within the governance of natural resource, influencing: whose voices are heard, how representation operates and whether there is accountability, particularly downwards to resource users. The absence of explicit consideration of power in the frameworks reflects the view of some observers (see, for example, Raik *et al.* 2008) that analyses of natural resource management and governance rarely explore the intricate workings of power.

Scale and levels

The scale of natural resource and social systems is of importance in an analysis of governance for several reasons:

1   Natural resource systems do not always fit neatly into the administrative boundaries of government structures and within country boundaries, requiring governments, decentralized governance bodies and other actors to cooperate across such boundaries.
2   Policies and organizational structures at multiple levels affect how a natural resource is managed, from international agreements made under the auspices of international organizations to national governments or other national governing bodies to provincial/regional structures and policies.
3   Given the nature of any natural resource system, there are likely to be multiple agencies that have some interest in the system. For example, the management of a forest may concern the ministries concerned with wildlife and land as well as forestry, and would benefit from coordination of policy and action.

The frameworks set out above enable an analysis of how governance systems and processes respond to scale and levels within natural resource systems. Frameworks examined in other chapters of this book have also been used to examine the impact of scale for natural resource governance, including interactions across scales and levels, such as the Institutional Analysis and Development and Social-Ecological System frameworks in Chapter 3.

In an important contribution to the social science conceptualization and literature on scale in relation to natural resources, Gibson *et al.* (2000: 218) use the term 'scale' to refer to 'the spatial, temporal, quantitative, or analytical dimensions used to measure and study any phenomenon', with levels referring to 'the units of analysis that are located on the same position on a scale'. These definitions are widely referred to in literature that considers the nature and impact of scale for natural resource governance. A particular concern within studies of scale and levels is the nature of interactions, within and between scales and levels. Cash *et al.* (2006: 2) define 'cross-level' interactions as 'interactions among levels within a scale', whereas 'cross-scale' refers to 'interactions across different scales, for example, between spatial domains and jurisdictions'. Interactions are likely to be *dynamic*, that is, they will change over time and space, in strength and direction. The usage of terms such as 'multi-scale' and 'cross-scale' can be confusing, as they can be used in slightly different ways. A useful review of such terms is provided by Poteete (2012), who urges caution in using terms such as 'multi-scale' and 'cross-scale' linkages and puts forward the idea of 'multi-dimensions linkages' as a broader frame of analysis that allows for multiple arenas and dimensions of linkages within a social-ecological system.

Research on scale in relation to natural resource governance is often concerned with how information is shared or exchanged between levels and how people, or groups of people, participate in structures and processes at multiple levels of governance. Participation will very likely involve representation of some kind, perhaps through democratic elections at different levels, and systems and norms to enable information flow will be important within and between levels. There are two key analytical lenses that have been developed to examine how structures and processes enable a flow of information and representation of interests. These are analyses of nested structures and of polycentricity:

1   *Nested structures:* structures are present at multiple levels, with clear linkages between them. Representation and information flow between and within nested structures, where a structure at the lowest level sends representatives up to the next level and information and resources flow up and down and across. This raises challenges of genuine and effective representation, but provides a way of establishing structures and processes that have the potential to enable information and resource flow, accountability and decision-making.
2   *Polycentricity:* this refers to there being multiple authorities with overlapping jurisdictions, creating a need for coordination and cooperation. Andersson and Ostrom (2008: 77) explain that a polycentric analyst 'considers relationships among governance actors, problems and institutional arrangements at different levels of governance'.

The concepts of nested structures and polycentricity respond to the challenges of scale within many natural resource systems, with a broad range of actors, power, institutions and issues.

Coping with change and uncertainty: adaptive governance

It has been noted at many points in this book that relationships, institutions and processes should be seen as dynamic – changing over time in response to a range of factors. Governance has, at times, been seen in a rather static way, which has led natural resource governance literature to examine the scope for adaptation. The concepts of 'adaptive co-management' and 'adaptive governance' have been developed to examine how governance and management systems have, and can, respond to change and what some of the challenges might be in this response (Armitage *et al.*, 2007; Folke *et al.*, 2005; Nunan, 2010). Being adaptive implies that actors and structures within a governance system learn by doing, are able to deal with uncertainty and complexity and have management flexibility (Nunan, 2010). Very often this adaptive approach will take place within a collaborative governance framework. Such an approach can be seen as challenging for responding to the governance agenda of inclusiveness, accountability and empowerment. Government reform initiatives within natural resource settings often focus on creating new structures, constitutions, guidelines and policies, whereas an adaptive approach would call for much more concern with building capacity – capacity to be flexible and responsive. This requires that consideration is given to information generation and sharing and decentralized powers of decision-making that can respond to new information and concerns.

Summary of key points

1   Governance is considered to be an elusive concept but can usefully be broken down into principles to enable analysis and intervention.
2   Analysis of governance can take descriptive and prescriptive forms. Descriptive forms describe the governance arrangements without seeking to impose norms of behaviour and practice, whereas prescriptive approaches seek approved norms of governance, particularly in relation to accountability and transparency.
3   Governance in relation to poverty–environment relationships is influenced by the nature and performance of governance at other levels and within other spheres. It would be unreasonable to expect forest governance to fully display features of good governance in a country where there is 'poor' governance at the national level.
4   Governance matters for natural resource situations because it influences who benefits and how, what revenue is generated from natural resources, how the revenue is used and who makes decisions on the use of, and benefits from, natural resources.
5   Principles of governance of particular concern for poverty–environment relationships include accountability and inclusiveness. Representation of stakeholder groups will be necessary in many natural resource governance situations. How representation is undertaken in terms of selection, consultation and accountability will impact on the effectiveness of both representation and natural resource governance.
6   Within the natural resource context, decentralization of management has been undertaken in many countries and for many different types of renewable natural resources, particularly fisheries and forestry. Decentralized systems face many challenges including lack of resources, power to make and enforce decisions and elite capture.
7   Frameworks developed for the analysis of natural resource governance do not always have a clear concern with outcomes for people, including in terms of poverty reduction or livelihoods. They are generally concerned with an analysis of who is involved in the process of governing, what mechanisms are used, what formal and informal rules inform the nature and performance of governance, and how accountability and transparency are enabled or constrained. These components of an analysis of governance can generate insight into who benefits from natural resources and why, and why the natural resource system is in the condition it is in, demonstrating potential to generate understanding of poverty–environment relationships.
8   The scale of natural resources presents challenges in terms of the number and plurality of actors and dimensions of the natural resource. Natural resources may cut across administrative boundaries, requiring cooperation across multiple administrative levels and sometimes the formation of nested structures that facilitate representation of interests upwards, downward accountability and the flow of information and resources. There may be multiple centres of power and authority, requiring analysis of the 'polycentric' nature of the governance system.

Further reading

Kjær, A.M. (2004) *Governance*, Cambridge: Polity Press.
Kjær provides a general introduction to the concept of governance, investigating its origins in theory and practice, examining how the concept has been used within public administration and public policy, international relations, European studies and comparative politics. The concept of 'good governance' and governance of the World Bank are also reviewed. Kjær concludes by reviewing key areas of debate within the different sub-fields in relation to governance, namely networks, reciprocity, accountability and democracy. The text is a useful and accessible introduction to this elusive concept.

Barnes, G. and Child, B. (2014) *Adaptive Cross-Scalar Governance of Natural Resources*, London: Earthscan.
An excellent contribution to literature on natural resource governance which introduces the theoretical and conceptual foundations of natural resource governance before examining more specific concerns such as property rights, scale and elite capture. Further topics include measuring and monitoring governance and participatory and adaptive governance. Drawing on case studies from Africa and Latin America the edited collection brings together theory, concepts and case studies on natural resource governance.

References

Agrawal, A. and Ribot, J. (1999) 'Accountability in decentralization: A framework with South Asian and West African cases', *The Journal of Developing Areas*, 33(4): 473–502.

Andersson, K.P. and Ostrom, E. (2008) 'Analyzing decentralized resource regimes from a polycentric perspective', *Policy Sciences*, 41: 71–93.

Armitage, D., Berkes, F. and Doubleday, N. (eds) (2007) *Adaptive Co-management: Collaboration, Learning, and Multi-Level Governance*, Vancouver: University of British Columbia Press.

Barnes, G. and Child, B. (2014) *Adaptive Cross-scalar Governance of Natural Resources*, London: Earthscan.

Batterbury, S.P.J. and Fernando, J.L. (2006) 'Rescaling governance and the impacts of political and environmental decentralization: An introduction', *World Development*, 34(11): 1851–1863.

Béné, C. and Neiland, A.E. (2006) 'From participation to governance: A critical review of the concepts of governance, co-management and participation, and their implementation in small-scale inland fisheries in developing countries', *WorldFish Center Studies and Reviews 29*. Penang: The WorldFish Center.

Béné, C., Belal, E., Baba, M.O., Ovie, S., Raji, A., Njaya, F., Andi, M.N., Russell, A. and Neiland, A. (2009) 'Power struggle, dispute and alliance over local resources: Analyzing "democratic" decentralization of natural resources through the lenses of Africa inland fisheries', *World Development*, 37: 1935–1950.

Cash, D.W., Adger, W.N., Berkes, F., Garden, P., Lebel, L., Olsson, P., Pritchard, L. and Young, O. (2006) 'Scale and cross-scale dynamics: Governance and information in a multilevel world', *Ecology and Society*, 11(2): 8.

Chhotray, V. and Stoker, G. (2009) *Governance Theory and Practice: A Cross-disciplinary Approach*, Basingstoke: Palgrave Macmillan.

Chuenpagdee, R. and Jentoft, S. (2009) 'Governability assessment for fisheries and coastal systems: A reality check', *Human Ecology*, 37: 109–120.

Cleaver, F. and Franks, T. (2008) 'Distilling or diluting? Negotiating the water research-policy interface', *Water Alternatives*, 1(1): 157–176.

Cleaver, F. and Hamada, K. (2010) '"Good" water governance and gender equity: A troubled relationship', *Gender & Development*, 18(1): 27–41.

Collinson, S. (ed.) (2003) 'Power, livelihoods and conflict: Case studies in political economy analysis for humanitarian action', *HPG Report 13*, London: Humanitarian Policy Group, Overseas Development Institute.

Duncan, A. and Williams, G. (2012) 'Making development assistance more effective through using political-economy analysis: What has been done and what have we learned?', *Development Policy Review*, 30(2): 133–148.

Evans, J.P. (2012) *Environmental Governance*, London: Routledge.

Folke, C., Hahn, T., Olsson, P. and Norberg, J. (2005) 'Adaptive governance of social-ecological systems', *Annual Review of Environmental Resources*, 30: 441–473.

Franks, T. and Cleaver, F. (2007) 'Water governance and poverty: A framework for analysis', *Progress in Development Studies*, 7(4): 291–306.

Gibson, C.C., Ostrom, E. and Ahn, T.K. (2000) 'The concept of scale and the human dimensions of global change: A survey', *Ecological Economics*, 32: 217–239.

Gisselquist, R.M. (2012) 'Good governance as a concept, and why this matters for development policy', *Working Paper No. 2012/30*, Helsinki: UNU-WIDER.

Grindle, M. (2004) 'Good enough governance: Poverty reduction and reform in developing countries', *Governance: An International Journal of Policy, Administration and Institutions*, 17(4): 525–548.

Grindle, M. (2007) 'Good enough governance revisited', *Development Policy Review*, 25(5): 553–574.

Hyden, G., Court, J. and Mease, K. (2004) *Making Sense of Governance: Empirical Evidence from Sixteen Developing Countries*, London: Lynne Reiner.

Jentoft, S. and Chuenpagdee, R. (2009) 'Fisheries and coastal governance as a wicked problem', *Marine Policy*, 33: 553–560.

Jentoft, S., Mikalsen, K.H. and Hernes, H-K. (2003) 'Representation in fisheries co-management' in Wilson, D.C., Raakjær Nielsen, J. and Degnbol, P. (eds), *The Fisheries Co-management Experience: Accomplishments, Challenges and Prospects*, Dordrecht: Kluwer Academic Press.

Kjær, A.M. (2004) *Governance*, Cambridge: Polity Press.

Kooiman, J. (2003) *Governing as Governance*, London: Sage.

Kooiman, J. and Bavinck, M. (2005) 'The governance perspective', in Kooiman, J., Bavinck, M., Jentoft, S. and Pullin, R. (eds), *Fish for Life: Interactive Governance for Fisheries*, Amsterdam: Amsterdam University Press, pp. 11–24.

Kooiman, J., Bavinck, M., Jentoft, S. and Pullin, R. (2005) *Fish for Life: Interactive Governance for Fisheries*, Amsterdam: Amsterdam University Press.

Kooiman, J., Bavinck, M., Chuenpagdee, R., Mahon, R. and Pullin, R. (2008) 'Interactive governance and governability: An introduction', *The Journal of Transdisciplinary Environmental Studies*, 7(1).

Larson, A.M. and Ribot, J.C. (2004) 'Democratic decentralisation through a natural resource lens: An introduction', *European Journal of Development Research*, 16(1): 1–25.

Larson, A.M. and Soto, F. (2008) 'Decentralization of natural resource governance regimes', *Annual Review of Environment and Resources*, 33: 213–239.

Larson, A.M., Pacheco, P., Toni, F. and Vallejo, M. (2007) 'The effects of forestry decentralization on access to livelihood assets', *The Journal of Environment & Development*, 16(3): 251–268.

Lockwood, M., Davidson, J., Curtis, A., Stratford, E. and Griffith, R. (2010) 'Governance principles for natural resource management', *Society and Natural Resources*, 23(10): 986–1001.

Mo Ibrahim Foundation (2014) *Ibrahim Index of African Governance*, http://www.moibrahimfoundation.org/iiag/ (Accessed 25/01/2014).

Mohan, G., Brown, E., Milward, B. and Zack-Williams, A.B. (2000) *Structural Adjustment: Theory, Practice and Impacts*, London: Routledge.

Nunan, F. (2010) 'Governance and fisheries co-management on Lake Victoria: Challenges to the adaptive governance approach', *Maritime Studies (MAST)*, 9(1): 103–125.

Poteete, A. (2012) 'Levels, scales, linkages, and other "multiples" affecting natural resources', *International Journal of the Commons*, 6(2): 134–150.

Poteete, A. and Ribot, J.C. (2011) 'Repertoires of domination: Decentralization as process in Botswana and Senegal', *World Development*, 39(3): 439–449.

Raik, D.B., Wilson, A.L. and Decker, D.J. (2008) 'Power in natural resources management: An application of theory', *Society and Natural Resources*, 21: 729–739.

Ratner, B.D., Cohen, P., Barman, B., Mam, K., Nagoli, J. and Allison, E.H. (2013) 'Governance of aquatic agricultural systems: Analyzing representation, power, and accountability', *Ecology and Society*, 18(4): 59.

Ribot, J.C., Lund, J.F. and Treue, T. (2010) 'Democratic decentralization in sub-Saharan Africa: Its contribution to forest management, livelihoods, and enfranchisement', *Environmental Conservation*, 37(1): 35–44.

Song, A.M. and Chuenpagdee, R. (2010) 'Operationalizing governability: A case study of a Lake Malawi fishery', *Fish and Fisheries*, 11: 235–249.

Tacconi, L. (2007) 'Decentralization, forests and livelihoods: Theory and narrative', *Global Environmental Change*, 17: 338–348.

Thoms, C.A. (2008) 'Community control of resources and the challenge of improving local livelihoods: A critical examination of community forestry in Nepal', *Geoforum*, 39: 1452–1465.

World Bank (1989) *Sub-Saharan Africa: From Crisis to Sustainable Growth*, Washington DC: World Bank.

World Bank (2014) *Worldwide Governance Indicators*, http://info.worldbank.org/governance/wgi/index.aspx#home (accessed 25/01/14).

8   Conclusion

Reflections on investigating poverty–environment relationships

Introduction

This book began by stating that it matters how poverty–environment relationships are understood and portrayed, suggesting that the 'vicious circle' and 'downward spiral' portrayals of poverty–environment relationships are misleading and unhelpful. Reviewing a diverse range of frameworks and approaches that enable a much deeper, nuanced analysis of poverty–environment relationships has shown how much the internal and broader political economy, governance and power context matters. An examination of the broader context implies that questions should be asked concerning why people are poor; why people have the access they do, or do not, to resources; and, why they have the capacity to manage resources or, indeed, have such limited capacity to manage the natural resources in question. This may lead analysts to investigate the governance context or to investigate who has power and what the implications of such power are for how people gain and maintain access, or how, and why, that access is so limited and complex.

It is not enough, and perhaps even detrimental, to think that reducing poverty is the answer to addressing environmental degradation and vice versa. Assuming a direct relationship between poverty and the environment may neglect the wider context and causal factors. Situations are generally more complicated and, indeed, by portraying poverty–environment relationships in this way, it is possible that attention to the role of wealthier groups in environmental degradation may be averted. Corruption, elite capture or inadequate governance may limit the scope that people have to make decisions that reduce pressure on, or misuse, environmental resources. Governance matters. Power matters. International economic and trade regimes impact on how people access and use environmental resources. The political economy of poverty–environment relationships matter for how and whether people have the capacity and capability to benefit from natural resources and to use those resources sustainably.

The previous chapters reviewed a broad range of frameworks and approaches, each having different roots, drawing on different concepts and seeking to address different questions. There are, however, many cross-cutting themes and concepts that emerge time and again. These are identified and discussed in this chapter. The cross-cutting themes and concepts are identified from Table 8.1, which provides a reminder of the main frameworks and approaches reviewed in the book, together with the examples of questions from the chapters that may be addressed using those frameworks and approaches.

A key theme emerging from the frameworks and approaches set out in Table 8.1 is a concern with what people *have* rather than what they do not. This may include access to land, having access to social capital within kinship and friendships, skills and knowledge. This comes across in an interest throughout the frameworks and approaches in resources, assets, capabilities and wellbeing. This suggests that the frameworks and approaches tend to have a constructive, positive outlook, concerned with building on what people have, recognizing the skills and knowledge of people who live and work with the natural environment, and their agency, that is their capacity and scope to make decisions and take action. However, how people can actually use what they have in forming livelihood strategies and improving wellbeing is affected by a wide range of factors, policies and institutions. These include cultural norms, local rules, national legislation and international agreements, including trade agreements. The use of resources, assets and capabilities is *mediated* by these – people are not free to do as they will; there are constraints on their agency. That is why it is important to understand exactly what 'access' means in a given situation and how it is shaped, recognizing that access to natural resources can change over time.

The discussion on the cross-cutting themes and concepts follows Table 8.1 and examines the following in detail: power, institutions, access to natural resources, poverty, livelihoods and wellbeing, gender, narratives/myths and scale. Several of these themes (power, institutions, access, poverty and gender) were introduced in Chapter 1. Their consideration in this chapter builds on the introduction and brings out key points from a comparison of the frameworks and approaches included in the book. Table 8.1 also lists the types of data collection and analysis methods that are most closely associated with the frameworks and approaches. These are introduced later in the chapter, with particular attention given to ethnography, mixed-methods research and participatory approaches. The chapter concludes with observations on frameworks and approaches.

Key themes arising from a comparison of frameworks and approaches

Key concepts and variables that arise in Table 8.1 are now considered in turn, bringing together different strands of thinking and situating the concepts within broader literature. The concepts considered are: power, institutions, access to natural resources, poverty, livelihoods and wellbeing, gender, narratives/myths and scale.

Power

Power was introduced as a recurring cross-cutting theme in Chapter 1, where it was stated that power manifested through power relations impacts on how people

Table 8.1 Summary of approaches and frameworks

Approach and frameworks	Focus and key variables	Examples of questions that could be addressed by the framework/approaches	Methods for data collection and analysis
Political ecology	Narratives; power; knowledge(s); scale – with multiple levels of concern; equilibrium and non-equilibrium ecology; social justice; neo-Malthusian arguments; tragedy of the commons	Why was a decision made to demarcate strict boundaries around a national park and how are people living in the area affected by this decision? Why were nomadic pastoralists evicted from an area and prevented from grazing their livestock and accessing water in that area? How have people living in an area responded to environmental change over time and why have they responded in that way? Are there reasons why other decisions could not be, or were not, made?	Natural and social science data collection methods; longitudinal, multi-method data collection; ethnographic approaches, with observation and key informant interviews; documentary analysis
Institutional analysis			
Critical Institutionalism	'Rules of the game'; institutions constrain or enable access to, use of and control over natural resources Bureaucratic and socially embedded institutions; importance of social structures and power dynamics; institutions evolve; institutional bricolage	How does governance function in an area and with what implications for different types of resource users? How are bureaucratic and socially embedded institutions drawn on in the governance of natural resources?	Ethnographic approaches: observation, interviews, life histories; documentary analysis
Environmental Entitlements framework	Entitlements, endowments, capabilities	How do different social actors gain access to and control over specific natural resources? How does natural resource use by different social actors transform different components of the environment?	Ethnographic approaches; observation; key informant interviews; focus group discussion; surveys; participatory approaches

(Continued)

Table 8.1 (Continued)

Approach and frameworks	Focus and key variables	Examples of questions that could be addressed by the framework/approaches	Methods for data collection and analysis
Institutional Analysis and Development	Physical/material conditions; community attributes; rules-in-use; action arena, patterns of interactions; evaluative criteria; outcomes	What types of rules would lead to the sustainable use of fisheries in a given context?	Mixed-methods research; experimental, in the field and in the laboratory
Social-Ecological System framework	Resource systems; resource units; governance systems; actors; focal action situations; multiple tiers of variables	Why are some social-ecological systems sustainable whereas others collapse?	Mixed-methods research; experimental, in the field and in the laboratory
A gender lens	Gendered lens; gender as power relations; intra-household relations; repoliticizing gender; access to and control over natural resources; forms of social differentiation	In what ways and why is access to land influenced by gender relations within households and the wider society? How and why do women and men benefit differently in a given context from access to natural resources?	Ethnographic approaches; key informant interviews; participatory approaches
Livelihoods and wellbeing	Capabilities, assets		
Sustainable Livelihoods framework	Livelihood assets, vulnerability context, policies, institutions and processes, livelihood strategies and outcomes	How are household livelihood strategies constructed? Which policies, institutions and processes constrain and enable livelihood strategies?	Participatory methods; surveys; key informant interviews
Millennium Ecosystem Assessment framework	Ecosystem services, constituents of well-being, human well-being and poverty reduction, direct and indirect drivers of change; all within local, regional and global arenas and over time	How do coastal ecosystem services underpin coastal community wellbeing? What are the key drivers of change affecting ecosystem services and wellbeing? What trade-offs should be considered in examining options for management measures?	Mixed-methods research; interdisciplinary, drawing on natural sciences to investigate ecosystem services; surveys; key informant interviews; participatory approaches; focus group discussions

Wellbeing in developing countries (WeD)	Material resources (assets, welfare and standard of living); relational – social relations and human (capabilities, attitudes to life and personal relationships); subjective – people's perceptions of their positions	What would people consider to be important for their wellbeing and what challenges do they experience in securing their wellbeing?	Mixed-methods research, collecting quantitative and qualitative data; surveys; key informant interviews; participatory approaches
Social network analysis	Social relations between actors, measures of centrality within networks, accessing resources through networks	Who has influence within a forest users' network and with what implications for governance outcomes? How does a person's personal network affect their access to irrigation water?	Largely quantitative surveys, collecting data that can be mapped and statistically analysed; qualitative data collected through interviews to seek interpretive and contextual data
Governance	Multiple actors involved in governing natural resources; accountability, representation, participation, transparency	Who makes decisions in relation to how natural resources are used and who benefits? Why were certain decisions reached?	Participatory approaches; key informant interviews; documentary analysis; focus group interviews; ethnographic approaches
Framework for analysing water governance and poverty	Resources drawn on to construct mechanisms for water governance, shaping outcomes for the poor and for ecosystems		
Interactive governance	Governability, system to be governed (socio-economic and natural), governing interactions	Why is the natural resource system in the condition it is in? How effective is the governing system and why?	Documentary analysis; key informant interviews

gain and maintain access to, and control over, natural resources, thereby influencing poverty–environment linkages. The concept of power is apparent in every chapter of this book, from political ecology, where power relations are a focus of concern in investigating whose knowledge and narrative counts, to governance, where the nature and degree of power-sharing influences the effectiveness and equity of governance arrangements in a natural resource setting. Power relations are intrinsic within a gendered lens taken to the analysis of poverty–environment relationships and forms part of the 'transforming structures and processes' box of the Sustainable Livelihoods framework. Within social network analysis, power is manifested through connections and resources. It seems then that power really does matter for how people gain and maintain access to natural resources and how those resources are governed.

What is power though? Power is a slippery, complex and contested concept. Theory and literature on power are particularly informed by the writings of Michel Foucault and Stephen Lukes. From Foucault, amongst other lessons, we can learn that power is diffuse, not necessarily held by a specific person. Someone may have power in relation to some people but not to others, or in some settings but not in others. Power may come with position and resources but may be dynamic, i.e. change in nature and degree over time and space, and be difficult to identify. Foucault (1980: 98) advises that 'power must be analyzed as something which circulates, or rather as something which only functions in the form of a chain. It is never localized here or there'. The idea of power being apparent within relations is advocated by Scott (2001: 2), who suggests that 'at its simplest, power is a social relation between two agents' with 'intention to produce a particular effect or the desire to see a particular effect occurring'. Such 'intention', though, may be unconscious as well as conscious.

Scott's definition is reflected in the way that Lukes sees power. Lukes (2005: 29) defines power as '*A* exercises power over *B* when *A* affects *B* in a manner contrary to *B*'s interests', noting that such power not may be consciously or deliberately exercised. Lukes goes further though to identify three dimensions of power:

1   *One-dimensional view:* power is observable, 'involves a focus on *behaviour* in the making of *decisions* on issues over which there is an observable *conflict* of (subjective) *interests*, seen as express policy preferences, revealed by political participation' (Lukes, 2005: 19).
2   *Two-dimensional view:* 'setting the agenda', with analysis of decision-making and non-decision-making. The two-dimensional view 'of power involves a *qualified critique* of the *behavioural focus* of the first view . . . and it allows for consideration of the ways in which *decisions* are prevented from being taken on *potential issues*' (Lukes, 2005: 24–25).
3   *Three-dimensional view:* this view sees power as manipulating the views of others, critiquing the first two dimensions as being too individualistic. It 'allows for consideration of the many ways in which potential issues are kept out of politics, whether through operation of social forces and institutional practices or through individuals' decisions' (Lukes, 2005: 28).

According to Lukes, then, power can be manifested and investigated in different ways; it is not always observable, going on 'behind the scenes', influencing knowledge, belief and attitudes. We can conclude from these observations from Foucault, Scott and Lukes that power is diffuse, not concentrated; it is embodied and enacted, not possessed; and power is everywhere. It should also be noted that power is not necessarily a negative thing. After all, much development effort is concerned with 'empowerment'; enabling people to become more powerful within their own lives and situations.

Within research related to poverty–environment relationships using the frameworks and approaches reviewed in the previous chapters, analysis relating to power has involved recognition that:

1   Power influences how knowledge about the environment is gained, interpreted and used. People with greater power in a particular setting are more able to get their views across and the explanations they support of environmental change become the 'dominant narratives' that explain people–environment relations. Political ecology seeks to investigate how and why such narratives have come to dominate explanations of environmental change and with what implications for natural resource users. Political ecology also seeks alternative explanations, drawing on a wide range of data sources, including resource users, over a long period of time.

2   Power relations form part of the institutional landscape that influences the distribution of benefits from natural resources. How people gain and maintain access to natural resources through institutions will be influenced by power relations. Power relations may be exercised beyond the natural resource context and still be of influence, as reflected in Critical Institutionalism and in the Sustainable Livelihoods framework.

3   Changes in the management or governance arrangements of natural resources often aim to redistribute power – power to make decisions relating to access to resources and sanctions and to raise and spend revenue moving from central government to local government and/or resource users, for example. In Chapter 7, it was observed that research on the decentralization of natural resource governance (with many forms of decentralization noted) has found that power is rarely adequately shared or redistributed effectively, so that those with power – whether government officers and/or more powerful people within an area – find ways of holding onto that power. Poteete and Ribot (2011) refer to people with power using 'repertoires of domination' to hold onto that power despite the apparent decentralization of power and responsibility. Social network analysis has also been used to show why leaders within a community resist change in governance arrangements (Crona and Bodin, 2010).

4   Even where there are no obvious attempts to hold on to power, governance reforms may result in reproducing existing power structures, with elite capture of the new governance arrangements securing decision-making and benefits for the elite few. Béné *et al.* (2009) and Njaya *et al.* (2012) observe

how fisheries co-management arrangements have often enabled the 'elite' within localities to capture the leadership of co-management committees, with consequences for equity, justice and accountability.

Despite this apparent concern with power in much literature on natural resource governance and livelihoods, it has been suggested that studies rarely investigate the 'workings of power itself' (Raik *et al.*, 2008: 730). Whilst power dynamics and relations may be alluded to, the nature and processes of power are rarely the focus of analysis. Jentoft (2007: 426) observes in relation to literature on fisheries and coastal management that 'with a few notable exceptions, power is an understated and understudied concept'. Raik *et al.* (2008) put forward a way of addressing this gap by taking a 'realist' view of power, which recognizes that 'power is thus the capacity to act within preconditioned, structured social relations' (2008: 736). This approach would reflect findings from research on natural resource governance where the lack of room to act and make decisions by those without power has been observed.

Institutions

An investigation of the nature and influence of power within poverty–environment relations suggests that attention should be given to institutions. Chapters 1 and 3 set out definitions of an institution, beginning with the classic definition from North (1990). From Table 8.1 it can be seen that institutions form part of the analytical investigation of many of the approaches and frameworks. The identification of social and power relations, norms, rules and policies at multiple levels is integral to a political ecology analysis. Gender relations present a particular form of institution, interacting closely with other manifestations of social differentiation and therefore other social relations/institutions. Institutions mediate how people can use their assets in developing and maintaining livelihood strategies and in enhancing their well-being. Institutions influence the nature and extent of social and personal networks. Finally, the governance of natural resources is infused with and influenced by institutional arrangements, as seen in the analytical frameworks reviewed in Chapter 7. The perceived failure of so many decentralization initiatives of natural resource governance in achieving greater sustainability of natural resources and equity in the share of benefits can be analysed with reference to institutional arrangements. Such arrangements will influence how the decentralization approach is designed and implemented and how people behave and respond to the opportunities arising from, and constraints imposed by, governance reform.

Institutions matter. They really matter for poverty–environment relations. From social norms, taboos, gender relations, beliefs, formal policies and legislation to global agreements, institutions have a bearing on who makes decisions, what kinds of decisions are made, who gets access to natural resources and what that access looks like, and how decision-making, decisions and outcomes change, or do not, over time.

Access

The nature of 'access to and control over' natural resources is a further recurrent theme. As noted in Chapter 1, access has been defined within literature on natural resources as 'the ability to benefit from things' (Ribot and Peluso, 2003: 153). The concept does not suggest ownership or rights, but that a complex range of institutions and factors will influence the nature of access people have to resources at a given point in time. Access is not straightforward – it does not suggest that if someone has access they can take what they like, when they like. Access may be for a certain period of time, in relation to a certain area of land or forest, or for particular resources and will vary between people for many reasons. The question of access relates not only to natural resources, but access to labour and capital, for example, matters, influenced by a range of social institutions (Berry, 1989). Ribot and Peluso (2003:160–161) put forward an analysis of access that would entail:

> 1) Identifying and mapping the flow of the particular benefit of interest; 2) identifying the mechanisms by which different actors involved gain, control, and maintain the benefit flow and its distribution; and 3) an analysis of the power relations underlying the mechanisms of access involved in instances where benefits are derived.

All of the frameworks and approaches reviewed in the book can facilitate an investigation and understanding of the nature of access to natural resources. Political ecology would investigate the norms, policies and political-economic context of people–environment relations to identify who has access, what that access is, how access has changed over time and with what consequences for the environmental resources and for people's livelihoods. Institutional analysis offers a very clear route into an investigation of access to benefits from natural resources, whether taking a Critical Institutionalism approach, using the Environmental Entitlements framework or the Institutional Analysis and Development framework. A gendered lens would illuminate how gender relations in multiple spheres influence access to benefits from natural resources. A livelihoods or wellbeing approach would recognize the influence of institutions, assets and capabilities on the nature of access, whereas social network analysis could investigate how connections within personal and social networks facilitate or constrain access. The nature of governance arrangements has clear implications for how, and whether, people access benefits from natural resources, noting that such access may be through illegal, or illegitimate, as well as legal means.

Poverty, livelihoods and wellbeing

Most of the approaches and frameworks focus more on livelihoods and wellbeing than poverty *per se*. Very few of the frameworks and approaches are explicitly concerned with an understanding, or measurement, of poverty or with how poverty can be prevented or reduced. There is, though, a clear concern with the involvement or voice of poorer people in natural resource decision-making and governance. A political ecology approach and governance analyses in particular can facilitate investigation into such involvement and voice. There is clear recognition of the multiple dimensions and interpretations of poverty in the frameworks and approaches, with scope for reflecting on the views and experience of the subjects of the research in relation to the nature and extent of poverty. Investigation into coping mechanisms and sources of vulnerability are encouraged, but also into the assets and capabilities that people have in a much more positive way than a focus on deprivation might suggest.

The lack of explicit focus on poverty may reflect the concern with the frameworks and approaches with understanding broader people–environment relations. They are not principally concerned with investigating the 'poverty–environment nexus', where poverty is reduced and the environment improved. Many of the frameworks and approaches could, however, enable investigation into such potential 'win–win' situations. The relevance of the frameworks and approaches to investigating and understanding poverty–environment relations is apparent in many of their applications in developing country contexts. Undertaking research in a developing country does not imply that there is necessarily a poverty focus, but the frameworks and approaches have the potential to be used to investigate the experience and context of poverty and many have been used in that way.

Gender

Gender does not come out strongly as a key perspective within many of the frameworks and approaches, often viewed as one area of social difference rather than a key theme in itself. Gendered relations are often seen, however, as a mediating influence on people's access to and benefits from resources in many of the chapters. Within political ecology, a feminist perspective was introduced, noting that feminist political ecology as a distinct approach to analysis has not been widely taken, but rather gender is often taken as one area of social difference alongside others, such as race and age. With the interest in political ecology in the role and distribution of power, gender relations form an important area of investigation within a broader analysis. Gender relations may also constitute part of the institutional landscape in institutional analyses, whether undertaken within a Critical or Mainstream Institutional approach, or within the 'transforming structures and processes' box of the Sustainable Livelihoods framework. Wellbeing analyses have the potential to explore aspects and influence of gender in studying perceptions and experience of wellbeing of individuals, households and communities. Social network analysis may incorporate gender concerns in the design and analysis of data and governance analyses could involve a gendered perspective, whether through analyses of gendered relations or analysis of participation and representation of men and women in governance structures and processes. A gendered analysis can be incorporated into all of the frameworks and approaches, together with other dimensions of social difference where appropriate.

Narratives/myths

Chapter 1 began by expressing deep concern that a view still exists that poverty necessarily leads to environmental degradation and such degradation leads to greater poverty, portrayed in a 'vicious circle' or 'downward spiral'. This portrayal reflects the recurrence of 'myths', 'narratives' and 'received wisdom' about poverty and the environment, which are apparent in a range of explanations of environmental change and the role of local resource users. Challenging dominant narratives and received wisdom is a characteristic of many frameworks and approaches, whether explicit or implicit, but particularly of political ecology. Institutional analysis, taking a gender lens perspective and livelihoods, wellbeing and governance analyses can all contribute to generating evidence in challenging received wisdom and offering alternative explanations and narratives of environmental change and of people–environment interactions.

Scale

The question of scale was discussed in Chapter 7 in relation to natural resource governance, where a multi- and cross-level and scale perspective was observed in many approaches to the analysis of governance. Recognition of the place and importance of scale – whether temporal (over time) or spatial (over space) – is apparent in other frameworks and approaches as well. This includes political ecology investigating the political economy of the global, regional, national, sub-national and local situation in relation to environmental change. Approaches to the analysis of institutions in relation to natural resources differ considerably in how they approach the question of scale. A Critical Institutionalism approach would reflect more of a social network analysis perspective – that institutions, as do social relations, cross administrative and geographic boundaries, making a focus on levels and places within scales unhelpful and inappropriate. People may have connections that cross levels and boundaries – through kinship, political connections or other relations – that may not emerge through a concern with scale. If social networks were to be investigated within determined levels and spaces, important connections could be missed and different types of boundaries may be more appropriate than those offered by an analysis of scale. A more 'mainstream' approach to institutional analysis would, however, recognize scale and pay attention to cross- and multi-level and scale interactions and to the nesting of structures and institutions within broader arrangements.

In contrast, a gendered lens calls for attention to be given to an analysis of intra-household relations, as well as other locations and spaces that influence gender relations. A livelihoods and wellbeing perspective would call for investigation into institutions and resources at all levels and in all spaces of relevance, and for people's perspectives on the role and importance of these. Coming back to a more formal recognition of multiple levels, governance analyses tend to give clear recognition to there being a range of structures and levels within any governance arrangement and that reform of such arrangements may alter, or try to alter, the distribution of power and resources between and within these levels and structures.

How the issue of scale is addressed by, and reflected in, an analysis of poverty–environment relations will depend then on the framework or approach being used and the nature of the research problem being investigated.

What do these common themes add up to?

These common themes from the broad range of frameworks and approaches are encapsulated within political ecology, which provides an overarching approach to the analysis of poverty–environment relationships. The themes reflect the defining characteristics of political ecology of investigating power and the nature of access to resources, challenging myths and narratives, seeking social justice, including from a gender perspective, and through that reduced poverty and improved livelihoods and wellbeing, through an analysis of institutions and within the context of multi-scale and levels of governance. There are clear connections then between the field of political ecology and the other frameworks and approaches reviewed in this book, which could, depending on how and why they are used, feed into a political ecology analysis.

Methods for data collection and analysis

Table 8.1 also identifies the main data collection methods associated with each analytical framework and approach. The chapters have not considered in detail the types of data that would need to be collected or how the data could be collected and analysed. Some of the chapters touch on data, data collection and analysis more than others. The examples given in the chapters provide insights into the types of data collected when certain frameworks and approaches have been used and how researchers have gone about the analysis. This has not been done systematically, as the purpose of the examples was to show how the frameworks and approaches have been applied and what they have revealed. There are, fortunately, many excellent books available on a range of social science research approaches and methods. A good social science research textbook such as Bryman (2012) provides an excellent introduction to a wealth of quantitative and qualitative methods. This section will not, then, set out when a survey or a focus group would be most appropriate and how to design relevant data collection tools and develop a plan for the analysis. Rather, this section highlights key methods of data collection and analysis that deserve particular attention within the context of investigating poverty–environment relationships, using the frameworks and approaches covered in previous chapters.

Reviewing the range of methods listed in Table 8.1, it can be seen that many of the frameworks and approaches encourage a number of methods to be used, reflecting the multi- and inter-disciplinary nature of development studies

(Desai and Potter, 2006) and the use of mixed-methods approaches in development studies research (Sumner and Tribe, 2008). In addition to employing a number of methods in a research investigation, recognition of the dynamics of change and scale over time and place is needed, creating challenges for some of the frameworks and approaches that might not readily appear to capture a dynamic perspective on the research problem. Investigating the historical context, as well as very often the political and economic context, of poverty–environment relations is key to informing the design of research and interpreting findings.

Studies related to investigating poverty–environment relationships are very often multi- or inter-disciplinary, that is they draw on a number of disciplines, such as economics, sociology, ecology and geography. Multi- and inter-disciplinary research differ in terms of whether the streams of research are undertaken quite separately or are integrated to some degree. Multi-disciplinary research involves research drawing on several disciplines that may bring different types of evidence and insights to a research problem but the strands of the research remain quite separate. Interdisciplinary research, meanwhile, involves a level of integration between the research methods and approaches. There remains debate as to what constitutes 'interdisciplinarity' but integration is seen by many as central to an interdisciplinary approach. Repko (2012: 3–4) describes integration in relation to interdisciplinarity as 'a process by which ideas, data and information, methods, tools, concepts, and/or theories from two or more disciplines are synthesized, connected, or blended'. Repko (2012: 16) goes on to provide a definition of inter-disciplinary studies as

> a process of answering a question, solving a problem, or addressing a topic that is too broad or complex to be dealt with adequately by a single discipline, and draws on the disciplines with the goal of integrating their insights to construct a more comprehensive understanding.

Given the focus of this textbook, on how poverty–environment relationships can be investigated, it is inevitable that multiple disciplines will need to be drawn on in seeking to answer many research questions. There will, however, be examples of disciplinary, multi-disciplinary and interdisciplinary research, reflecting the questions being asked, the context being studied and the expertise available. Three key approaches to research identified from Table 8.1 are now discussed in more detail: an ethnographic perspective, mixed methods and participatory approaches.

An ethnographic perspective

Ethnography should be viewed as a perspective towards research rather than as a method or set of methods. Within the remit of ethnography, there are certain characteristics that are associated with an ethnographic approach and certain methods that are more likely to be used than others. Taking an ethnographic approach would not generate research data that could be taken as representative of a given population or data that could be replicated under identical circumstances. Rather, an ethnographic approach involves interpretive research, where the researcher seeks to understand meaning ascribed to phenomena by the subject. Such research entails interaction between the researcher and the research subject(s), with subjective research undertaken, seeking to delve into the complexity of situations and developing hypotheses that can be tested in similar circumstances. An ethnographic approach requires that the researcher gains access to a real situation, studying life as it unfolds, and that trust is developed between researcher and subject(s). Gaining access, building trust and collecting the data means that an ethnographic approach can take many months or even years to undertake. Blommaert and Dong (2010) provide an introduction into an ethnographic perspective, setting out how to approach observation, make recordings of different kinds, take fieldnotes and collect all kinds of relevant pieces of information, such as photographs, drawings and examples of students' work, for example. Interviews may be undertaken, with interviews seen as a conversation rather than a list of questions for which answers should be sought.

From Table 8.1 it can be seen that an ethnographic approach to fieldwork is associated with a number of the frameworks and approaches, namely political ecology, Critical Institutionalism, the Environmental Entitlements framework and applying a gendered lens. These frameworks and approaches share a concern with gaining an in-depth understanding of the experience, perspectives and knowledge of the research subjects, that is, taking an interpretivist approach, with observation of practices, relations and behaviour in relation to how and why people seek benefits from natural resources in the way they do or how they are affected by environmental change. There is a clear link between taking an ethnographic approach and situations where identifying and understanding the complexity of institutions that mediate people–environment relations matters. Being able to identify and understand institutions requires time and good access to a situation and would be difficult to achieve through a questionnaire survey.

Mixed methods

Many of the frameworks and approaches have a number of research methods associated with them. This may mean that different methods have been used by different researchers based on their preferences, resources or the research questions being asked. It may alternatively suggest that a mixed-methods approach is often used, drawing on a range of qualitative, quantitative, modelling and experimental methods. A mixed-methods approach can be undertaken in different ways: taking either a sequential approach so that the findings from the use of one method feeds into the design and application of another; or, different methods may be used to generate data in response to different research questions or contexts. There has been much debate concerning how mixed-methods research should be defined, with Creswell and Plano Clark (2011) setting out defining characteristics of mixed-methods research, rather than defining the term itself. Such characteristics include the collection and analysis of qualitative and quantitative data, acknowledging that such data and data collection can be mixed concurrently, sequentially or embedded. It is sometimes argued that mixed-methods research is inappropriate, given the different assumptions underlying methods, but mixed-methods research has considerable support and uptake, with due consideration required for appropriate use, planning and interpretation.

Many of the frameworks and approaches reviewed encourage a mixed-methods approach to research, reflecting the natural and social science components of some of the approaches, such as political ecology, the Social-Ecological System framework and the frameworks associated with the Millennium Ecosystem Assessment, and the need to generate quantitative and qualitative data. The Institutional Analysis and Development framework, the livelihoods and wellbeing analysis frameworks and social network analysis call for the use of mixed methods, reflecting the need to generate quantitative data alongside deeper explanations and perspectives in relation to people–environment relations. Mixed-methods research may then require a team of researchers, bringing different disciplinary backgrounds, skills and experience.

Participatory approaches

Participatory research methods stem from the broader participatory approach and philosophy associated with the work of Robert Chambers. Chambers (see, for example 1983, 1997) challenged top-down, professional-led approaches to development research and practice, arguing that a more bottom-up, people-led approach is needed, in which researchers and professionals facilitate and listen but do not lead and impose. Within the broad approach of participatory development, certain methods are used that enable a more listening, people-led approach. There are certain norms of behaviour and practice that are expected as well as the use of certain methods. Such norms and behaviour include the use of appropriate language and tools for the exercises, consideration of the time exercises may take, where and when during a day/week they are undertaken, who may be able to participate given their availability of time and their status and what happens to the data resulting from the exercises – should it be stored and used by the people involved as well as the researcher, for example? The people (or research subjects) take more control of the investigation and analysis than they would for other research methods.

The approach promoted by Chambers was originally referred to as 'Rapid Rural Appraisal', becoming 'Participatory Rural Appraisal' (PRA) and then 'Participatory Learning and Action' (PLA). Methods for the collection of data that fall within the broad area of PRA/PLA methods include participatory mapping to show a range of information on locations, including information on natural resources; transect walks to gain a cross-sectional view of the area and activities; producing a seasonal calendar to show significant events and conditions over the course of an annual cycle; wealth or wellbeing ranking, with criteria and categories being defined as part of the exercise; and the use of Venn diagrams to show key institutions, individuals and organizations and their relationships with people, enabling an analysis of the importance and nature of those relationships. While there are guidelines for the use of such methods (see, for example Mikkelsen, 2005; Narayanasamy, 2009), part of the philosophy of the approach is that there should be innovation, improvisation and empowerment associated with PRA/PLA.

The application of livelihoods approaches are particularly associated with participatory research approaches, though such approaches can also be used to support the application of the Environmental Entitlements framework and in undertaking an analysis of natural resource governance. Participatory approaches are useful when local knowledge, understandings and perspectives are sought and where it is appropriate for such information to be generated through a group exercise, though very often men will undertake the exercises separately to women, and there may be other groupings, perhaps in relation to age or occupation.

A note on frameworks and approaches

In Chapter 1, the rationale for focusing on frameworks and approaches was set out, explaining that what is reviewed in this book are the tools that have been developed and used to investigate poverty–environment relationships. In each chapter, the background of the frameworks and approaches has been introduced, key characteristics and components analysed and examples of applications reviewed. In addition, the sections on 'further reading' provide readers with lists of essential literature which should be drawn on to enable more effective understanding and application of the frameworks and approaches. The chapters provide an introduction to the frameworks and approaches, but to use them effectively, more specialized literature should be drawn on, reflected in the lengthy lists of references at the end of each chapter.

A few general observations can be made about the frameworks and approaches:

1   The frameworks and approaches reviewed in the book are constantly being adapted, reviewed and critiqued. The chapters provide background to the frameworks and approaches, significant developments and examples, but further versions and applications have been, and will be, developed.
2   In analysing relations between poverty and the environment, multiple frameworks and approaches may be drawn on, bringing together critical concepts, variables and perspectives. Researchers should be aware, however, of the different conceptual underpinnings and assumptions within the frameworks and approaches, as there could be conflicting assumptions between some concepts and theories.
3   The selection of frameworks and approaches, or elements of them, in research will be at least in part informed by the questions being asked and the nature of the research problem and context. Such selection will also be informed by the interests and expertise of the researcher(s) and by the resources available for the research.
4   In some cases, researchers will draw on just part of a framework rather than use the entire framework. This enables a much deeper analysis of one aspect,

but cannot capture the complexity of a situation that the use of the whole framework would enable.

5   How good or useful the frameworks and approaches are will depend in part on how they are used and the findings interpreted, though all frameworks and approaches have their limitations.

6   The issue of 'change' in poverty–environment relationships should be considered in how frameworks and approaches are used and findings interpreted. A 'dynamic' approach is needed that can capture and investigate changes over time and space.

The book should be seen as providing a way in to diverse areas of literature that can each bring tools and insights to an analysis of poverty–environment relationships. This is a dynamic and complex field of analysis, requiring innovation and cooperation between and within disciplines. By bringing together examples of diverse frameworks and approaches that can each contribute to deeper understanding of poverty–environment relationships, the book aims to contribute to cross-fertilization between the frameworks and approaches, with an expectation that such innovative research approaches will lead to stronger and more effective commitment to both poverty reduction and environmental sustainability.

Further reading

Angelsen, A., Larsen, H.O., Lund, J.F., Smith-Hall, C. and Wunder, S. (eds) (2011) *Measuring Livelihoods and Environmental Dependence: Methods for Research and Fieldwork*, London: Earthscan.

This innovative book is an output of the Poverty Environment Network (PEN) coordinated by the Center for International Forestry Research (CIFOR). One of the aims of forming the network was to promote better practices in collecting data to quantify the role of environmental resources in rural livelihoods. The book takes a broader perspective than that by covering the entire research process, from the formulation of hypotheses to the collection, analysis and presentation of data. The main method addressed in the book is the use of quantitative surveys. The chapters cover many dimensions for researchers to consider in planning for and undertaking field research, with a more specific chapter given the context of their research interests on valuing non-marketed environmental products. This is a unique text of value to students, researchers and practitioners engaging with research in a rural setting in developing countries, particularly those undertaking more quantitative surveys.

Poteete, A.R., Janssen, M.A. and Ostrom, E. (2010) *Working Together: Collective Action, the Commons, and Multiple Methods in Practice*, Woodstock, NJ: Princeton University Press.

The focus on research methods used to investigate common pool resources and collective action makes this book particularly useful for researchers concerned with investigating people–environment relationships. The book is principally concerned with exploring the potential for, and practical challenges of, multiple method and collaborative research, observing that there is no single research method that can overcome all challenges faced in social research and that employing a multiple method approach is a way of responding to the range of challenges, or shortcomings, associated with specific methods. The text introduces a range of methods commonly employed in common pool resources and collective action research, from case studies and meta-analyses to laboratory and field-based experiments and agent-based modelling, identifying challenges experienced by each category of method. The authors link debates concerning methods with theoretical development and so go on to review theory on collective action along three lines: individual decision-making, microsituational conditions and the broader social-ecological context, drawing on the social-ecological systems framework.

References

Angelsen, A., Larsen, H.O., Lund, J.F., Smith-Hall, C. and Wunder, S. (eds) (2011) *Measuring Livelihoods and Environmental Dependence: Methods for Research and Fieldwork*, London: Earthscan.

Béné, C., Belal, E., Baba, M.O., Ovie, S., Raji, A., Malasha, I., Njaya, F., M.N. Andi, Russell, A. and Neiland, A. (2009) 'Power struggle, dispute and alliance over local resources: Analyzing "democratic" decentralization of natural resources through the lenses of Africa Inland fisheries', *World Development*, 37(12): 1935–1950.

Berry, S. (1989) 'Social institutions and access to resources', *Africa*, 59(1): 41–55.

Blommaert, J. and Dong, J. (2010) *Ethnographic Fieldwork: A Beginner's Guide*, Bristol: Multilingual Matters.

Bryman, A. (2012) *Social Research Methods*, Oxford: Oxford University Press.

Chambers, R. (1983) *Rural Development: Putting the Last First*, London: Longman.

Chambers, R. (1997) *Whose Reality Counts? Putting the First Last*, London: Intermediate Technology Publications.

Creswell, J.W. and Plano Clark, V.L. (2011) *Designing and Conducting Mixed Methods Research*, London: Sage.

Crona, B. and Bodin, Ö. (2010) 'Power asymmetries in small-scale fisheries: A barrier to governance transformability?', *Ecology and Society*, 15(4): 32.

Desai, V. and Potter, R. (eds) (2006) *Doing Development Research*, London: Sage.

Foucault, M. (1980) *Power/Knowledge: Selected Interviews and Other Writings, 1972–1977*, London: Harvester Wheatsheaf.

Jentoft, S. (2007) 'In the power of power: The understated aspect of fisheries and coastal management', *Human Organization*, 66(4): 426–437.

Lukes, S. (2005) *Power: A Radical View*, London: Palgrave Macmillan.

Mikkelsen, B. (2005) *Methods for Development Work and Research: A New Guide for Practitioners*, 2nd edition, New Delhi: Sage Publications.

Narayanasamy, N. (2009) *Participatory Rural Appraisal: Principles, Methods and Application*, New Delhi: Sage Publications.

Njaya, F., Donda, S. and Béné, C. (2012) 'Analysis of power in fisheries co-management: Experiences from Malawi', *Society and Natural Resources*, 25: 652–666.

North, D.C. (1990) *Institutions, Institutional Change and Economic Performance*, Cambridge: Cambridge University Press.

Poteete, A.R. and Ribot, J.C. (2011) 'Repertoires of domination: Decentralization as process in Botswana and Senegal', *World Development*, 39(3): 439–449.

Poteete, A.R., Janssen, M.A. and Ostrom, E. (2010) *Working Together: Collective Action, the Commons, and Multiple Methods in Practice*, Woodstock: Princeton University Press.

Raik, D.B., Wilson, A.L. and Decker, D.J. (2008) 'Power in natural resources management: An application of theory', *Society and Natural Resources*, 21: 729–739.

Repko, A.F. (2012) *Interdisciplinary Research: Process and Theory*, 2nd edition, London: Sage.

Ribot, J.C. and Peluso, N.L. (2003) 'A theory of access', *Rural Sociology*, 68(2): 153–181.

Scott, J. (2001) *Power*, Cambridge: Polity Press.

Sumner, A. and Tribe, M. (2008) *International Development Studies: Theories and Methods in Research and Practice*, London: Sage Publications.

Index

I Love you Faye